T0364608

Seeking Middle Ground

Seeking Middle Ground

Land, Markets, and Public Policy

Edited by
Sanjoy Chakravorty
Amitendu Palit

OXFORD
UNIVERSITY PRESS

OXFORD
UNIVERSITY PRESS

Oxford University Press is a department of the University of Oxford.
It furthers the University's objective of excellence in research, scholarship,
and education by publishing worldwide. Oxford is a registered trademark of
Oxford University Press in the UK and in certain other countries.

Published in India by
Oxford University Press
2/11 Ground Floor, Ansari Road, Daryaganj, New Delhi 110 002, India

First Edition published in 2019

ISBN-13 (print edition): 978-0-19-949545-0
ISBN-10 (print edition): 0-19-949545-9

ISBN-13 (eBook): 978-0-19-909767-8
ISBN-10 (eBook): 0-19-909767-4

Typeset in Bembo Std 10.5/13
by The Graphics Solution, New Delhi 110 092
Printed in India by Replika Press Pvt. Ltd

Contents

Figures and Tables

FIGURES

TABLES

Abbreviations

AIADMK	All India Anna Dravida Munnetra Kazhagam
BBMP	Bruhat Bengaluru Mahanagara Palike
BJD	Biju Janata Dal
BJP	Bharatiya Janata Party
BMC	Brihanmumbai Municipal Corporation
BSP	Bahujan Samaj Party
CBD	Central Business District
CEPT	Centre for Environment Planning and Technology University
CERSAI	Central Registry of Securitisation Asset Reconstruction and Security Interest
CIDCO	City and Industrial Development Corporation Ltd
CMD	Chairman and Managing Director
CMIE	Centre for Monitoring Indian Economy
CPR	Common Property Resource
DCR	Development Control Regulations
DILRMP	Digital India Land Records Modernization Programme
DMK	Dravida Munnetra Kazhagam
DP	Displaced Persons
FAO	Food and Agriculture Organization
FAR	Floor Area Ratio
FDI	Foreign Direct Investment
FORRAD	Foundation for Rural Recovery and Development
FSI	Floor Space Index
GDP	Gross Domestic Product

GIDC	Gujarat Industrial Development Corporation
GIS	Geographic Information System
GST	Goods and Services Tax
IAAP	Intensive Agricultural Areas Programme
IADP	Intensive Agricultural Development Programme
IDF	India Development Foundation
IIM	Indian Institute of Management
ISAS	Institute of South Asian Studies
ITI	Industrial Training Institute
JLL	Jones Lang Lasalle
JNNURM	Jawaharlal Nehru National Urban Renewal Mission
JPC	Joint Parliamentary Committee
KEIPL	Khed Economic Infrastructure Private Limited
LAA	Land Acquisition Act 1894 (India)
LAL	Land Administration Law 1998 (China)
LARR	Right to Fair Compensation and Transparency in Land Acquisition, Rehabilitation and Resettlement Act 2013 (India)
LTV	Loan-to-value
MIDC	Maharashtra Industrial Development Corporation
MNREGA	Mahatma Gandhi National Rural Employment Guarantee Act
MSRDC	Maharashtra State Road Development Corporation
NBFC	Non-banking Finance Companies
NDA	National Democratic Alliance
NGO	Non-governmental Organization
NICE	Nandi Infrastructure Corridor Enterprises
NITI Aayog	National Institution for Transforming India
NLRMP	National Land Records Modernisation Programme
NSDP	Net State Domestic Product
NSSO	National Sample Survey Office
ONGC	Oil and Natural Gas Corporation Ltd
PAC	Public Affairs Centre
PAP	Project Affected People
PDS	Public Distribution System
PPP	Public–Private Partnership

RIS	Research and Information System for Developing Countries
ROR	Record of Rights
RSS	Rashtriya Swayamsevak Sangh
RTC	Record of Tenancy and Crops
SEZ	Special Economic Zone
SIDCO	Tamil Nadu Small Industries Development Corporation Limited
SIPCOT	State Industries Promotion Corporation of Tamil Nadu
SP	Samajwadi Party
ST	Scheduled Tribe
TCPO	Town and Country Planning Organisation
TDRs	Transfer of Development Rights
TIDCO	Tamil Nadu Industrial Development Corporation
TMC	Trinamool Congress
UK	United Kingdom
ULB	Urban Local Body
ULCRA	Urban Land Ceiling and Regulation Act
UPA	United Progressive Alliance
US	United States
USSR	Union of Soviet Socialist Republics
VLW	Village Level Worker

Introduction

Reframing the Land Debate in India: Bringing the Market Back into a Political Discussion

Sanjoy Chakravorty and Amitendu Palit

Land is a subject of great conflict and debate in India. Over the past decade, the debate has focused on land acquisition, which some have called India's 'biggest problem'. Land issues, especially those related to acquisition, have heavily influenced electoral verdicts and political fortunes in various parts of the country. A new law for acquisition was created by the left-of-centre Congress-led United Progressive Alliance (UPA) government in 2013, a few months before the parliamentary elections of 2014, as a major plank of its re-election agenda. But the elections were won by the right-wing Bharatiya Janata Party (BJP)-led National Democratic Alliance (NDA), which immediately sought to amend the new land law it had voted in favour of a few months earlier, for facilitating greater availability of land for industry and businesses. The amendment attempt was unsuccessful at that time but may be tried again. These differing visions on acquisition are often simplified into binaries or opposing camps: people-friendly versus business-friendly; or 'populist' versus 'neoliberal'. Much of the general discourse on land remains similarly polarized.

At the core of the debate are serious issues of justice and history intertwined with politics and economics. These debates are not just prominent now, but are expected to become more robust in the coming decade given the anxieties over rural distress and the problem of livelihoods. Social, economic, and political turmoil over land is likely to become more visible as India struggles to address the serious challenges of satisfying the aspirations of a burgeoning young population with a continuing lack of sufficient work. Political assurances of doubling farmer incomes within a few years also bring into sharp focus the issues of productivity, livelihood, and sustainable returns accruing from occupations that are fundamental to land. As land-based incomes stagnate for rural communities, alternative options remain vague and limited, and changing land use from agriculture to more productive alternatives remains fraught with conflict, popular politics and public policies in India will have to stay engaged with the debate on land at their core.

This book is a contribution to this discourse on land. It does not claim to be the last word on the subject given that the struggle over land is as old as recorded time. Nonetheless, it is a serious scholarly attempt to shed light on a subject that seems to generate only heat.

Our primary argument is simple: The land debate must be refocused from its current preoccupation with acquisition and politics (that is, state actions) to include land markets and public policies. We argue that the focus on politics and political solutions to a deep-rooted problem of political economy has deflected attention from market-oriented approaches that, in many situations, could be more effective, especially because of the booming land and real estate markets in the country. Land markets have become ever more salient as more of India urbanizes and produces new political actors sustained by real estate, land brokerage, and mobile constituencies. We argue that good welfare outcomes—including outcomes addressing social justice issues—can materialize if land markets are integral to the discussion and policy framework. Neither politics nor markets are by themselves solutions to a serious problem of political economy. We, therefore, aim to nudge the discourse towards a better understanding of the complementary strengths of state- and market-led approaches to the many problems of land in rural and urban India.

We also emphasize scale, particularly the local scale. Much of the current discourse is engaged with the national scale (as is about half the material in this volume) for undoubtedly good reasons. Land is an issue of national importance. But, as many of our contributors note, the local scale may be just as important for pragmatic welfare outcomes. Sub-national local bodies, whether it is the Brihanmumbai Municipal Corporation (BMC) or a gram panchayat in Ratnagiri district, do matter in the matter of land, as do local bureaucracies, communities, and political actors, by ultimately managing compromise or escalating conflict. The land debate in India must include the local scale at which the action actually takes place for the discourse to be more enlightening.

An improved discourse on land is urgently needed, not least because no one in India is immune from the need for land. Half the labour force (and population) still derives some or all of its income from working on land. They, and much of the remaining half, the working and struggling classes, spend most of their lives and precious savings, hunting for land and housing. The better off tend to use the land and housing markets as locations for parking savings (investments); the nefarious are attracted to land and housing for the high returns which their dubious uses can yield (considerably higher than the old standards—the smuggling and sex trades); and the political class thrives and prospers on (black) money that land and real estate generates. The latter sustenance continues, notwithstanding radically disruptive state interventions like demonetization in 2016.

At the same time, the old struggles of domination and alienation between majorities and minorities, the powerful and the marginalized, not only persist, but may also have intensified. These are expressed through innumerable caste and tribal conflicts over land in various parts of the nation, most sharply in what is euphemistically called the 'Maoist' insurgency, but what by other interpretations might be described as an Adivasi uprising for control of traditional land and land-based resources. Given these conditions, it is necessary to get away from the binaries of good versus evil and state versus market, and to work from solid information and case studies to move to a realistic middle ground. *That middle ground is what we seek in this volume.*

It is not easy to find the middle ground. The polarization of the discourse, the intellectual grounds staked out at the far left ('no land acquisition or conversion under any circumstances because it is always unjust') and far right ('acquire or convert as much land as quickly as possible to ride the fickle winds of development'), tend to command great intellectual loyalty. These dug-in positions are often explained by using extreme illustrations—of disastrous acquisition processes (like

Singur, in West Bengal) or 'everybody wins' stories (like Sanand, in Gujarat, the metaphorical *yang* to Singur's *yin*). The reality is that most situations fall somewhere between disaster and glory and create both losers and winners. Some analysts choose to see only what their ideology permits: disasters and losers or glories and winners. We differ in our perspective and choose to look at the vast middle by drawing lessons from a range of case studies and examining the possibilities in law and policy that can enable more winners to emerge in a variety of ways.

Many doubts and uncertainties persist—as they must because both states and markets are better at ensuring some things and less effective in ensuring others. The state can take land and also give it away. The market can make the rich richer at the same time it empowers the marginalized. It is unwise to rely entirely on either one of these institutions to deliver both growth and justice. These doubts and uncertainties are expressed by most of the authors in this volume. But there is far less doubt among the authors—who range from academic disciplines like economics, geography, political science, sociology, and urban planning to the senior end of the bureaucracy and the media—that there are better ways of moving forward that include both state and market solutions.

We have organized the ideas into three baskets. In Part 1, we look at 'The Challenge of Land'. Four chapters cover some of the key material on the unique challenge of land in India, and the efforts of policy-makers and legislators in dealing with this in different periods after independence. In Part 2, we look at the last decade and 'A Variety of Land Markets' emerging in different regions of the country using case studies of acquisition and other forms of land conversion (such as land pooling) from Gujarat, Tamil Nadu, Uttar Pradesh, Chhattisgarh, and Maharashtra. These are among the most solidly grounded field studies of land-use change in India. Finally, in Part 3, we discuss 'A Range of Land Policies' that extend well beyond the usual limits of the discourse on land, and include analyses of land as a source of credit, land information systems, taxes, urban land-use regulations, and the limits and distortions of land laws.

THE CHALLENGE OF LAND

We begin with some background material on the distribution of land in India. This may be known to readers who are familiar with land issues but may be new for others. Some of these data are shown in Figures I.1 and I.2.

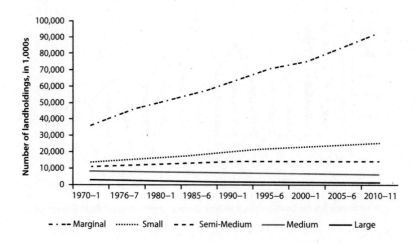

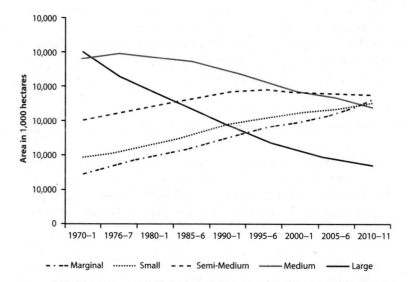

FIGURE I.1 Distribution of Landholdings by Size, 1970–1 to 2010–11
Source: Agriculture Census Report 2010–11.

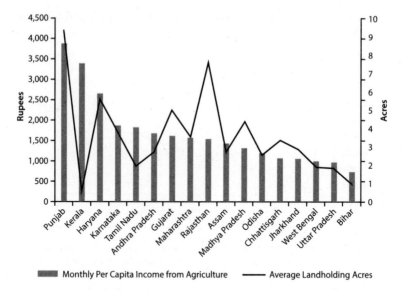

FIGURE I.2 Agricultural Income and Landholding by State, 2010–11
Source: Income data from Chakravorty, Chandrasekhar, and Naraparaju, 'Income Generation and Inequality in India's Agricultural Sector' (2018). Landholding figures calculated from data in Table 6.9 in the Agriculture Census Report 2010–11.
Note: The landholding data are combined for Andhra Pradesh and Telangana, but the income data are for Andhra Pradesh alone.

- India's total land area is about 812 million acres (one acre is roughly two-thirds of a regulation football field).[1] Of the total, in 2007–8, about 348 million acres (or 43 per cent) was under cultivation. The remaining land was forested, steep, urban, fallow, sandy, under water, or in use for transportation and other infrastructure.
- The most productive land is irrigated land, which is roughly twice as productive as dry land in the same region. About 154 million

[1] The figures in this section are compiled from different sources for cultivation and ownership; they differ slightly because not all privately owned land is cultivated. The cultivation data are from 'Agricultural Statistics at a Glance 2010', http://eands.dacnet.nic.in/. The data on operational holdings or ownership are from the 'Agricultural Census of 2010–11', http://agcensus.nic.in/document/agcensus2010/agcen2010rep.htm.

acres or roughly 44 per cent of India's cultivated land area is irrigated. Much of this is also land on which more than one crop is grown annually. These 'multi-crop' lands cover about 136 million acres or around 39 per cent of the land under cultivation.

- According to the most recent agricultural census of 2010–11, the agricultural land in the country (not all of it cultivated) covers about 395 million acres divided into 138 million discrete land parcels: an average of 2.86 acres per holding. In contrast, the average landholding size in France is 110 acres, in the United States (US) it is about 450 acres, and even more than that in much of South America.

- This average is, not surprisingly, the lowest ever recorded. Data from previous agricultural censuses show that the average landholding size was 5.63 acres in 1970–1 (in the first census), 4.55 acres in 1980–1, 3.83 acres in 1990–1, and 3.04 acres in 2005–6. In the 40 years that the agricultural census has been undertaken, the average landholding size has decreased by about half. During that period, there has been a massive growth in the number of marginal farms (tripled in 40 years) and an equivalent decline in the area covered by farms larger than 10 acres (down to one-third in 40 years).

- The nationwide average of 2.86 acres masks the reality that small holdings (92 million of the 138 million landholdings in the country) averaged just 1 acre per holding. In several major states, the average landholding size was less than 2.5 acres (which is roughly 1 hectare): Kerala (0.5 acres), Bihar (1 acre), Uttar Pradesh and West Bengal (1.9 acres each), and Tamil Nadu (2 acres); together, these states cover close to one-quarter of all the agricultural land in the country.

- Largely as a result of this abysmally low size of landholding, income from cultivation is abysmally low. Chakravorty, Chandrasekhar, and Naraparaju find that in 2012–13, monthly per capita incomes from agriculture varied widely between states, from INR 3,872 in Punjab down to INR 736 in Bihar (a fivefold difference); incomes from cultivation alone (that provides about half of all agricultural income) varied even more widely, from INR 2,311 in Punjab to INR 250 in West Bengal (a ninefold difference). Most disturbing is the finding that monthly expenditures exceeded income in three of the most populous states in the country—West Bengal, Uttar Pradesh, and Bihar—and, correspondingly, that the average income of households with less than 2.5 acres of land was less than consumption.[2]

- These findings are confirmed in the Socio Economic and Caste Census of 2011: In almost 75 per cent of rural households, the monthly income of the highest earning member was less than INR 5,000; this condition existed for over 83 and 86 per cent of Dalit and Adivasi households, respectively. Thirty per cent of rural households were landless; these and another 20 per cent of rural households derived their primary income from manual casual labour.[3]

- These conditions are unambiguous and unrelenting: Agricultural land in India continues to fragment into increasingly unsustainable sizes as a result of the continuing growth of the agricultural population, the intergenerational subdivision of already-small holdings, the inability to move enough of the farming population into salaried jobs in the formal sector (instead of casual labour) or business or other non-farm occupations, and the inability of the urban sector to absorb low-skill rural labour (caused principally by the slow growth of urban jobs, the failure to create a labour-intensive manufacturing base, and the appalling quality of life for the urban poor). At the same time, incomes from agriculture and agricultural land remain the lowest of all occupations, are not sufficiently supplemented with off-farm income, and continue to fail to provide sustainable livelihoods for millions of families.

- There are two productivity stories in Indian agriculture: Land is intensely used and very productive, but labour is abundant and very unproductive. Simply put, there is just not enough land per family in most of the country for agriculture to generate liveable incomes. The conclusion is unavoidable that the fragmentation of agricultural land is the root cause of poverty in India.[4]

[2] Sanjoy Chakravorty, S. Chandrasekhar, and Karthikeya Naraparaju, 'Income Generation and Inequality in India's Agricultural Sector: The Consequences of Land Fragmentation' (2018), http://www.igidr.ac.in/pdf/publication/WP-2016-028.pdf.

[3] The figures are the author's calculations reported in Sanjoy Chakravorty, 'Land Acquisition and the Rent-Seeking State', *Seminar* 674 (State of Democracy; October 2015): 35–9, 38.

[4] This argument is made by many scholars, including Sukhamoy Chakravarty, *Development Planning: The Indian Experience* (New Delhi: Oxford

This condition of unremittingly low labour productivity, income, and capital formation in agriculture inspires Abhirup Sarkar's identification of 'The Indian Malady' in Chapter 1 in this volume: To increase productivity, it is necessary to build large irrigation facilities, which are likely to displace people and increase poverty. Similarly, transformation of land from agriculture to industry and infrastructure displaces people from their traditional livelihood, and may temporarily increase poverty. In other words, development causes displacement. The absence of development deepens poverty. At least, that has been the Indian way.

The current politics and policy on land is squarely focused on land acquisition and displacement, but that is not how things were in the initial years and decades after Independence. At that time, the politics and policy were focused on land reform and raising agricultural productivity. Two chapters in this volume tackle these themes separately. In Chapter 2, Subrata Mitra looks at the various reform measures that have been implemented—such as abolishing zamindari, tenancy reform, land ceiling laws—and the policy tools—especially the Green Revolution—that were used in the post-independence period. In Chapter 3, Ronojoy Sen looks at the 'land question' as it has been debated in the Indian Parliament from independence to contemporary times. He looks at the Constituent Assembly deliberations, the First Amendment debates, and subsequent parliamentary interventions, including the Right to Fair Compensation and Transparency in Land Acquisition, Rehabilitation and Resettlement Act (LARR) passed in 2013, and the BJP government's attempt to amend it.

It is necessary to understand the differences between these two periods and their foci—that is, the current period (beginning roughly around 2000) in which the emphasis is on land acquisition and displacement versus the earlier period (roughly from independence to the early 1980s) in which the emphasis was on land reforms and agricultural productivity. One way to think about the difference between the periods is what preceded them. The discourse in the current period can be seen as a reaction to six to seven decades of rapacious and pauperizing land acquisition by the independent Indian state, topped

University Press, 1987); and Sanjoy Chakravorty, *The Price of Land: Acquisition, Conflict, Consequence* (New Delhi: Oxford University Press, 2013).

up by a quarter century of economic liberalization. Similarly, the previous (post-independence) period of reforms were a reaction to the agricultural mess that had been inherited from the colonial authorities.

Land was the primary source of revenue during colonial rule—more under the pre-1857 Company raj, and less later under the Crown raj. Land revenue was the primary reason for colonization, not, contrary to popular belief, trade or British industrialization. The revenue was extracted by a variety of agents of expropriation, like zamindars and 'kings'. After World War I, there came, for the first time in Indian history, a rapidly rising population and consequent land fragmentation (this was the beginning of the demographic transition in India and its population explosion), expanded tenancy rights which led to exchange rights, a feudal ownership structure with numerous intermediaries and subinfeudation, and informal credit markets run by usurious local moneylenders. At independence in 1947, soon after the devastating Bengal famine in 1943, four-fifths of the Indian labour force worked in agriculture, under conditions of widespread poverty, exploitation, illiteracy, and landlessness. It is worth noting that India's population at independence was about 330 million. In the little over 70 years since, it has more or less quadrupled to about 1.3 billion.

As a result, land reform was one of the most important items on the large and difficult agenda of the newly independent nation. The First, Fourth, and Seventeenth amendments to the constitution created the legal basis for key land reforms. The abolishment of intermediaries (zamindars, *inamdars*) was the first reform attempted, and its success led to some decrease in inequality in land ownership in the first decade after independence. Tenancy reform had mixed outcomes—it was successful under communist administrations (in Kerala and West Bengal), but far less so under other regimes, especially Congress regimes. Land ceiling reform was generally unsuccessful and very possibly counterproductive. All the land reforms together led to the redistribution of less than 6 per cent of cultivable land. Inequality in landownership remained virtually unchanged from the 1960s, and may have increased markedly in the last two decades.

The Fifth Five Year Plan document (1974) had the following blunt statement: 'A broad assessment of the programme of land reform is that ... legislation has fallen short of the desired objectives, and implementation of the enacted laws has been inadequate.'[5] Maitreesh Ghatak and Sanchari Roy have concluded: 'Overall, land reform legislation seems to have had a negative and significant effect on agricultural productivity in India.... Decomposing by type of land reform, the main driver for this negative effect seems to be land-ceiling legislation. In contrast, the effect of tenancy reform, averaged across all states, turns out to be insignificant.'[6] We still do not have a solid accounting of the negative effects of many land reforms—tenant eviction, benami transactions, endless litigation, land fragmentation, increased inequality, lowered productivity, and so on. One must agree with the conclusions of numerous observers of land reforms in India that, other than eliminating the zamindari system, they failed. To be fair, it is difficult to see how successful they could have been with redistribution even if there were sincerer efforts, given the extreme scarcity and fragmentation of land.

It may well be that the more important policy/action by the independent Indian state on land was acquisition rather than reform. No new law was created for it. The existing colonial Land Acquisition Act of 1894 (LAA) was retained, unchanged. This Act was vital for enabling the massive industrialization and modernization programme of the Nehruvian state. Over the 70 years after independence, much agricultural land was acquired for infrastructure and industry. The state took land it deemed necessary for development using the language of public purpose—for dams, irrigation, defence, factories, townships, power, roads, rails, and so on—this time in the national interest, as opposed to the colonizer's interest. The economic geography of modern India was created by the LAA. Sanjoy Chakravorty has written that 'the independent Indian state's policies on land were fundamentally contradictory. It gave (or redistributed) land with one hand, and took (or acquired) land with the other. It took more than it gave, and the giving stopped long ago, whereas the taking intensified in recent years.'[7]

[5] Reported in Timothy Besley and Robin Burgess, 'Land Reform, Poverty Reduction, and Growth: Evidence from India', *Quarterly Journal of Economics* 115, no. 2 (2000): 389–430, 394.

[6] Maitreesh Ghatak and Sanchari Roy, 'Land Reform and Agricultural Productivity in India: A Review of the Evidence', *Oxford Review of Economic Policy* 23, no. 2 (2007): 251–69, 253.

[7] Chakravorty, *The Price of Land*, xxiii.

No entity kept track of how much land was acquired or how many people were affected. In the absence of official data, independent scholars have reconstructed the impacts from sources like government gazettes. Their findings can be treated as reasonably reliable estimates.[8] It is possible that as much as 50 million acres, or about 6 per cent of all the land in the country, was either acquired outright or converted from common use during 1947–2000. It is likely that as many as 50 million people were displaced or adversely affected. The land-losers were paid very little compensation (sometimes none at all), and few of the displaced were resettled or rehabilitated. Many others, perhaps more in number than the land-losers, were displaced without compensation because they did not own land. The socially marginalized groups were the worst affected: Dalits, because they lived on but often did not own land in project-affected areas; and Adivasis, because much of their land was community-held rather than privately owned (and could be taken lawfully without compensation).

There is little doubt that the land- and livelihood-losers

> effectively subsidized India's development, or, to be more accurate, its winners—that is, the populations that got power and roads and water…This regressive redistribution system lasted well into the 2000s. It was politically sustainable for many reasons, not least because the direct winners outnumbered and were more powerful than the direct losers. Even if the worst accounts of land takings are exaggerated, even if the highest numbers of affected people are overblown, this would have to be considered a deeply inequitable and significant state failure by today's standards.[9]

This regressive system existed for almost six decades without much resistance. No political parties emerged to champion the rights of the displaced. However, around the mid-2000s, the system started breaking down. There were well-known cases of very troubled and violent acquisition processes (in Nandigram, Singur, Kalinganagar, Posco, Vedanta, and the Yamuna Expressway, for example), plus hundreds of

---

[8] See Walter Fernandes, 'Sixty Years of Development-Induced Displacement in India: Scale, Impacts, and the Search for Alternatives', in *India Social Development Report 2008: Development and Displacement*, ed. H.M. Mathur (New Delhi: Oxford University Press, 2008), 89–102.

[9] Chakravorty, *The Price of Land*, xxiii–xxiv.

small and large cases of land acquisition processes facing resistance, many in the new economic spaces that were enabled by the Special Economic Zones (SEZ) Act of 2005.[10] The seeds of resistance may have been sown by the Narmada Bachao Andolan (NBA), a social movement that began in the mid-1980s to resist the displacement created by the Sardar Sarovar dam project in Gujarat and Madhya Pradesh. But the seeds were able to bloom because of fundamental changes in India's information system, with new media and information agents acting in an environment of increasing political competition. Land acquisition became a wedge issue in Indian politics. And there was a new land market. This is the subject of Sanjoy Chakravorty's contribution in Chapter 4 in this volume: how a political non-problem (land acquisition) became a problem.

Resistance to land acquisition became so widespread that some called it India's 'biggest problem'. It became a major issue in state-level politics. In West Bengal, the 34-year rule of the communists was upended by Mamata Banerjee and the Trinamool Congress (TMC) because of it. In Uttar Pradesh, the Mayawati government of the Bahujan Samaj Party (BSP) may have been defeated by the Samajwadi Party (SP) of Mulayam Singh Yadav for the same reason. So important was this issue that the Congress-led UPA government made it a major plank of their national re-election campaign in 2014, and enacted a new land acquisition law, framed in terms of the rights of land-losers, just before the elections.

The law has five important elements: (1) Increased compensation—market prices are doubled in urban and quadrupled in rural areas; (2) Expanded coverage—non-owners facing livelihood loss are compensated; (3) Rehabilitation and resettlement is made compulsory above certain thresholds with minimum set standards; (4) Informed consent of land-losers—using referenda, specifically when the acquisition has any private sector involvement; and (5) A new process, involving social impact assessments and a new multilayered bureaucracy. All major parties voted for the new law, including the BJP.

But, within months of coming to power in the 2014 Lok Sabha elections, the BJP tried to amend the law, specifically by diluting

---

[10] Amitendu Palit and Subhomoy Bhattacharjee, *Special Economic Zones in India: Myths and Realities* (Delhi: Anthem Press, 2008).

the 'informed consent' and 'social impact assessment' elements, initially through ordinances and later by making an unsuccessful attempt to amend the law in parliament. The main goal surely was to make land acquisition easier in what appears to be the BJP's primary development thrust—the creation of industrial corridors near and between key cities, because, in their view, this is where the investment action is concentrated, and this is how urbanization and the economy are likely to grow. It would be a mistake, however, to see the failure of the BJP amendment as the end of the legal manoeuvres. This is a long-running epic, and India is nowhere near the end of the story.

A VARIETY OF LAND MARKETS

During the same time that resistance to land acquisition was growing, fundamental changes were taking place in India's land markets. Land prices more than quintupled between 2000 and 2013 (and stabilized after that in most places), so much so that India now has arguably the highest land prices in the world. The global peak prices—as in central Hong Kong, Shinjuku and Shibuya in Tokyo, or midtown Manhattan in New York—are not reached in India yet, though south-central Mumbai comes very close (at around INR 250 crore/ acre for large plots). However, the average prices in metropolitan areas are extremely high; they are far in excess of equivalent US urban land prices (see Figure I.3). Especially remarkable is the gap between the peak prices and the average incomes expressed in terms of the 'Penthouse Index' in Figure I.4. Moreover, everywhere else— from near-suburban to far-suburban, peri-metropolitan to midsized and small towns, prosperous well-connected rural regions to strug- gling poorly-connected rural regions—land prices in India appear to be unmatched in the world (with the possible exception of China, which does not, however, have an individualized agricultural land market like India).

In peri-urban regions (around all the megacities and most major cities) and prosperous rural regions in states like Punjab and Haryana, farmland prices are easily INR 1 crore per acre (over USD 160,000/ acre); often they are much higher. Almost nowhere in the country is it possible to find farmland that costs less than INR 10 lakh per acre

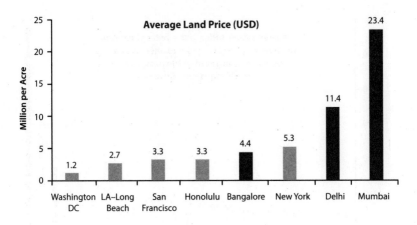

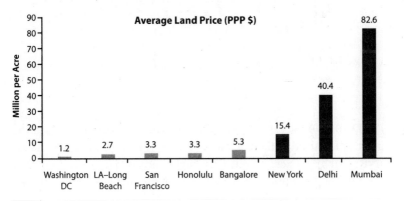

FIGURE I.3 Average Price of Urban Land in India and the US

Sources: US data from David Albouy, Gabriel Ehrlich, and Minchul Shin, 'Metropolitan Land Values' (2017). Indian data are calculated from Chakravorty, *The Price of Land*.

Note: 'PPP' here stands for Purchasing Power Parity, which is an exchange rate based on a basket of consumption that includes both tradable and non-tradable goods and services. This is similar to but more comprehensive than say the 'Big Mac Index' used by *The Economist*. 'PPP' provides a more realistic sense of what USD 1 is worth in rupees inside India, and is considerably lower than the official exchange rate. The conversion rate used here is PPP$ 1 = INR 17 (rather than USD 1 = INR 65 or 70). It is taken from the OECD estimates in 2014–15 (reported in https://data.oecd.org/conversion/purchasing-power-parities-ppp.htm).

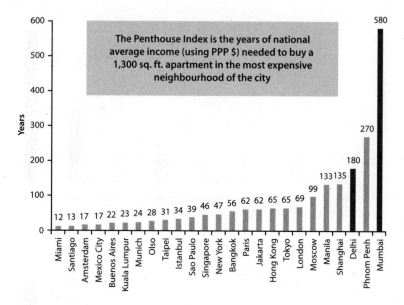

FIGURE I.4 The Penthouse Index
Source: Calculated from Chakravorty, *The Price of Land*, Table 13.

(USD 16,000) today.[11] To put these prices in context, consider that the price of farmland in the US state of Kansas is about USD 1,300 (about INR 1 lakh) per acre. This is what highly productive agricultural land should cost if the price was based only on productivity. Therefore, one must conclude that the price of farmland in India is a dozen to a hundred times more (or higher) than can be justified by agricultural productivity.

---

[11] This is confirmed from a number of localized studies. A good example is Sai Balakrishnan, *Shareholder Cities: Agrarian to Urban Land Transformations along Economic Corridors in Liberalizing India* (Philadelphia, PA: University of Pennsylvania Press, 2019; forthcoming). She shows that land prices have spiked 15-fold or more in western Maharashtra to levels up to INR 10–30 lakh (USD 16,000–50,000) per acre for waste land (which cannot be used for farming or pasture). Similar data are shown for several states in India by M. Rajshekhar, 'Great Rural Land Rush: 3 to 100-Fold Rise in Farm Land Prices May Not Bode Well', *The Economic Times*, 12 November 2013.

Chakravorty argues in *The Price of Land* that some of the explanation for this unprecedented rise comes from a mismatch between supply and demand. The supply is more or less fixed, whereas the demand from *all* parties (industrial users, the service sector, farmers, homebuyers) is increasing. There is a lot more money in the system. Home mortgage loans alone grew 40-fold (in nominal terms) in 2001–13, bringing millions more homebuyers into the market, not to mention the unquantified growth in non-resident Indian (NRI), black, and criminal money in the country. Land was always an important status good; its status value probably increased further with scarcity. In addition, rising income and wealth inequality enabled India's upper-class and proto–upper class families to drive up prices for everyone else. This new price regime is a new condition, and seems to be not a bubble but a structural transformation (that has lasted for close to two decades, through a global economic recession in 2008–10 and a radical demonetization in 2016).[12]

The Indian government's response to this structurally transformed market in which prices quintupled in a decade was to create a new acquisition law that would further double or quadruple prices. Several analysts have argued that the pricing mechanism of the new law— and any pricing system that is based on an arbitrary multiplication of 'market price'—would severely constrain the provision of public goods, urbanization, and industrialization. The constraints would not be evenly spread between states, but would additionally disadvantage states that are land-poor and/or more urbanized. There would be new windfall gainers—specifically landowners (including absentee owners), whose income would multiply by 20- to 400-fold and more in many settings. This would impose a social tax on the remaining citizenry. The political problem of resistance to land acquisition would probably be diminished—which is what the lawmakers wanted, no doubt—but an even bigger economic problem would be created. Chakravorty noted that the new law on land acquisition 'carries within it the seeds of its own destruction'.[13]

---

[12] Sanjoy Chakravorty, 'A New Price Regime: Land Markets in Urban and Rural India', *Economic & Political Weekly* XLIII, no. 7 (2013): 45–54.

[13] Sanjoy Chakravorty, 'On Land, No Lessons Learnt', *The Indian Express*, 30 August 2013, http://indianexpress.com/article/opinion/columns/

Let us examine this statement, beginning with the assumption that such a thing as 'development' is possible. If this cannot be agreed on, no further discussion is possible. Let us agree that development is progressive, marked by rising standards of education and health, enabled by a growing economy that makes possible higher levels of investment in human capital and social infrastructure. Development, thus defined, cannot take place without changing the use of some land. If all of India's agricultural land is frozen in its current use, as the country's population inexorably rattles towards 1.5 billion, the consequences cannot be but miserable for most people, not least the poor and near-poor.

Is it possible to change land use without acquisition? Certainly. A big majority of land transactions take place without the use of any acquisition law. But without a land acquisition law, it is very difficult if not impossible to collate large, contiguous areas, especially when the land is as fragmented as it is in India. (For example, the infamous Singur case in West Bengal involved the acquisition of about 1,000 acres from around 1,600 landowners.)[14] Without such collations, it is not possible to undertake large-scale public works in irrigation, transportation, energy, and so on, or make private investments in plants that rely on scale economies. This is why every country has some legal acquisition process. India is not so unique that it can be an exception to this. The problem is not with acquisition per se, but with unjust acquisition. That is what had taken place for decades, at massive scale, by the state, for state projects. The injustice had many dimensions, the most important of which were the use of force and the utter inadequacy of the compensation.

The balance between 'force' and 'compensation' is one that has not been examined at much analytical depth. We suggest that there is a continuum between feeling forced to part with one's land to the point of resisting it with violence (in extreme cases) and feeling happy that one's land is being acquired (to the extent that one would be unhappy if a

---

on-land-no-lessons-learnt/. Also see Maitreesh Ghatak and Parikshit Ghosh, 'The Land Acquisition Bill: A Critique and a Proposal', *Economic & Political Weekly* XLVI, no. 41 (2011): 65–72.

[14] Maitreesh Ghatak, Sandip Mitra, Dilip Mookherjee, and Anusha Nath, 'Land Acquisition and Compensation in Singur: What Really Happened?' (2012), http://personal.lse.ac.uk/ghatak/singur.pdf.

neighbour's land was taken and one's was not). The difference between the two feeling states, we suggest, is the level of compensation (which is a combination of money, jobs, length and reliability of support, and social status).

The argument here is that every landowner has a reservation price for his land, a price below which he will not part with it unless under duress (such as the force of the state or crippling debt). This reservation price is not based on the productivity of the land, but a host of other reasons.[15] As long as the acquisition or market price does not match the reservation price, the land should remain unacquired or unsold. If it is acquired at below reservation price, the compensation is inadequate and imposes a cost on the landowner; this can, and as seen in the last two decades, does lead to conflict. This was the old system and the costs on landowners were often devastating. We believe that a strong case can be made for the argument that the massive rise in the price of land (in both rural and urban regions) has fundamentally changed this dynamic in most of India.[16]

[15] In theory, an agricultural landowner should be open to the idea of selling his land if the income generated from it is exceeded by the price on offer (which should be the net present value of all future incomes). This would be true if income was the only utility provided by land. In reality, in many settings, agricultural production and the income generated from it is not the only source of utility from landownership; in fact, it may not even be the most important source of utility. Agricultural land is also viewed as an asset, an insurance, and a status good. It provides satisfaction or utility not only from the income it generates but as the source of the *only* income a typically unskilled farmer can earn, as a hedge against disaster, as a basis to access credit, as an inheritance for future generations, as insurance for old age, and as a source of social status (and identity and personhood). This element of the utility of land—that is, as an asset, insurance, and status good rather than a source of income—is subjective and contextual. The context varies with the landowner's access to other assets, insurance, and status goods than land, and the local social norms on land.

[16] Are there situations in which no amount of compensation can be higher than the reservation price? At an individual level this is undoubtedly true, but can it be true at a community scale? It may indeed be that way in some communities. We are not referring to heritage lands (like Niyamgiri in Odisha) that should always be off-limits. Rather, there may be communities in India that are so far removed from what many would consider 'modernity', that

The rise in the price of land opens up a range of new possibilities. Most of these possibilities result in considerably superior compensation for landowners. But there are significant regional differences in how affected people perceive their specific situations, the social relations between communities in the specific localities, the ideology of the local state, and the operation of the bureaucracy. This itself is a sea change in conditions. As recently as 2000, the state could simply notify an acquisition and take the land with minimum fuss and minimal compensation almost anywhere in the country. Now, with the new information and land markets, it is simply impossible to do so. It is important to note that this happened well before the new law (LARR) kicked in. Consider the four examples in this volume.

The most famous of these is the case of Sanand in Gujarat where, in 2008, the Nano small car project was relocated by Tata Motors after it faced stiff resistance to land acquisition in Singur, West Bengal (a resistance movement that later toppled the Communist Party of India (Marxist) (CPI(M))-led government that had been in power for 34 uninterrupted years). A ground-level study by Yinghong Huang in Chapter 5 in this volume shows that landowners in Sanand were paid INR 45–75 lakh per acre (USD 75,000–125,000 per acre) and were happy to part with their land. He writes that landowners got adequate compensations and, in some instances, even a share in the developmental benefit of the acquired land, and thus welcomed rather than resisted the developmental projects. Most displaced landowners bought cheaper land elsewhere with this windfall; some even became movie producers.[17]

Similar positive win-win findings are reported by Sojin Shin, in Chapter 6 in this volume, who finds that a bargaining process between the state, society, and foreign capital for land acquisition for a tyre-manufacturing foreign company in a special economic zone met the needs of citizens (especially those from 'lower' castes) in the Thervoy

---

money may mean little to them if getting it meant the end of a way of living (as pastoralists or agriculturists). This is a difficult discussion that, for reasons of staying on point, we set aside for another occasion.

[17] M. Pathak, 'Gujarat Farmers Turn Film Producers', *Mint*, 11 November 2010.

region of Tamil Nadu. Both Huang and Shin credit bureaucratic capacity, innovation, and adaptability for enabling these transitions.

More complicated is the comparative situation studied by Manjusha Nair in Chapter 7 in this volume (with some of the fieldwork undertaken after the passage of LARR). She reports on Bhatta–Parsaul in Uttar Pradesh (where thousands of acres were acquired for the explosive Yamuna Expressway project), and coal mining projects in Raigarh district in Chhattisgarh. She shows how more money has pacified the situation in Bhatta–Parsaul (where compensation demands of INR 2 crore per acre are now 'normalized' for land that should not be 'worth' more than INR 5 lakh by productivity alone) but less so in Chhattisgarh. Nair locates the changes in the land market in a new 'moral economy' of the Indian peasant.

Sai Balakrishnan has worked on three cases along the Mumbai–Pune highway in Maharashtra (Lavasa, Khed, and Magarpatta) in which new townships were created using a range of tactics from force to accommodation. In Chapter 8 in this volume, she reports on Khed, where a new urban area was created largely by commodifying what had little or no market value earlier—wasteland. She identifies the nuanced forms of land conversion in Khed, where no acquisition took place, and among other issues, shows how caste relations are being recalibrated as a result of the land market. There are many 'winners' in Khed now, but some communities have won more than others.

A RANGE OF LAND POLICIES

What our case studies do not address (because they are not meant to do so) is the future of land acquisition with the new law in this new land market. Let us briefly consider the possibilities. The new law has made it nearly impossible to acquire land in most metropolitan and many urban settings. The prices are simply too high (see Figures I.3 and I.4), even before the doubling imposed by the new acquisition law. After the highest prices in the world are doubled, it is well-nigh impossible to legally acquire land, especially for public agencies tasked with providing affordable housing (which, at INR 15 lakh or USD 25,000, is tantamount to a cruel joke in metropolises like Mumbai), or open space/parks/recreation (all endangered species in urban India), or linear projects (like transportation or water supply). The only real players in this new land market are private property developers (like Lodha and DLF) that can profitably build apartments worth a million dollars and more for a microscopic elite.

If acquisition is almost impossible in much of urban India, it has also become very difficult in much of rural and semi-urban India, especially for projects with large land needs, such as infrastructure and new towns. The reason is the same: Market prices have skyrocketed to perhaps the highest levels in the world, and these would need to be quadrupled in cases of acquisition. The net result is that different methods than acquisition are beginning to be deployed to change land use in parts of rural and much of urban India. At least two of these methods (land pooling and land leasing) have been around for decades, but are being 'rediscovered' now, and one emerging method (shareholding) may work well in some settings. Two of these methods (pooling and shareholding) change land ownership, but turn the landowners into stakeholders or partners (rather than land-losers); the third method (leasing) does not change ownership (therefore, there are no land-losers) and provides a guaranteed income (and removes the uncertainties of farming).

Land pooling allows the government to collate small plots, develop them (working with private developers in some instances), and return a portion of the developed land back to the erstwhile landowners. This returned portion can be as large as 60 per cent of the original land (for instance, in some schemes of the Delhi Development Authority) and more than 80 per cent in some schemes in Gujarat. The incentive for the landowner is that he keeps some or most of his land which is worth much more than before. This method was widely used in the Bombay Presidency in colonial India, was continued in Gujarat after independence, and is now being revived or newly legislated in many cities and states. The most famous (or notorious) use of land pooling is for the new state capital of Andhra Pradesh, Amaravati, being built on around 38,000 acres of land pooled from 29 villages. Amaravati is massive and controversial (and based on a site visit by Sanjoy Chakravorty in mid-2018, probably a significant overreach that could turn into a planning disaster). We tried but unfortunately could not get a case study done on it.

Land leasing is an old method in the agricultural sector, much despised by many (because it was associated with the feudal zamindari system in colonial India that led to infeudation and subinfeudation and absentee landlordism), and much regulated in the different states of independent India (to the extent of being banned in Kerala and Jammu and Kashmir). However, the idea of leasing agricultural land for non-agricultural use has returned in a big way, and new laws are being created at the state level to enable it (for instance, in Madhya Pradesh, Maharashtra, Uttarakhand, and Uttar Pradesh). Large new projects are beginning to use this model; for example, a solar power project in the driest region of Karnataka for which 12,000 acres have been leased at INR 21,000 per acre (USD 350) for 25 years (with inflation adjustments).[18] The annual cost of leasing is about INR 25 crore (USD 4 million). It would have cost between INR 300 and 500 crore (USD 50–80 million) to acquire this land.

Shareholding is a new idea that is a version of the land pooling method, with the major exception that the pooling is initiated by the landowners themselves (led by some prominent local personality or community). In this method, more of the benefits of the land price increase (before and after land improvements) are captured by the landowners. Good examples are in the case studies of Khed and Magarpatta on the Mumbai–Pune Expressway done by Sai Balakrishnan.[19]

But it is vitally necessary to look beyond land acquisition and other forms of land conversion (like pooling and leasing) and consider other significant policy possibilities of India's new political economy of land. Some of the most important of these are outlined in Chapter 9 in this volume by K.P. Krishnan, Venkatesh Panchapagesan, and Madalasa Venkataraman in their discussion of structural, regulatory, and information-driven distortions, and their negative effects on developing a credit market in land in India. They argue that one of the main reasons for the vitality of developed nation economies is their policy structure that transforms a 'dead asset' like land into 'live capital'. They go on to outline a range of policy interventions to unlock the full value of land, something that is necessary for continued economic growth.

Not only are there serious policy issues on land to consider at the national scale as Krishnan, Panchapagesan, and Venkataraman show, there are major issues that operate at the local urban scale and have

---

[18] https://en.wikipedia.org/wiki/Pavagada_Solar_Park.

[19] Balakrishnan, *Shareholder Cities*.

serious implications for urban planning and development. Kala Sridhar discusses two of the most significant of these urban land issues—the FAR (or Floor Area Ratio that determines urban density) and rent control—with two case studies using rare ward-level data in Bengaluru and Mumbai in Chapter 10 in this volume. She shows how strongly interventionist land-use controls in urban India have had counterintuitive effects—removing valuable land from the market and distorting private incentives—and calls for a more clear-headed approach to land-use planning in Indian cities.

In Chapter 11 in this volume, Subhomoy Bhattacharjee focuses on a core paradox on land in India—that state actions themselves create new problems and unleash a range of negative reactions at the scale of both marginal farms and large land blocks that are government owned. This, he argues, is again the case with LARR, the unintended effects of which include problems of price-setting, inefficient welfare outcomes, and corruption.

In Chapter 12, as a bookend to this volume, Amitendu Palit completes the circle with a clear assessment of the serious challenges of converting agricultural land to non-agricultural use, especially after the passage of the new acquisition law (LARR). This law has made the already difficult issue of land conversion close to impossible, so much so that several states—irrespective of ideology—are creating laws to work around it. He concludes that the law has had perverse effects—mainly by making the state an even bigger player and thereby a major hindrance to the development of a well-functioning land market in India.

In the end, it is fair to say that India's new land markets, especially their extraordinary prices, are beginning to generate multiple institutional, community, and individual responses (some of them contradictory). If the national-level response was an old-style, over-inclusive, paternalistic, and purely political new acquisition law that seemed to be oblivious to the market changes that were taking place, local and regional governments are being more imaginative and adaptable (and sometimes regressive). Some state governments appear to be more active, especially of those states in which the demand for land-use change is more insistent. These include Maharashtra, Gujarat, Tamil Nadu, Karnataka, Delhi, Haryana, and Uttar Pradesh (in particular, the region adjoining Delhi). Other states like West Bengal (which has taken a complete 'hands-off' approach to acquisition) appear to be blind or clueless. It is possible that the future of regional development and urbanization in India will hinge on how state governments comprehend and react to the new ground reality.

This new ground reality is that scarcity of land is finally leading to its commodification. Exactly why it is happening now when land has been scarce for decades is a serious question without a clear answer. Not everyone is in favour of commodification. Sai Balakrishnan, for instance, appears to be ambivalent about its distributive impacts, whereas K.P. Krishnan and his associates argue that it may finally provide what the poor farmer needs most: access to credit. Subhomoy Bhattacharjee shows how the state, as the largest landowner, is itself deeply implicated in the land market, to no good effect—a deterrent, really—argues Amitendu Palit.

The question of the state continues to loom large over all land matters. Whether it is through law or policy, the state makes the rules. There is justifiably much discussion on the rules at the national scale: why and how they are framed (Sarkar, Chapter 1 in this volume; Mitra, Chapter 2 in this volume; Sen, Chapter 3 in this volume; and Chakravorty, Chapter 4 in this volume) or not framed, and their large-scale consequences (Krishnan, Panchapagesan, and Venkataraman, Chapter 9 in this volume; Palit, Chapter 12 in this volume). But a case can be made that what matters most at the ground level is how the rules are implemented and received—what the bureaucracy does, what local communities and their leaders do. As Huang and Shin (Chapter 5 and Chapter 6 in this volume, respectively) show, an engaged and responsive state can enable welfare-enhancing land conversion outcomes; as Nair shows (Chapter 7 in this volume), the local state can be ham-handed yet adaptable.

There are many land markets in India, and many local states and bureaucracies and communities. It is necessary to pay attention to them all. Therefore, our call to reframe the land debate in India not only demands that the market be brought back into what is too often an overwhelmingly political discussion, but also that the local state and its operatives be invited to the discourse, and, if at all possible, the national state be disinvited.

PART I

The Challenge of Land

1   Land, Poverty, and Displacement

The Indian Malady

Abhirup Sarkar

There is a general perception that excess population is the main cause of Indian underdevelopment and poverty. The perception is not confined to the man in the street alone. Even policy-makers, entrusted with the task of formulating long-run paths of development, are often inclined to believe that their toil would be substantially saved if the pressure of population could be reduced in the country. The perception is somewhat problematic. How does one know if there is excess population or not? Surely, absolute population figures do not reveal much. To make population figures meaningful and comparable across countries or regions, one must express them relative to some available resources. One resource that is commonly used for this purpose is land. It is indeed common to look at population densities, that is, habitation per unit of land, to determine whether a country is over-populated. Thus, for instance, the available land in the United States (US) is three times that of India while the population is less than one-third. This makes India more than nine times as densely populated as the US. But this difference in population density can hardly explain the difference between the living standards of the two countries. Some European countries like the Netherlands or Belgium, and some Asian countries like South Korea or Japan have comparable population densities to India, but living standards much above the Indian level. On the other hand, there are some African countries which are poor but thinly populated. Population densities are not accurate indicators of development.

In a modern economy, land no longer occupies the important position it used to 200 years ago. While there is very little scope for increasing the land endowment of a country, except perhaps by cleaning up jungles at an early stage of settlement, there is virtually a limitless prospect of growth through capital accumulation. Therefore, ever since the Industrial Revolution, the most important driving force in the process of development has been capital accumulation. Consequently, a much better indicator of development can be had if one looks at population (or the size of the labour force) relative to the physical stock of capital. The capital stock should include not only machines and implements installed in various units, but also public infrastructure. If one considers the volume of population of a poor country relative to its capital stock and compares the ratio with that of rich countries, in general, the former would look overpopulated. Evidently, by this measure, India's population would also appear to be excessive. One can, therefore, argue that our backwardness is caused not so much by our inability to reduce population growth, but more by a low rate of investment and capital accumulation in the past.

Fortunately, of late, Indian policy-planners are becoming increasingly aware of the importance of capital accumulation. In particular, since the last decade of the last century, India has opted for a more open and market-oriented development strategy, which has clearly enhanced the rate of growth of the economy. The services sector, and more recently, the manufacturing sector, have been growing spectacularly, even during a period when the rich countries of the world are passing through a phase of deep recession. One can call this a process of vigorous industrialization. But industrialization and capital accumulation cannot be pulled out of thin air. They involve building of factories and infrastructure; of roads and highways; bridges; seaports and airports; dams and irrigation canals; and also townships, shopping malls, and entertainment centres for the emerging professional class. In a globalized world, no investor would consider investing in the country if basic infrastructure is not available. Clearly, to build all this capital and infrastructure, one needs land, which is in general scarce. In other words, one has to perceive land as a constraining factor to growth and development. How severe is the land constraint?

Broadly speaking, two objections have been raised against an unrestricted use of land for building up industries and infrastructure. First, the transformation of agricultural land to industrial use has been viewed as a likely threat to food security. Second, transformation of agricultural land for the purposes of building industries and infrastructure evicts millions of people from their traditional homes and livelihoods. This displacement often takes place against the will of the displaced, and without proper compensation and rehabilitation. Recently, this development-induced displacement has led to deep social unrest throughout the country, jeopardizing the process of industrialization itself. The purpose of this chapter is to consider each of these aspects of unrestricted land use in the context of a developing country like India.

FOOD INSECURITY AND AGGREGATE SCARCITY OF FOOD

It is certainly a matter of great concern that even after seven decades of independence, at least a quarter of the Indian population lives in poverty. While differences of opinion regarding the exact measure and incidence of poverty might persist, there cannot be any controversy over the fact that a sizable number of Indians still subsist in a state of hunger and undernourishment. Would the transformation of agricultural land into industrial use reduce the supply of food, increase food prices, and worsen the condition of this vulnerable section?

Like in many other less developed countries, poverty and destitution in India are intimately related to the consumption of food. People are placed below the poverty line by virtue of the fact that they do not get enough to eat. The scarcity of food, in turn, shows up in insufficient calorie consumption. Traditionally, therefore, the so-called poverty line is constructed on the basis of calorie intake; people with less than a prescribed level of calorie intake are identified as poor, those with a calorie intake more than the prescribed level are called non-poor.

Scarcity of food can occur due to two distinct reasons. First, the economy may not be in a position to supply the food required to feed its population. This is a situation of aggregate scarcity. In contrast, one can conceive of situations where there is abundance of food in the aggregate, but due to the lack of adequate purchasing power, some sections of the population are unable to acquire enough food. In this second situation, poverty arises due to distributional problems. In what follows, we shall argue that in India, both aggregate scarcity and distributional problems are responsible for the existence of a large number of poor.

First we talk about aggregate scarcity. At the outset it must be pointed out that aggregate scarcity does not necessarily happen when there is a lack of production. Similarly, adequate or near adequate domestic production does not necessarily guarantee that all sections of the population will have enough food. There are countries in the world like Japan, South Korea, or Belgium, which significantly substantiate their domestic production by imports to maintain the overall adequacy of food supply within the country. In 2009, for Japan, domestic production of cereals was only 30 per cent of net imports of cereals. In the same year, for South Korea and Belgium, these figures were 42 per cent and 85 per cent, respectively.[1] Food supply in all these countries has been adequate because these countries had enough purchasing power to supplement their domestic production by imports. There are, on the other hand, countries like India and Bangladesh, where domestic production of food is much higher compared to imports, yet there is an aggregate food scarcity. For Bangladesh, domestic production of cereals was 11 times net imports of cereals in 2009. In India, though there was an overall scarcity of cereals in 2009, there was a net outflow of cereals from the country in the form of net exports amounting to 2.5 per cent of the total domestic production in the same year. Indeed, there was not enough purchasing power in these countries to supplement domestic production by imports. In the case of Bangladesh, imports were inadequate. For India, domestic purchasing power was insufficient to create a large enough market to keep domestic production within the country.

How do we know if there is a problem of food shortage in a country? The traditional method is to look at the consumption of calories. In Table 1.1, we present FAO statistics on per capita intake of calories per day in different countries over the period 2000–9.[2] Though India

[1] FAOSTAT, www.fao.org/economic/ess/ess-fs/ess-fadata/en/#.XKoSL ZgzbIU.

[2] FAOSTAT, www.fao.org/economic/ess/ess-fs/ess-fadata/en/#.XKoSL ZgzbIU.

TABLE 1.1 Consumption of Kcal Per Person Per Per Day in Different Countries during 2000–9

Country/Year	2000	2001	2002	2003	2004	2005	2006	2007	2008	2009
India	2,264	2,227	2,241	2,312	2,240	2,252	2,309	2,344	2,326	2,321
China	2,867	2,878	2,890	2,884	2,912	2,950	2,950	2,957	3,008	3,026
Bangladesh	2,309	2,378	2,359	2,396	2,435	2,417	2,421	2,455	2,376	2,481
Sri Lanka	2,332	2,375	2,351	2,348	2,324	2,378	2,411	2,399	2,448	2,426
Uganda	2,270	2,283	2,340	2,367	2,347	2,334	2,294	2,269	2,261	2,260
Burundi	1,674	1,701	1,704	1,696	1,700	1,674	1,667	1,656	1,604	1,607
Japan	2,902	2,892	2,859	2,851	2,855	2,842	2,793	2,821	2,768	2,723
South Korea	3,090	3,078	3,078	3,059	3,095	3,101	3,124	3,145	3,176	3,200
Belgium	3,724	3,728	3,732	3,724	3,728	3,700	3,706	3,736	3,751	3,721
UK	3,372	3,418	3,437	3,421	3,455	3,437	3,433	3,453	3,453	3,432
Brazil	2,882	2,894	2,929	3,070	3,085	3,081	3,100	3,110	3,177	3,173
US	3,804	3,756	3,829	3,821	3,853	3,799	3,804	3,794	3,733	3,688

Source: www.fao.org/economic/ess/ess-fs/ess-fadata/en/#.XKoSLZgzbIU.

is the focus of our analysis, we have reported the calorie consumption of 12 other countries for the sake of comparison. Among four countries—India, China, Bangladesh, and Sri Lanka—India's performance in terms of calorie intake is the worst. In fact, China's calorie intake is closer to those of Brazil and Japan than to those of its eastern neighbours. Calorie intakes of advanced countries like Belgium, the United Kingdom (UK), or the US are understandably significantly higher. Only very poor African countries like Uganda or Burundi have calorie intakes less than that of India.

In Table 1.2, we present the minimum calorie requirements of different countries as prescribed by the Food and Agriculture Organization (FAO).[3] These requirements vary across countries depending upon the average body mass index (BMI) and other structural and historical features of the population. For India, the minimum calorie intake has

TABLE 1.2　Minimum Kcal Requirement Per Person Per Day in Different Countries as Specified by the FAO

Country/Year	2000–2	2006–8
India	1,760	1,780
China	1,890	1,910
Bangladesh	1,760	1,780
Sri Lanka	1,810	1,800
Uganda	1,710	1,710
Burundi	1,730	1,760
Japan	1,890	1,890
South Korea	1,890	1,900
Belgium	1,980	1,980
UK	1,940	1,940
Brazil	1,840	1,860
US	1,980	1,980

Source: www.fao.org/economic/ess/ess-fs/ess-fadata/en/#.XKoSLZgzbIU.

[3] FAOSTAT, www.fao.org/economic/ess/ess-fs/ess-fadata/en/#.XKoSL ZgzbIU.

been fixed at 1,780 Kcal in 2006–8. Clearly, the per capita availability of calories for each year during 2000–9 satisfies this minimum calorie requirement. From this, can we conclude that India does not have any food shortage? We shall argue that we cannot.

Now, a person can get his calorie requirement from various sources. A quick glance at Table 1.3 will tell us that on an average, Indians obtain a very high percentage of their calorie requirement from the consumption of cereals. Indeed, of the 12 countries for which this proportion is reported in Table 1.3, the percentage of calories obtained from cereals in India is second only to that in Bangladesh. This high percentage comes mostly from the high dependence on cereals of the poorer section of the population. The rich can supplement cereal consumption by other more expensive nutrients which the poor cannot. Therefore, before we can draw any conclusions regarding the adequacy of food availability in India, we must look separately at the availability of cereals.

In Table 1.4, we present the per capita availability of cereals in the 12 countries.[4] The per capita availability is arrived at by subtracting net exports, net purchase of stocks by the government, wastage, seed requirement, animal feed, and the amount going for processed food from production, and then dividing the residual by the population. We find that per capita availability of cereals is higher in India than in all other countries except Bangladesh. But this does not tell us whether this is enough because the dependence on cereals is also high in India. In Table 1.5, per capita availability of cereals is expressed in days rather than years, and apart from the FAO estimates, we present the estimates provided by the Government of India. As we can see, the two estimates are not remarkably different. If we take the average cereal availability over these 10 years, it comes to somewhere between 406 grams and 411 grams per day. The question is: Is this enough?

In 2009, an Expert Group of the Indian Council of Medical Research (ICMR) brought out a report on nutrient requirements and recommended dietary allowances for Indians.[5] The report specified

---

[4] FAOSTAT, www.fao.org/economic/ess/ess-fs/ess-fadata/en/#.XKoSL ZgzbIU .

[5] Nutrient Requirements and Recommended Dietary Allowances for Indians: A Report of the Expert Group of the Indian Council of Medical Research (2009), www.pfndai.com/draft_rda-2010.pdf.

TABLE 1.3 Percentage of Kcal Obtained from Cereals in Different Countries during 2000–9

Country/Year	2000	2001	2002	2003	2004	2005	2006	2007	2008	2009
India	60	60	61	61	61	60	60	58	57	57
China	54	53	52	51	50	50	49	49	48	48
Bangladesh	82	81	83	82	81	79	78	79	79	78
Sri Lanka	52	53	54	55	55	55	52	52	52	55
Uganda	22	20	21	22	22	23	23	22	22	22
Burundi	16	15	15	17	17	17	17	18	19	16
Japan	38	38	38	38	38	38	38	38	38	39
South Korea	49	48	46	44	45	44	44	43	43	44
Belgium	21	21	22	22	23	23	23	23	22	23
UK	25	24	26	26	25	25	25	26	26	26
Brazil	29	31	30	32	32	33	31	31	30	30
US	23	23	22	22	21	22	22	22	22	22

Source: www.fao.org/economic/ess/ess-fs/ess-fadata/en/#.XKoSLZgzbIU.

TABLE 1.4 Per Capita Availability of Cereals (kg/year) in Different Countries during 2000–9

Country/Year	2000	2001	2002	2003	2004	2005	2006	2007	2008	2009
India	147.9	145.1	148.5	155.9	148.6	147.6	150.1	149.7	145.1	143.7
China	162.1	160.2	158.2	155.3	154.2	153.7	152.8	150.9	151.5	151.4
Bangladesh	192.7	196.3	199.5	201.5	200.7	193.8	194	198	190.7	197.5
Sri Lanka	137.9	144.8	144.8	146.4	147.5	149.1	142	142.2	143.2	150.3
Uganda	60.7	56.4	60.5	62.5	63.6	66.3	64.4	61.9	60.6	62.6
Burundi	30.6	29	29.2	32.7	33.6	32.6	31.8	33.6	30.6	34.7
Japan	122.6	120.8	120.5	118.4	117.8	118.3	116.1	116.9	115.1	114.7
South Korea	160.3	158.4	153.6	146.9	148.5	146.1	144.4	143.3	142.2	146
Belgium	107.8	111.9	112.8	112.6	116.5	115.9	116.3	115.9	114.2	117.4
UK	107.9	104.7	114.7	114.6	112.1	113.0	112.5	113.8	115.9	114.7
Brazil	98.8	106.1	105.3	117.5	115.5	117.9	114.7	114.4	114.4	114.6
US	117.6	115.2	112.2	112	110.5	111.2	112	112.7	110.2	108.2

Source: www.fao.org/economic/ess/ess-fs/ess-fadata/en/#.XKoSLZgzblU.

TABLE 1.5 Government of India and FAO Estimates of Per Capita Availability of Cereals (gm/day) in India during 2000–9

	2000	2001	2002	2003	2004	2005	2006	2007	2008	2009	Average
FAO Estimates	405.9	397.5	406.8	427.1	407.1	404.3	411.2	410.1	397.5	393.6	406.1
GOI Estimates	422.7	386.2	458.7	408.5	426.9	390.9	412.8	407.4	394.2	407.0	411.5

Source: www.fao.org/economic/ess/ess-fs/ess-fadata/en/#.XKoSLZgzblU.

that for an Indian adult, a balanced diet requires 2,734 Kcal apart from other nutrients. Therefore, a quantity of 400 grams of cereals per day was recommended for an Indian adult who does moderate work and who can afford to buy other food items like vegetables, fruits, milk products, meat, and fish to supplement his or her diet. Therefore, the 1,780 Kcal requirement specified by the FAO is for mere survival, not for a hearty and healthy life.

These findings would lead us to a number of observations. First, in India, the average per capita calories available per day are less than those specified by the ICMR for a healthy life as is clear from Table 1.1. Hence, in India there is indeed an aggregate shortage of food. Second, as is clear from Table 1.5, even the 400-grams-per-day requirement of the ICMR is not met by cereal availability in some of the years under study, and only marginally met for some other years. Third, for persons who are poor and cannot afford to buy more expensive food items like fruits, vegetables, or milk, the cereal requirement is higher. More so, because these are the people who are usually engaged in hard manual work, and therefore, need more calories than the others. This increases the food shortage problem. Fourth, the ICMR report mentions that 100 grams of rice or wheat in India gives 345 Kcal. Hence, if a poor person wants to get all his daily requirement of 1780 Kcal (prescribed as the minimum requirement by the FAO) through the consumption of cereals alone, he or she needs to consume 516 grams of cereals per day. This is a tall order as far as the current cereal availability in India is concerned.

The National Sample Survey Office (NSSO) of India divides the rural and urban households of the country into 10 groups according to the monthly per capita consumption expenditure (MPCE) of the households. For the year 2009–10,[6] these groups are described in Table 1.6. The average consumption of cereals per person per day for each group in the year 2009–10 is given in Table 1.7. From Table 1.7, it is clear that the requirement of 400 grams of cereals per day of the ICMR is met only by the highest decile group in the rural sector. The upper decile groups of both rural and urban sectors might be supplementing their cereal intake with more expensive nutrients; for the lower decile groups, certainly food is inadequate. In general, therefore, we may conclude that there is aggregate food scarcity in India.

[6] *Level and Pattern of Consumer Expenditure 2009–10*, NSS Report No. 538 (66/1.0/1), National Sample Survey 66th Round (December 2011).

TABLE 1.6 Monthly Per Capita Consumption Expenditure (MPCE) across Decile Classes of MPCE in India, 2009–10

Decile Class of MPCE (Rural)	Upper Limit (INR/ month)	Average (INR/ month)	Decile Class of MPCE (Urban)	Upper Limit (INR/ month)	Average (INR/ month)
0–10	537	452.98	1	753	599.27
10–20	631	584.40	2	926	830.96
20–30	718	675.35	3	1,101	1,011.84
30–40	804	760.79	4	1,293	1,196.08
40–50	895	848.07	5	1,502	1,397.99
50–60	1,001	944.35	6	1,773	1,633.42
60–70	1,133	1,062.93	7	2,097	1,930.96
70–80	1,322	1,220.59	8	2,603	2,329.87
80–90	1,653	1,470.33	9	3,665	3,050.69
90–100	–	2,516.69	10	–	5,863.25
All Classes	–	1,053.64	All Classes	–	1,984.46

Source: *Level and Pattern of Consumer Expenditure 2009–10*, NSS Report No. 538 (66/1.0/1), National Sample Survey 66th Round (December 2011).

FOOD INSECURITY AND THE PROBLEM OF DISTRIBUTION

We just saw in Table 1.7 that for lower decile groups, food is inadequate. In other words, distribution of income matters as far as food entitlement is concerned. One necessary step to reduce food insecurity is to increase the production of food. But even adequate production does not necessarily reduce starvation and hunger. As has been repeatedly pointed out by Amartya Sen and his frequent collaborator Jean Dreze, *entitlement failures* can occur for one or more vulnerable groups, which can compel them to starvation in a period and location of abundant aggregate supplies.[7] Entitlement failures can occur due to various reasons of which the most important is low purchasing

[7] Amartya Sen, *Poverty and Famines: An Essay on Entitlement and Deprivation* (Oxford: Clarendon Press, 1981); Amartya Sen, *Commodities and Capabilities* (Amsterdam: North Holland, 1985); Jean Dreze and Amartya Sen, *Hunger and Public Action* (New Delhi: Oxford University Press, 1990).

TABLE 1.7 Distribution of Consumption of Cereals (gm/day/person) across Decile Classes of MPCE in India, 2009–10

Sector/Class	0–10	10–20	20–30	30–40	40–50	50–60	60–70	70–80	80–90	90–100	All Classes
Rural	342.5	358.6	368.7	378.5	377.6	381.2	390.4	387.8	392.2	404.1	378.3
Urban	307.1	318.5	318.3	322.1	318.6	322.9	308.1	312.4	306.3	290.2	312.4

Source: Level and Pattern of Consumer Expenditure 2009–10, National Sample Survey 66th Round.

power. A region or state might be producing adequate food, but that does not mean everyone in that region would have enough purchasing power to buy that food. If purchasing power is inadequate, food produced in the region will flow out to other places where purchasing power is high, keeping the poor in the food-producing region hungry. By a similar argument, a region producing little food but much else is always capable of buying food from outside and avoiding starvation. As indicated by Tables 1.1 and 1.4, Japan, South Korea, and Belgium fall in the class of these countries. In short, per capita food production might not have high correlation with the level of poverty and starvation.

In Table 1.8, per capita production of food grains for the year 2003–4, which was available for consumption in 2004–5, are presented for 28 Indian states along with poverty ratios in each state for 2004–5. There are states like Chhattisgarh and Madhya Pradesh where relatively high per capita production coexisted with high poverty. Again, there is Kerala where in spite of extremely low per capita production, poverty level was low. Finally, there are states like Punjab and Haryana, where high per capita production coincided with low poverty, as one would expect.[8] From all this it is clearly hard to conclude that increased per capita production of food grains leads to lower levels of poverty and starvation *per se*.

ON INCREASING THE PRODUCTION OF FOOD GRAINS

We can identify two ways of solving the problem of food security in India. First, one can try to increase the production of food grains within the country. Second, by increasing the pace of industrialization, one can

---

[8] When poverty is regressed on per capita food grain production taking into account all the 28 states, the coefficient of the regressor turns out to be small but negative ($\beta = -0.00461$), and significant ($t = 7.87$). However, the two outliers in terms of per capita production, Punjab and Haryana, are certainly responsible for this overall negative relationship. If we drop these two states, then the relationship becomes positive ($\beta = 0.015624$), and significant ($t = 2.88$). In both cases, however, the R square values are small, being 0.04 in the first case, and 0.06 in the second case.

TABLE 1.8   Food Grain Production Per Capita in 2003–4 and Poverty in
Indian States in 2004–5

State	Gross Food Grains Production Per Capita (gm per day)	Poverty
Andhra Pradesh	474	15.8
Arunachal Pradesh	582	17.6
Assam	390	19.7
Bihar	346	41.4
Chhattisgarh	796	40.9
Goa	336	13.8
Gujarat	335	16.8
Haryana	1,606	14.0
Himachal Pradesh	605	10.0
Jammu & Kashmir	376	5.4
Jharkhand	279	40.3
Karnataka	326	25.0
Kerala	48	15.0
Madhya Pradesh	673	38.3
Maharashtra	277	30.7
Manipur	427	17.3
Meghalaya	264	18.5
Mizoram	407	12.6
Nagaland	534	19.0
Orissa	510	46.4
Punjab	2,655	8.4
Rajasthan	811	22.1
Sikkim	480	20.1
Tamil Nadu	187	22.5
Tripura	454	18.9
Uttarakhand	524	39.6
Uttar Pradesh	678	32.8
West Bengal	521	24.7
All India	535	27.5

Source: planningcommission.gov.in/data.

shift people from the overburdened agricultural sector to the newly
emerging industrial sectors, thereby increasing their purchasing power so
that they can buy food from the world market. As we shall see below, both
endeavours need additional land, and involve displacement of the poor.

First we consider the constraints to increasing agricultural production. In Table 1.9, we find acreage and yield of food grains (that is, cereals and pulses) in India since the beginning of the present century. As for acreage, recalling that the total land of India is 328.7 million hectares, and noting that the numbers within brackets represent the percentage of total land devoted to the production of food grains, one has to come to the conclusion that a fairly high proportion of Indian land, more than one-third, is engaged in food-grain production. Moreover, though the yield of cereals has exhibited a threefold increase over the last five decades, productivity of Indian agriculture in cereals is still far below the world standard. World Development Indicators of the World Bank reveal that in terms of yield of cereals (kilograms per hectare), India ranks 90 among 172 countries. Comparison of Indian yields with those of some densely populated countries of the world can be made from Table 1.10.

From all this, a basic fact about production conditions in India becomes immediately clear. It becomes apparent that output in India is reached mainly through high acreage, and not so much by achieving a high level of productivity. This would imply that if there is a marginal fall in acreage, due to land being taken away from food-grain production and put to industrial use, a compensating increase in productivity is eminently feasible to keep the total output constant. This is particularly feasible for the following reason. A significant part of

TABLE 1.9 Acreage and Yield of Food Grains in India

Year	Acreage* (million hectares)	Yield (kg/hectare)
2000–1	121.0 (36.8)	1,626
2001–2	122.8 (37.3)	1,734
2002–3	113.87 (34.58)	1,535
2003–4	123.45 (37.49)	1,727
2004–5	120.1 (36.5)	1,652
2005–6	121.6 (37.0)	1,715
2006–7	123.7 (37.6)	1,756
2007–8	124.1 (37.7)	1,860
2008–9	123.2 (37.4)	1,898

*Percentage of total available land given within brackets.
Source: https://rbi.org.in.

TABLE 1.10   Yield and Acreage of Cereals in Some High Population-Density Countries in 2005

Country	Yield (kg per hectare)	Acreage (percentage of total available land)	Density (population/ sq. km)
South Korea	6,283	10.8	492
Netherlands	8,154	5.2	395
Belgium	8,414	10.5	340
Japan	6,028	5.3	337
India	1,684	36.7	329
UK	7,229	11.9	247

Source: World Development Indicators 2009 (Washington, DC: World Bank).

Indian agriculture is characterized by fragmented landholdings. In fact, due to fragmentation of land, it often becomes difficult to use modern mechanized technology and large-scale farming in the agricultural sector, and this is one major hindrance to increasing productivity. With industrialization, as more and more people shift to the industrial and services sectors, pressure on agricultural land will fall, and average land-holding will increase as some of the emigrants going away from the rural sector will sell off their land to the people who would stay back. An increase in average landholding in the agricultural sector would, in turn, help consolidate fragmented pieces of landholding, which would make possible the use of modern technology, and exploit the advantages of increasing returns to scale.

As we have argued above, there is an urgent need for increasing food production in India. In fact, increased aggregate food production can help the vulnerable in two important ways. First, a rise in the supply of food makes the public distribution system easier to function. If output is high, the government can procure stocks with relative ease and distribute it to poor areas. This is one important way in which regional differences in purchasing power can be counterbalanced.

Second, given the uncertainty in the world market for food grains in terms of supplies and prices, it is prudent to ensure enough food supply from within the country. In other words, as an insurance against this uncertainty, it is necessary to increase the domestic production of food. However, since India is a vast country with large regional variations in the productivity of agriculture, it is always possible to locate food production in areas where land is fertile, and build up the new industries on less fertile land. This will cause minimum harm to agricultural production. Therefore, if regions can specialize according to their comparative advantage, efficient specialization can be implemented within the country, and enough less fertile land can be released for building up industries, services, and infrastructure without jeopardizing internal food security.

PRODUCTIVITY, IRRIGATION, AND DISPLACEMENT

One of the conclusions that emerged from the previous section is that to reduce hunger and to ensure food security, it is necessary to increase the level of productivity of Indian agriculture. Many policy-makers believe that the most formidable hindrance to increasing productivity is the lack of irrigation and the dependence on natural rainfall for cultivating the soil. In 2007–8, only 54.3 per cent of the total land of the country producing cereals was irrigated. The corresponding figures for pulses and total food grains were 16.2 per cent and 46.8 per cent, respectively.[9] It seems that substantial productivity gains can be had by extending irrigation to unirrigated land. Now, irrigation can come from ground water, ponds, and small as well as big dams. India is a large builder of dams, and in terms of building dams ranks third in the world (after China and the US). Of the total irrigated land, dam irrigation accounted for 38 per cent in 2000, and of the fourfold increase in the production of food grains between 1951 and 2000, up to a quarter took place in dam-irrigated areas.[10] Again, confining oneself to dam-irrigated areas alone, attempts have been made to ascertain how much of the increase in production is due to mechanization, and how

[9] *Statistical Year Book of India, 2018*, Ministry of Statistics and Programme Implementation, Government of India.

[10] See H. Thakkar, 'Assessment of Irrigation in India', in World Commission on Dams, *Dams and Development: A New Framework for Decision Making* (London: EarthScan Publications, 2000), http://www.internationalrivers.org/files/world_commission_on_dams_final_report.pdf; Satyajit Singh, *Taming the Waters: The Political Economy of Large Dams in India* (New Delhi: Oxford University Press, 2002).

much due to dam irrigation. The results have varied widely: The World Commission on Dams attributes 10 per cent of the increase to dam irrigation while Gopalkrishnan has estimated the contribution to be 50 per cent.[11] The Commission has observed that the economic internal rates of return of irrigation dams all over the world have varied from more than 12 per cent to less than 4 per cent, with the return being more than 10 per cent in the majority of cases under study. Therefore, it is generally felt that dam irrigation has played an important role in increasing agricultural production in general, and food-grain production in particular, in India as well as in the rest of the world.

But apart from increasing production, building of dams has led to massive displacements. Again, estimates of the extent of displacements vary widely. According to the World Commission on Dams, an average Indian dam displaces 31,340 persons, and submerges 8,748 hectares of land. Estimates of total persons displaced by the construction of dams over the second half of the last century varied from 16 million to 40 million. The World Commission on Dams has estimated that around 40–50 per cent of the displaced people belonged to the traditionally disadvantaged tribal community.[12] The report also reveals that the situation in other less developed countries of Asia, Africa, and Latin America with respect to dam-related displacement is similar. In other words, in other less developed countries also, the burden of displacement is borne disproportionately by tribals and other historically disadvantaged groups.

More recently, even the economic desirability of large dams has been questioned. Duflo and Pande, on the basis of data spanning from 1970 to 1999, evaluate the performances of Indian dams.[13] When a dam is built, its effect is felt both upstream, where it is built (the so-called catchment area), and downstream (the so-called command area). When a dam is built, a large part of the catchment area is submerged, salinity of water in the area increases, and diseases like malaria spread

[11] E. Gopalkrishnan, 'ICOLD Comment on Report of World Commission on Dams' (2000), www.dams.org/report/reaction/icoldindia.htm.

[12] Gopalkrishnan, 'ICOLD Comment on Report of World Commission on Dams'.

[13] Esther Duflo and Rohini Pande, 'Dams', *Quarterly Journal of Economics* 122, no. 2 (2007): 601–46.

out from still water. The command area, on the other hand, gains from the construction of the dam. Not surprisingly, Duflo and Pande find that after the dam is built, in the catchment area, agricultural production does not increase but there is a rise in poverty. On the other hand, there is an increase in agricultural production and a decline in poverty in the command area. However, on the basis of their estimates, the authors conclude that the net financial gain from large dam construction is marginal, about 1 per cent, and it is associated with a rise in poverty in the aggregate.

One problem, however, remains with the existing cost–benefit approach. This is the problem of evaluating the benefits of increasing agricultural production, consequent to the building of a dam, in terms of market prices. Market prices are determined by forces of demand and supply. Prices are low either because supplies are high or because demand is low. If supplies are already high and consequently prices are low, the market price would rightly indicate that the benefit from an extra unit of production is low. However, this is not necessarily the case when prices are low because of low demand. If demand is low just because the society has a low preference for the product, then again a low market price rightly indicates low social benefit. But if low demand is due to poverty or low purchasing power, then the consequent low market price does not necessarily mean that the social benefit from an extra unit of production is low.[14]

This is especially true for food grains in a country like India. As Amartya Sen has argued, famines and starvation often occur due to entitlement failures which in turn may be caused by low purchasing power.[15] In fact, starvation can coexist with low local prices. In such cases, more production might be required in spite of prices being low.

Be that as it may, one cannot deny that big dams in India have displaced millions. This poses the uncomfortable question as to whether we can hurt one group of Indians, who are usually poor and vulnerable, to feed the rest of the countrymen, many of whom are also poor. If we cannot then the inevitable question is: How are we to increase

[14] Abhirup Sarkar, 'Development, Displacement and Food Security: Land Acquisition in India', in *Oxford Handbook of the Indian Economy*, ed. Chetan Ghate (New York: Oxford University Press, 2012).

[15] Sen, *Poverty and Famines*.

productivity in the agricultural sector? One possibility is to switch to other forms of irrigation like small dikes, wells, or ground water. However, several analysts argue that these alternative forms of irrigation are cost ineffective, and are incapable of meeting the huge demand for irrigation in a vast country like India, where rainfall is highly fluctuating.[16] The other way out is mechanization. Here again there are two major problems. First, mechanization might require more inputs like fertilizers, electricity, and high-yielding variety (HYV) seeds which, in turn, are complementary to irrigation. In other words, mechanization might not be feasible without adequate irrigation. Second, as we have argued above, landholding in Indian agriculture is fragmented, which itself is a big hindrance to mechanization. Therefore, large-scale irrigation and consolidation of landholdings, both of which seem essential for increasing agricultural productivity, would imply displacement, and the displaced persons need to find occupations elsewhere. For making this possible, industrialization seems to be the only feasible option. But then, industrialization itself requires land. We are indeed faced with a non-trivial problem of choice.

DISPLACEMENT DUE TO INDUSTRIALIZATION

Though land has not found its proper place in the theoretical literature on economic development, the problem of industrialization leading to displacement is by no means new. Indeed, history is full of such examples. The enclosure movement in pre-Industrial Revolution England probably gives the earliest instance where landlords, the village gentry, and a newly emerging merchant class, aided by royal power, evicted people from their traditional land and livelihood.

By the beginning of the seventeenth century, England had almost come out of her demographic debacles of earlier centuries caused by bubonic plague epidemics commonly known as Black Death, and by sustained agricultural repression. The growing population was creating pressure on land. At the same time international trade, especially maritime trade, opened up new possibilities. In particular, the market

---

[16] Asit Biswas and Cecilia Tortajada, 'Development and Dams: A Global Perspective', *Water Resources Development* 17, no.1 (2001): 9–21; B. Dhawan, *The Big Dams: Claims and Counter Claims* (New Delhi: Commonwealth, 1989)

for manufactured woollen cloth was expanding at a spectacular pace. This, in turn, increased the demand for land further, not for cultivation but for grazing sheep.

The emerging wool trade led to deep-rooted social and economic changes. While land was relatively plenty and labour was relatively scarce throughout the fifteenth up to the mid-sixteenth century, leading to low rents and high wages, from the middle of the sixteenth century the scenario reversed, leading to land shortage, labour surplus, high rents, and declining wages. Landlords, who found it difficult to get either tenants or labour to cultivate land and as a consequence left the land fallow, could now profitably convert land into grazing grounds for their sheep. The result was the enclosure movement.

Prior to enclosures, there was common land in the manor, which was under a medieval system of land tenure, and which was cultivated on a communal basis. Following the enclosure movement, the common land in the manor was divided up and fenced in, and the peasant farmer who held his tenure either by copy (a document recorded in the manor court) or by unwritten custom was evicted. This was an extremely convenient arrangement for yeoman farmers and gentlemen sheep rearers, who could have a huge saving on labour costs, for one shepherd and his dog could now do the work of half a dozen men who had previously tilled the same land. The arrangement was further supported by urban cloth manufacturers and merchant adventurers, who bought fleece from sheep raisers, took it to cottagers for spinning and weaving, and finally sold the finished product to Europe.

According to some estimates, 2.76 per cent of the total land was enclosed, and 50,000 persons were forcefully evicted. This was no small number in a country where the total population around 1600 AD was about four million. As Sir Thomas More pointed out in his famous book *Utopia* (1515), the enclosure movement and the consequent eviction of tillers from land led to the large-scale conversion of farmers into a mass of vagrant labour, gradually turning into beggars and thieves. The same sentiment was expressed by Polanyi more than 400 years later in his book *The Great Transformation* (1944).[17]

---

[17] Karl Polanyi, *The Great Transformation: The Political and Economic Origins of Our Time* (Boston: Beacon Press, 2001 [1944]).

The enclosure movement changed British society permanently and beyond recognition. The timeless quality of village life was gone forever. The immediate beneficiaries of this change were, of course, the village gentry and the newly emerging merchant class. The sufferers were the evicted peasants, who lost not only their livelihood, but also their age-old knowledge of cultivating land. Even the conditions of those who found employment in the newly emerging industrial sector did not improve for almost 100 hundred years.[18]

That was just a beginning. Instances of expropriation and displacement abound in the history of world development since the Industrial Revolution. In the US, during 1870–1910, vast areas of land were acquired by the state governments to subsidize private enterprises in railway construction, milling, and mining. State legislation supported these acts. As we have already pointed out, in Brazil, Argentina, Mexico, Panama, Colombia, as well as other places on the American continent, and in Indonesia, Malaysia, Thailand, Pakistan, Bangladesh, and other Asian countries, the building of dams alone has displaced millions of people. The interested reader is referred to the report of the World Commission on Dams for further details.[19] The important point to note is that be it the Chakmas of the Chittagong Hill tracts in Bangladesh, the Waimari–Atroari tribe of Northern Brazil, or the native Indians of the Missouri River basin in the US, the traditional dwellers of the soil have been the main victims of development-related displacement. Clearly these displacements have increased poverty.

A more recent account of development-led displacement can be found in the story of the unprecedented industrial growth in China. As is well known, reliable data on China is not easy to come by, especially on controversial issues like eviction and land riots. According to a paper contributed to the World Commission on Dams, since the 1950s, 10 million people have been displaced in China due to hydraulic and hydroelectric projects alone.[20] According to more radical estimates,

[18] Eric Hobsbawm, *The Age of Capital, 1848–1875* (New York: New American Library, 1975).

[19] World Commission on Dams, *Dams and Development: A New Framework for Decision Making* (London: EarthScan Publications, 2000), http://www.internationalrivers.org/files/world_commission_on_dams_final_report.pdf.

[20] Jun Jing, 'Displacement, Resettlement, Rehabilitation, Repatriation and Development: China Report', Contributing Paper to World Commission on Dams (2000).

between 1992 and 2005, 20 million farmers were evicted from agriculture due to land acquisition, and between 1996 and 2005, more than 21 per cent of arable land in China has been put to non-agricultural use.[21] An article by Joseph Kahn in *The New York Times* of 20 January 2006 quotes a government statement admitting that 5 per cent of the total arable land in China has been grabbed for non-agricultural use between 1998 and 2004. Another statement made by China's Ministry of Public Security acknowledges that 87,000 public order disturbances broke out in the country in 2005 alone, a large chunk of which were due to land grabs.

India is not free from the curse of development-related displacement either. Since Independence, between 20 and 40 million people have been displaced on account of dam construction alone. According to a recent report of the World Commission on Dams, 4.5 million hectares of forest land has been submerged by dam construction in India between 1980 and 2000, and on an average, the construction of each dam has displaced more than 31,000 people. Notably, about half of the displaced people are tribals or Adivasis, the oldest dwellers of the soil, though their proportion in the Indian population is not more than 8 per cent. Apart from dams, other developmental projects have also displaced a sizeable number of people from their land and livelihood since Independence. According to figures quoted in the Tenth Five Year Plan, mining has displaced 2.5 million, of whom 52.2 per cent are tribals; forest conservation has displaced 0.6 million, of whom 75 per cent are tribals; industry has displaced 1.25 million, of whom 25 per cent are tribals; and infrastructure building including road, bridge, and airport construction has displaced 0.5 million, of whom 25 per cent are tribals.

Of late, India has embarked upon a path of market-oriented industrialization. Evidently this will require a lot of natural resources, and among other things, transformation of agricultural land to non-agricultural use. This will lead to evictions, riots, and losses of human lives, like it has in China. This would suggest that more serious research needs to be steered towards the issue of development-related displacement and displacement-induced poverty.

[21] Bhaskar Goswami, 'Special Economic Zones: Lessons from China' (2007), countercurrents.org.

***

In this chapter, we have argued that to reduce poverty, there is a serious necessity of increasing the availability of food in India. This, in turn, may be done in two different ways. First, one may try to increase the domestic production of food. Since the proportion of total land already under cultivation is very high in India, there is no further scope for increasing acreage. On the other hand, the level of productivity in India is very low. Hence there is a lot of scope for increasing productivity in Indian agriculture. The problem is that the main channel through which productivity may be increased is large irrigation. But the chapter argues that large irrigation projects in the past have led to massive displacement of the poor, and have actually increased poverty. The other way out is industrialization. Through industrialization, the poor may be given employment in the urban sector, which would increase their ability to buy food from the international market. Indeed, this is what food deficit countries like Japan and South Korea have been doing. But again industrialization involves transformation of agricultural land, and hence loss of home and livelihood for the poor.

In other words, for a vastly populated country like India, land emerges as a major constraint to development and removal of poverty. The problem of displacement is not a new issue, but more research needs to be done on displacement in the context of poverty alleviation.

2 The Dilemma of Balancing Growth and Social Justice

A Retrospective View on Agriculture, Land, and Rural India

Subrata Mitra

In the demanding years following a century and half of economic stagnation during British colonial rule, India changed progressively from a colonial, agrarian economy into one where services and manufacturing have overtaken agriculture in terms of sectoral contribution to the gross domestic product (GDP). During this transition, the country's democratic institutions have held their own. Electoral competition has generated the political momentum that reinforces reform, without upsetting the democratic and judicial due processes. Many had maintained that radical changes in India's economy and welfare would be unlikely as long as both were constrained by the liberal democratic constitution and the capitalist mode of production.[1] India has defied

---

[1] Barrington Moore was most closely identified with this line of reasoning. See Barrington Moore, *Social Origins of Dictatorship and Democracy: Lord and Peasant in the Making of the Modern World* (Boston: Beacon Press, 1966). This pessimistic prognosis was sustained by Myrdal's concept that the 'soft state' would be incapable of taking urgent measures to reform the economy. See Gunnar Myrdal, *Asian Drama: An Inquiry into the Poverty of Nations* (New

those prognostications. However, the robust confidence in long-term, sustainable growth that one finds in sections of India's corporate sector has its critics. The diversity of India's political economy and the complex role of the state in balancing growth and justice call for a nuanced analysis. This chapter analyses how India has coped with the dilemma of 'democratic' land reforms—a key component of the Indian model of economic growth versus social justice—and the policy paralysis that has often resulted.

THE ECONOMY, POST-INDEPENDENCE POLITICS, AND POLICY

Those with painful memories of the Bihar famine and humiliating import of food grains from abroad in the 1960s will take comfort from the fact that contemporary India is self-sufficient in food, has large reserves and a good public distribution system (PDS) to cope with natural disasters, and is even able to export food without jeopardizing food security at home. India's food grain production has increased from around 50 million tonnes in 1950–1 to 285 million tonnes in 2017–18.[2] Food production has far outpaced population growth.

Though the contribution of agriculture to the GDP has come down to below 15 per cent, India still remains a predominantly agricultural country, with close to half the population still dependent upon agriculture for work and income. Most people engaged in agriculture are marginal peasants with small holdings or no land at all. The majority of these peasants draw their livelihood from rain-fed, subsistence

---

York: Pantheon, 1968). A new generation of commentators has taken Nehru to task for his failure to take hard decisions about crucial economic and political reforms on land, foreign trade, and entrepreneurship at a time when South East Asian states like South Korea were making their own breakthrough. See Gurcharan Das, *India Unbound: From Independence to the Global Information Age* (New Delhi: Penguin, 2002). The dilemma of democratic reform in a postcolonial context and the potential for neo-institutional solutions have been discussed at length in Subrata Mitra, *Politics in India: Structure, Process and Policy* (London: Routledge, 2017).

[2] See *Economic Survey of India 2013–14*, https://www.ibef.org/industry/economic-survey-2013-14.

agriculture. Those fortunate enough to have made a breakthrough into mechanized agriculture, in the absence of a system of comprehensive crop insurance, remain vulnerable to the risks of bankruptcy, as one can see in the cases of farmers' suicides, widely discussed in the Indian media.[3] In addition, there are widespread inadequacies in infrastructure, especially the transport and communication network.

These are long-standing gaps. Upon assuming power after Independence, the Congress government worked to create a mixed economy in which the state engaged in building infrastructure and key industries. The private sector was to focus on manufacturing and distribution. National planning, conceived by technocrats but under the guidance of key members of the central cabinet and the state chief ministers who constituted the National Development Council, was charged with balancing the needs of growth with the imperative of social justice and redistribution. Besides introducing new notions of entitlement, the Constitution promised a life of dignity and economic opportunity to the underprivileged, particularly to the former untouchables and the tribal population.

But while development was high on the agenda, it was not placed outside the political arena as occurred in 'developmental' states[4] like Japan or South Korea, where development policy became the preserve of a technocratic and financial elite. In India, not only was economic

---

[3] Farmer suicides in the country spiked by over 40 per cent between 2014 and 2015. While 2014 saw 5,650 farmer suicides, the figure crossed 8,000 in 2015; the state that registered the sharpest jump is Karnataka—from 321 in 2014 to more than 1,300 in 2015, the third-highest among all states. Other states that saw more than 100 farmer suicides in 2015 are Madhya Pradesh and Chhattisgarh; some states, such as Bihar, Jharkhand, West Bengal, and some North-eastern states, did not witness any farmer suicides. Sources: *Accidental Deaths & Suicides in India 2015*, National Crime Records Bureau, Ministry of Home Affairs, Government of India (2015); S. Rukmini, 'India's New Farm Suicides Data: Myths and Facts', *The Hindu*, 24 July 2015, http://www.thehindu.com/data/indias-new-farm-suicides-data-myths-and-facts/article7461095.ece.

[4] See Chalmers Johnson, *MITI and the Japanese Miracle: The Growth of Industrial Policy, 1925–1975* (Stanford, CA: Stanford University Press, 1983) for the concept of the 'developmental' state, where the agenda of economic growth was above and beyond the pale of partisan politics.

policy an integral part of national and regional politics, but institutions like the Planning Commission, and the adoption of a mixed economy as the framework of development, guaranteed that economic policy was not shifted outside public control and democratic accountability. This model of democratic planning was further reinforced by a number of reforms that protected the rights of workers, extended electoral democracy up to the village councils (as part of the integrated panchayati raj system that connects the locality to the region and the Centre), removed intermediary rights of large landlords (zamindars) and princely rulers, and attempted to introduce land ceilings and cooperative farming.[5]

As a consequence of these policies, Indian development during the early decades after Independence, though unspectacular in any specific area, nevertheless strengthened the country's modern political institutions, and eliminated famine and reliance on imported food in the span of one generation (despite a doubling of the population in that time). The first gains came in the 1950s through an expansion of the area under cultivation and irrigation works. The 1960s saw accelerated agrarian production through a series of technical innovations like seeds of a high-yielding variety (HYV), new pesticides, chemical fertilizers, and precise information on weather and market conditions. This 'Green Revolution' transformed India from a net importer of food to a country that was self-sufficient.

Through the 1970s, the government developed a complex system of storage and market interventions called 'Food Procurement' at guaranteed prices to maintain a steady flow of food production and supply to consumers. India's food policy, which evolved in reaction to chronic food shortages that created huge human, financial, and political costs, particularly during the Vietnam War when the Indian position was

---

[5] The Indian model of development most identified with Nehru has had sharp critics like Barrington Moore (*Social Origins of Dictatorship and Democracy*) who has described it as 'an out-an-out failure' (p. 395), 'rather long on talk and quite short on accomplishments' (p. 407). For a positive evaluation of Nehru's model of development see Jyotirindra Dasgupta, 'India: Democratic Becoming and Combined Development', in *Democracy in Developing Countries*, eds Larry Diamond, Juan Linz, and Seymour Martin Lipset (Boulder, CO: Lynne Rienner, 1989).

opposed to that of the United States (US), finally started yielding dividends in the 1980s. India's system of food security became so resilient that even the severe droughts of 1987 did not lead to significant fluctuations in the prices of agricultural commodities.[6]

The modernizing leadership around Nehru intended to raise the general standard of living and protect the country's newly won freedom through a mixed economy. This model, based on import substitution, planned economic development, and a policy of self-reliance did not leave much scope for integration with the international market. In part, this reflected a certain Gandhian nostalgia for *swadeshi*—the consumption of goods made in India—but also a basic distrust of the capitalist West. Bitter memories of colonial rule underpinned this deep antipathy.

FROM FOOD SHORTAGES TO THE GREEN REVOLUTION

The Green Revolution is seen by the advocates of agrarian modernization as a paradigm shift from subsistence farming to modern agriculture, involving the use of high technology and credit, in an integrated production system stretching from farming, distribution, and financing, to agri-business. It prompted a gradual shift from the classic problems of Indian agriculture—fragmentation of holdings, insecurity of tenure, uneconomic units of production, excessive dependence on the monsoon, low unit yield, and rack renting—to a modern agrarian economy. Scholarly opinion on the nature, extent, and durability of the Green Revolution remains divided.[7]

[6] See John Wall, 'Foodgrain Management: Pricing, Procurement, Distribution, Import and Storage Policy in India', Occasional Papers, World Bank Staff Working Paper No. 279 (Washington, DC: World Bank, 1978), 88–9.

[7] Is the 'Green Revolution' yet another example of the Indian penchant for catchy slogans, heady rhetoric, or as Barrington Moore put it, an Indian habit of being tall in talk and short in action? As Francine Frankel says: 'The phrase "green revolution" has all the qualities of a good slogan. It is catchy; it simplifies a complex reality; and most important, it carries the conviction that fundamental problems are being solved. Agriculture, it suggests, is being

A number of factors led to a re-appraisal of the agrarian policy in the 1960s. Massive food deficits in the early 1960s, famine in Bihar, and the difficulty of obtaining food from abroad without compromising the sovereignty of the country forced planners to question the marginal role accorded to agriculture in the overall economic model of India. Besides the half-hearted attempt to abolish *zamindari*, no comprehensive plan for agrarian development had been made in the immediate post-Independence years. Agriculture was seen only as an adjunct to the industry-infrastructure-led, mixed-economy-based planning process. Public intervention, in the case of agriculture, extended only to control over production, distribution, and financing. Planners believed in the Indian model which allocated the 'commanding heights' of the economy to industry, based on planning, and the trickle-down of resources and new ideas from the tip of the pyramid to the masses, based on the felt-needs model.[8] Agriculture, following the classic model of growth drawn from European experience, was seen as the source of surplus capital, to be invested for greater industrialization, not the object of transfer of investment from industry. In India's federal system, agriculture is a state subject, and as such, beyond the scope of central planning. In consequence, not much direct central investment was made, except in the form of initiatives like community development, zamindari abolition, land-ceiling legislation, and cooperatives.

As India went through its first three Five Year Plans, the main approach to agricultural development was dominated by two

---

peacefully transformed through the quiet workings of science and technology, reaping the economic gains of modernization while avoiding the social costs of mass upheaval and disorder usually associated with rapid change.' Francine R. Frankel, *India's Green Revolution: Economic Gains and Political Costs* (Princeton, NJ: Princeton University Press, 1971),V.

[8] 'The basic assumption of the Community Development Programme ... has been that the Indian peasant would of his own free will, and because of his "felt needs" immediately adopt technical improvements, the moment he was shown them' (Moore, *Social Origins of Dictatorship and Democracy*, 401). Moore explains why it did not happen that way. '"Felt needs" in any society are in large measure the product of the individual's specific social situation and upbringing. They are created; not simply the gift of nature' (Moore, *Social Origins of Dictatorship and Democracy*, 402).

irreconcilable goals: 'The economic aim of achieving maximum increases in agricultural output to support rapid industrialization; and the social objective of reducing disparities in rural life'.[9] One of the most difficult dilemmas arose from the obvious economic advantage of concentrating scarce inputs of improved seeds, fertilizers, pesticides, and equipment in irrigated areas of the country, where they could be expected to bring the greatest returns in output. Indeed, the selection of the first community projects in 1952 was guided by this consideration. They were allocated only to districts with assured water from rainfall or irrigation facilities. Almost immediately, however, serious social objections were raised to the practice of 'picking out the best and most favourable spots' for intensive development, while the largest part of the rural areas was left economically backward. Within a year, the principle of selective and intensive development was abandoned. The Planning Commission announced a programme for rapid all-India coverage under the National Extension Service and Community Development Programme, with special attention to backward and less favoured regions.

The social goal of reducing disparities also influenced the selection of methods of agricultural development. The planners were inclined to give only secondary importance to the introduction of costly modern inputs as a means of increasing agricultural productivity. Instead, they devised agricultural development programmes based on 'intensive cultivation of land by hand—and improving conditions of living in rural areas through community projects, land reforms, consolidation of holdings, etc.'[10] Indeed, the planners' strategy for agricultural development rested on the capacity of the Community Development Programme to mobilize more than 60 million peasant cultivators for participation in labour-intensive agricultural production programmes and community works, including the construction of capital projects. The crux of the approach—the major inducement for the greatest effort on the part of small farmers—was the promise of social reform, held out by large-scale initiatives for institutional change. The highest priority was assigned to rapid implementation of land reforms, including security of tenure,

[9] Frankel, *India's Green Revolution*, 3.

[10] P.C. Mahalanobis, *Talks on Planning* (Bombay: Asia Publishing House, 1961), 69.

lower rents, transfer of ownership rights to tenants, and redistribution of land. Meanwhile, state-partnered village cooperatives were created to fortify small farmers with cheap credit facilities and economies of bulk purchase and sale of agricultural commodities.[11]

In retrospect, it was probably inevitable that a development strategy requiring extensive land reform and institutional change as preconditions for success should meet with powerful opposition from landed groups; and that in a political democracy, where landowning interests are heavily represented in the legislatures, this resistance should manifest itself in a go-slow approach towards agrarian reforms. By the early 1960s, most legislation on tenancy reform and ceilings on land ownership had not been effectively implemented. Yet in the absence of agrarian reform it proved impossible to provide attractive incentives to the majority of small farmers for participation in labour-intensive agricultural production programmes.

There was, in fact, no dearth of policies. Following the recommendations of the Balwantrai Mehta Committee in 1957, panchayati raj was adopted as the overall administrative structure for rural development. The Congress party passed a resolution in 1959 proclaiming a modified version of cooperative farming as a goal for the future. But as Moore notes drily, the implementation was not at the same level as the rhetoric. The Community Development Programme took no note of the reality on the ground: '...official instructions to program officials in contact with the villagers made no mention of caste, property relationships, or surplus manpower in the village—in other words, any of the real problems.' Though local elections, in some parts of the country, had some effect on weakening the authority of hereditary social notables, as a whole, Moore found the experiment a dismal failure.[12]

---

[11] The problem from the Second Five Year Plan onwards was that there were significant organizational changes but little investment. This approach continued till the mid-1960s. See Francine R. Frankel, *India's Political Economy: The Gradual Revolution (1947–2004)* (2nd edition, New York: Oxford University Press, 2005).

[12] 'Fundamentally, the notion of village democracy is a piece of romantic Gandhian nostalgia that has no relevance to modern conditions. The premodern Indian village was probably as much of a petty tyranny as a petty republic; certainly the modern one is such. To democratize the villages without altering property relationships is simply absurd.... Finally, the real sources

As a matter of fact, as early as 1958, lagging growth rates in the agricultural sector became a serious limiting factor for the overall rate of economic advancement. By the middle of the Third Plan, years of relatively static production levels (1960–1 to 1963–4) convinced the Planning Commission that continuation of shortfalls in agriculture would jeopardize the entire programme of industrial development. Of necessity, some retreat from the social goals of planning had to be contemplated. In 1964, therefore, the planners announced 'a fresh consideration of the assumptions, methods, and techniques as well as the machinery of planning and plan implementation in the field of agriculture'.[13] Two major departures from previous policy were initiated as a result of this re-evaluation:

1. Development efforts would be subsequently concentrated in the 20–5 per cent of the cultivated area where supplies of assured water created 'fair prospects of achieving rapid increases in production'[14]; and
2. Within these areas, there would be systematic effort to extend the application of science and technology, including the adoption of better implements and more scientific methods to raise yields.

In October 1965, the new policy was put into practice when 114 out of 325 districts were selected for an Intensive Agricultural Areas Programme (IAAP). A model for the new approach already existed in the 15 districts taken up under the pilot Intensive Agricultural Development Programme (IADP), beginning in 1961. Initially pioneered by the Ford Foundation, the IADP emphasized the necessity of providing the cultivator with a complete 'package of practices' in order to increase yields, including credit, modern inputs, price incentives, marketing facilities, and technical advice.

---

of change, the factors that determine the fate of the peasantry, lie outside the boundaries of the village. Through the ballot box and through their pressure on state and national politics, the peasants can do something about those questions, but not within the framework of village politics.' Moore, *Social Origins of Dictatorship and Democracy*, 394.

[13] Hem Chandra Lal Das, *Agricultural Efficiency in India: An Inter-regional Analysis* (New Delhi: Mittal, 1993), 299.

[14] Frankel, *India's Green Revolution*, 5.

The economic rationale of an intensive agricultural areas pro-gramme was considerably strengthened by the technical breakthrough reported from Taiwan and Mexico in 1965 of the development of new varieties of paddy and wheat seeds with yield capacities of 5,000–6,000 pounds per acre—almost double the maximum potential output of indigenous Indian varieties—and also by the development at Indian research stations in the late 1950s of higher-yielding hybrid variet-ies of maize, *bajra*, and *jowar*. In all cases, the availability of controlled irrigation water and the application of the package of modern inputs, especially very high doses of chemical fertilizer and pesticides, were essential preconditions for realizing maximum yield potential. By November 1965, the Food Ministry was ready with a full-blown ver-sion of the new strategy: In essence it called for the implementation of an HYV Programme in districts that had already been selected for intensive development under the IADP and IAAP schemes, following the same extension concepts embodied in the package programme.

The missing link in the chain of agrarian production was soon iden-tified in the person of the 'progressive farmer'.[15] These link men, with some measure of literacy, contacts with the world outside, and enough status within the local society to engender the trust of their fellow men, caught the imagination of the bureaucracy responsible for pro-ducing results. Soon, in various parts of the country, the liaison of the progressive farmer and the VLW (Village Level Workers, also known as *gram sahayaks*) produced a critical mass which cut through the local 'bottlenecks'—to use a favourite term of Indian planners—and the Green Revolution was underway. The statistics of food production tell the story of the agrarian political economy in a nutshell. By 1966–71, food production had increased massively. In 1972–5, bad weather conditions led to the decline of food production to 101 million tons, causing imports of 7.41 million tons. By 1975–6, however, thanks to good weather, production went up to 116 million tons.[16]

The Green Revolution was marked by the introduction of a new group of actors—the 'bullock capitalists'—into the political arena. These agrarian entrepreneurs—often farmers from the middle and

---

[15] Frankel, *India's Political Economy*, 197–8.

[16] Subrata Mitra, *Politics in India: Structure, Process and Policy* (London: Routledge, 2011), 154.

backward castes—quickly learnt to combine their numbers, social networks, and political contacts to garner power in local institutions. They formed farmers' parties and movements to promote their interests: in subsidized energy, loans, agrarian inputs, and slowing down the trends towards collective farming.[17]

Overall, the Green Revolution is considered to have produced a mixed legacy. On the positive side, it certainly contributed to the improvement of the quality and quantity of food supply, self-sufficiency, and the PDS.[18] On the negative side, increasing volumes of agrarian subsidies have become a drain on the public exchequer. The increasing prosperity of the rural rich and their lifestyles based on conspicuous consumption have widened the gap between the rural haves and have-nots, exacerbating class conflict, both of the Right and the Left. However, *kisan* movements cutting across regions and social classes mitigated the worst possibilities. Finally, with technological progress came its pathology—in the form of growing pollution, terminal decline of local resources, and degradation of local biodiversity.[19] Most of all, many on the Left remain sceptical that agrarian problems of productivity can be solved through technology and capital investment without giving serious attention to land reform.

THE DILEMMA OF DEMOCRATIC LAND REFORM

The postcolonial state and popular democracy, with their commitment to fundamental rights—to property on the one hand, and social justice and empowerment of marginal groups on the other—have been both

---

[17] At least in the short run, the dominant landed castes were successful in manipulating the majority of subsistence cultivators and landless workers, fragmented by vertical factional structures, to capture the village institutions. They increased their access to scarce development resources and strengthened their position as strategic intermediaries, linking local markets and power structures to the state and national economic and political systems. Frankel, *India's Political Economy*, 200.

[18] Murray J. Leaf, 'The Green Revolution in a Punjab Village, 1965–1978', *Pacific Affairs* 53, no. 4 (Winter 1980/1981): 617–25, 620.

[19] Vandana Shiva, *The Violence of the Green Revolution* (London: Zed Books, 1991), 200.

a stimulant for and a constraint on land reform in India. In view of its centrality to India's political discourse, land reform is one of the most discussed problems of India's political economy. Every major author or policy-maker active in this field has felt obliged to respond to the reality of millions of insecure, indebted peasants under the constant threat of a bad monsoon, illness, and pestilence, by offering a diagnosis and a solution. Unlike capital, land is static, concrete, and visible, giving the impression of being more accessible to political control from above. As such, land reforms, already on the agenda of the British colonial government and the Congress movement that opposed it, have attracted the attention of all shades of reformers. This section defines the concept, summarizes the measures taken, engages in an evaluation, as well as develops broad questions about the political gains and economic costs of land reforms in India.

Though the rhetoric of land reform in India has consistently revolved around the slogan of 'land to the tiller', in practice, land reform has meant something different from the transfer of property rights to the poor. The broad range of meanings grouped together under this generic concept has included legislation aimed at (i) tenancy reform, (ii) abolition of intermediaries, (iii) ceiling on landholdings, and (iv) consolidation of landholdings. On the whole, however, India's land reforms have involved only limited efforts at land redistribution, implemented mostly through ceilings on landholding. Agrarian land belongs to the state list under the federal division of powers. As such, state-level legislation aimed at regulating tenancies, improving tenurial security, and reducing the power of absentee landlords and intermediaries has been the most common method.

Independent India inherited a complex and diverse system of land tenure from the British raj. In 1947, Indian agricultural land was administered under three systems: zamindari (57 per cent),[20] ryotwari (38 per cent), and *mahalwari* (5 per cent).[21] Between the zamindars and the tillers, there was a layer of intermediaries numbering up to 50 in some places. These zamindars used to collect several times the intended revenue, though they had a fixed tax to pay to the government which

---

[20] Zamindars were also known as *talukdars*, *jagirdars*, and *malguzars*.

[21] Pushpendra Kumar and B.K. Sinha, *Land Reforms in India: An Unfinished Agenda* (Vol. 5, New Delhi: Sage, 2000).

was permanently determined as land tax back in 1793 (leading to rack renting).

Life for most people engaged in agriculture under colonial rule was precarious at best. In addition to the exploitation by landlords and intermediaries, the moneylender was always in the background. What was left to the actual cultivator after the claims of various superior rights holders were satisfied was subject to the collection of unpaid debt by moneylenders. The mechanism for enforcement of this withdrawal of the great bulk of the product from the primary producers was provided by the new body of written law, the courts, the police, the promulgation of ordinances, and so forth.

The main goal of land reform after Independence was to generate both growth and justice in agriculture, as indeed in all areas of the economy. This meant, in practice, to establish a direct relationship between the state and the cultivator, and to provide the latter with optimal conditions of production. Following Independence, the autonomy to initiate legislation and enforce the new order, in view of the fundamentally political nature of the enterprise and the diversity of conditions prevailing in Indian states, ensured that there would be significant regional variations. The success of land reforms depended on a number of factors. In states like Kerala, there was a measure of success because the potential beneficiaries—the rural masses—were highly organized, politicized, and capable of fighting for their rights. However, as subsequent developments showed, under the watchful eyes of the Supreme Court defending the right to property, and the Central Government making sure that political unrest would not reach a level which would obstruct lawful governance, the autonomy of the states to undertake land reforms was quite limited.[22]

---

[22] The Uttar Pradesh Zamindari Abolition Act, 1950, which covered the most populated state of India, was the first act on this subject. However, the manner in which it was passed severely compromised its objectives. The bill was under preparation for a very long time. Since it was debated for years, it gave enough opportunity to most zamindars, talukdars, and other intermediaries to sell or dispose of their landed property to near relatives, family-controlled trusts, or through *benami* (false-name) transactions. Subsequently, the Act was struck down by the Allahabad High Court as ultra vires. Consequently, the Constitution was amended, for the first time, in early 1951, and the Act was incorporated in the Ninth Schedule of the Constitution itself, and only

Following Independence, all the states in the country enacted legislation for the abolition of zamindari. The main consequence of zamindari abolition was the creation of a new class of 'rich peasants', mostly from the cultivating castes, who took advantage of the provision for resumption of land under 'personal cultivation' (that is, transfer of property—*bhumidari*—rights to superior tenants) to displace tenants-at-will (inferior tenants). In addition, the capital that they gained through compensation helped them further consolidate their hold on agricultural operations, and went into the making of the Green Revolution and bullock capitalists at a later stage.

Lloyd and Susanne Rudolph describe the key policies that evolved in response to the double challenge of growth and justice, resulting from the interplay of local conditions and state and central legislation.[23] The first policy regime, characterizing the agricultural strategy of the Nehru era (1947–64), consisted of land reform (mostly, the abolition of intermediaries between the state and the peasant) and the centrally sponsored and funded Community Development Programme that saw the whole village as its unit of operation and strived to improve general welfare. The second strategy, geared mostly towards improving agrarian productivity through new technology, which began soon after Nehru's death, continued till 1971. The third strategy, focused on basic needs and income redistribution, began with Indira Gandhi's *garibi hatao* (abolish poverty) appeal in the 1971 parliamentary and 1972 state assembly elections. The fourth was launched in 1977 by the Janata Party's agrarian-oriented government. It emphasized rural employment and asset creation, paving the way for agri-business. However, the rhetoric of income redistribution and nostalgia for agrarian socialism continued to be voiced by vote-hungry politicians and intellectuals of the Left, and got a boost with the return of Indira Gandhi to power in 1980. More recently, in the wake of liberalization and the scramble for setting up new industries, land acquisition became the new focus of

---

thereafter became enforceable. By that time, the political context had changed significantly.

[23] Lloyd I. Rudolph and Susanne Hoeber Rudolph, *In Pursuit of Lakshmi: The Political Economy of the Indian State* (Chicago: The University of Chicago Press, 1987), 314.

the politics of land. The contemporary situation is a combination of all these initiatives and strategies.

In the absence of a large-scale rural exodus and of manufacturing to absorb surplus labour, a consensus has grown that India will need to solve the problem of rural poverty on land itself. Hence, 'land reform' continues to be on the political agenda still, after seven decades of independence. However, the consequences of various forms of land reform have left their stamp on the rural landscape. The attempt to abolish intermediaries has generated some surplus land that has been redistributed. One of the overall consequences of reforms appears to have been a general reduction in the number of large holdings and an increase in the number of small holdings.

As such, while reforms might have had some effect on poverty reduction, it is not clear if they have also contributed to the growth of agrarian productivity. As a production input, land has a particular limitation. Beyond a specific point, at a given level of technology, investment in agriculture reaches a point of decreasing marginal productivity. While industry also has a point beyond which additional investment brings in lower levels of output, factories can take in more investment than agriculture before diminishing returns set in. Besides, the technological environment in factory production is more dynamic, justifying the case for investment to be made on a regular basis.

The debate between the advocates of land reforms and agri-business as the better solution for India has intensified in recent years. The First Five Year Plan (1953) expressed the commitment to redistributive land reforms in terms of a recommendation to the state to 'reduce disparities in wealth and income, eliminate exploitation, provide security for tenants and workers, and finally, promise equality of status and opportunity to different sections of the rural population'.[24] These sentiments have been echoed by all successive plan documents. The fact that *implementation* turned out to be the fatal weakness in the causal chain built into the structure and process of plans did not deter the Planning Commission, given an opportunity, from coming up with similar recommendations. The key point here remains that, thanks to democratic empowerment and India's half-hearted land reforms, the

---

[24] Planning Commission, *First Five Year Plan* (Publications Division, Ministry of Information & Broadcasting, Government of India, 1953), 178.

message of a right to ownership, if not the capacity to make a profit out of the little parcels of land, has certainly spread all over India. However, this has also created the phenomenon of 'poor' landowners—people owning small parcels of land—who cannot put their land to profitable use, either because they do not have the means or because they do not see the need and hold on to their land merely as an investment, letting it lie fallow rather than renting it out, for fear of losing ownership altogether.

The debate on land reform has now become a part of the larger issue of the pace of liberalization of the economy. Some suggest that a more rational strategy for India's agrarian policy would be to create legal mechanisms that would facilitate renting out, so that one can retain tenancy in a rational and efficient form, while trying to avoid its exploitative dimensions. Seen from this angle, Indian agriculture can be positioned not necessarily as a drain on her economy but as a potential strength.[25]

RURAL POVERTY AND INDIA'S 'NEW' POLITICAL ECONOMY

The issue of continuing and large-scale rural poverty brings back, once again, the core problem of India's political economy, namely, growth versus redistribution. Many critics of the Indian model of development consider the continued existence of mass poverty as evidence of the shortcomings of Indian democracy and the political economy of development. Others point in the direction of the relative improvements in India's infrastructure, GDP, and rate of growth as a sign of progress. In theoretical and methodological terms, mass poverty raises issues of great complexity, including problems of

[25] Once agricultural capitalism gains legitimacy, the next step would be to think of land as *convertible*, depending on the *market opportunity*, and to let the logic of the market spread into lucrative fruits, vegetables, and other cash crops like cashew nuts. The Indian producer can then link up with the international market in a competitive way. India can ignore the 'niche-marketing' strategy at her own peril. However, as the successful resistance to the acquisition of agricultural land for special economic zones (SEZ) in West Bengal shows, the case for land rights of small peasants is far from lost.

politics and public policy against the moral issue of poverty in the midst of plenty. The issue raises a host of questions—specific to the Indian case—as well as problems of cross-cultural significance. First and foremost among these is how successful India has been in reducing poverty.

Though there is some controversy between Indian and external measurements, the fact remains that the poverty ratio has radically come down from nearly half the population to little over a quarter in the span of about two decades. In terms of numbers, since liberalization began, India has been able to reduce the number of people under the poverty line by over 100 million (see Figure 2.1). In contrast to China, where the combination of authoritarian policies and the expansion of manufacturing has achieved the breakthrough, in India, the progress has been achieved through the policies of redistribution and market forces.

Modest by the standards of the tiger economies of East Asia or China, India's achievements nevertheless question the pessimistic predictions of Moore that saw no possibility of a breakthrough for the country within the political and technological constraints that prevailed at

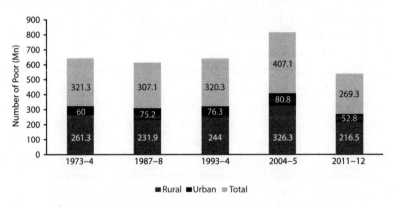

FIGURE 2.1   Population in Poverty, 1973–4 to 2011–12 (in millions)

Source: Tata Services Limited, Department of Economics and Statistics, *Statistical Outline of India 2007–8* (Mumbai, 2008), 235.

Note: Up to 1993–4, revised data are based on Planning Commission. The figures for 2004–5 and 2011–12 are based on the Tendulkar Methodology.

Independence.[26] Similar sentiments led Dandekar and Rath, at the
peak of the period of the populist rhetoric of Indira Gandhi, to suggest that poverty alleviation needed higher taxation and employment
generation through public works.[27] True, the new agrarian technology
that made the Green Revolution possible has certainly increased the
manoeuvring room of poor democracies struggling against mass poverty. Still, India has yet to lift a lot of people out of poverty, particularly
in the countryside. This population tends to have low human capital,
and is dependent, to some extent, on subsidies of various kinds for
their basic survival. Consequently, the radical politics and populist policies of vote-hungry politicians have found a niche in these sections of
the Indian population.

As a matter of fact, the struggle between the market and the state—
driven by the concern for social justice and populist politics—has been
characteristic of Indian development right from the outset. India's
five year plans directed public funds towards private enterprise and
infrastructure building, not employment generation. Nehru's model—
import substitution, industrialization, modernization of agriculture, and
planning—was based on the 'felt needs' and the trickle-down theories
of development. Zamindari abolition was followed by less enthusiastic
but not very effective land reforms. Cooperative village management
became the preferred jargon. By the late 1960s, the land situation was
getting polarized. Bullock capitalists on the one side and radicalized
peasantry on the other were producing an environment many thought
to be ripe for a Maoist revolution.

The splits among the communist parties and the rise of Naxalite
violence and political instability in many Indian states indicated the
deeper problems of the Indian model of development. The revolution
by the peasants did not materialize. What followed instead was a spate
of radical legislation, nationalization, and some overblown promises
under the 20-point programme, for example, land to the landless,
homestead land, and target-group programmes. These measures were
introduced by Indira Gandhi during the 21-month Emergency in the
mid-1970s. Many of these social-democratic policies were put on hold

[26] Moore, *Social Origins of Dictatorship and Democracy*, 410.

[27] V.M. Dandekar and Nilakantha Rath, 'Poverty in India', *Economic &
Political Weekly* VI, nos 1 and 2 (1971): 25–7, 29–48, 106–46.

when the Janata Party came to power after the end of the Emergency and the fall of Mrs Gandhi. Rich peasant parties dominated. Then came the stagnation of the late-1970s, and finally, the 'half-hearted' liberalization of the mid-1980s. Current poverty policy straddles between the target approach, subsidies, special election-oriented policies of state governments, and the programmes launched by non-governmental organizations (NGOs) and activist groups.

The poor in India have neither disappeared nor formed themselves into a political party or movement, but continue to exist as a 'demand group' whose presence is a brake on rapid and radical liberalization.[28] These demand groups have expressed themselves through sporadic violence, which has spurred the state—acting through the union, state, and local governments; central agencies; and NGOs—to generate anti-poverty policies and programmes. Following Independence, a Centre-dominated developmental model and a centralized federal system operated in a complementary fashion. The Constitution provided for several methods to transfer resources from the Centre to the states, such as assigning in full the net proceeds of certain taxes and duties like stamp duties, duties on toilet and medicinal preparations, estate duty on non-agricultural property, duties of succession to property other than non-agricultural land, and taxes on railway fares and freight; compulsory sharing of certain taxes like income tax; and permissive sharing of taxes like excise. Two conflicting principles govern these transfers: Should the productive and leading groups and regions be rewarded, or should the poor and lagging groups and regions be helped? Once again, we are faced with the dual challenge for the political economy in the context of a poor, postcolonial, democratic state which must balance the conflicting principles of accumulation and legitimacy.

The policies of liberalization which were launched in 1991, to start dismantling the draconian rules of the command economy, required a new regime—informal arrangements among sets of actors—to provide

[28] For an analysis of the concept of demand groups, see Rudolph and Rudolph, *In Pursuit of Lakshmi*, 247–58. As key actors in Indian politics, demand groups add a radical edge to India's parliamentary democracy. See Subrata Mitra, 'Democracy's Angry Crowds: Civil Society and Legitimacy in India', in *Seven Decades of Independent India*, eds Vinod Rai and Amitendu Palit (Gurgaon: Penguin Viking, 2018), 189–200.

coordination in a rapidly changing financial environment. By scaling down the involvement of the state in the developmental process and thereby reducing the functions of the Central Government, the process of liberalization risked generating opposition from the poorer state governments, which were dependent on central grants and subsidies. However, in practice it has not been so. Rob Jenkins even argues that part of the momentum for further liberalization actually comes from India's regions. The removal of subsidies and hand-outs has not produced an anti-reform coalition of Left parties, which must have been aware of the lack of popular support for reform. However, the effective management of the transition from the command economy to the market economy has helped India avoid the chaos that blighted liberalization in the post-communist states of Eastern Europe and Russia.[29] Still, the question remains: How to develop the economy, incentivize productivity gains, as well as secure distributive justice simultaneously? That poverty will continue to be a salient issue in the deliberations over economic policy in the foreseeable future is more than likely.

It is in the background of this stock image of mass poverty and dismal record with regard to indicators of human development that one can understand the pressing need for action. One solution has come in the form of the Mahatma Gandhi National Rural Employment Guarantee Act, 2005 (MNREGA) that is much discussed, and has achieved an iconic status among the legislative initiatives of the United Progressive Alliance (UPA) government, and has been retained by the successor National Democratic Alliance (NDA) government,

---

[29] Rob Jenkins, citing the case of windfall profits arising out of the ending of the monopoly of the Karnataka coffee board over the entire coffee crop, shows how in the new environment where the state government and provincial elites can make money, rather than ganging up on the Central Government, state governments have started competing against one another in order to enhance their incomes. Their ability to adapt themselves to the new political economy has further delinked states from one another—contributing to the pattern of 'provincial Darwinism' that has reduced the effectiveness of resistance among state-level political elites. The potential for Centre–state conflicts has thus been transformed into inter-state competition for investment by Indian and multinational capital. See Rob Jenkins, *Democratic Politics and Economic Reform in India* (Cambridge: Cambridge University Press, 1999), 132–3.

indicating yet another special feature of Indian democracy—policy continuity—despite party turnover.

The annual budget for the financial year that the NDA government presented in February 2016 to India's parliament provides some insights into how the state seeks to reconcile the exigencies of growth and need for short-term welfare, linked to the chances of re-election.[30] The UPA government had already set the trend of relating the budget to political exigencies. Measures to accelerate growth and respond to the financial crisis were supplemented with attempts to promote long-term investment and short-term welfare. For example, the allocation for Bharat Nirman, a rural infrastructure development plan, was raised to INR 313 billion, and the National Rural Employment Guarantee Scheme was to be implemented in all districts of the country with a budget provision of INR 160 billion. The government committed itself to increasing funds for education, and undertaking institutional measures to boost exchange-traded currency and bond markets. In response to the crisis affecting India's farming sector which reportedly led to 17,000 farmers' suicides in 2007, the government allocated the sum of USD 15 billion as a one-off loan waiver for farmers.

The 2016 budget of the NDA continued the trend of supporting rural interests in terms of continuing financial support for MNREGA, and instituting a comprehensive crop insurance scheme (the Pradhan Mantri Fasal Bima Yojna)[31] while providing some incentives to middle-class and corporate interests as well. Financial inclusion plans like the opening of bank accounts for sections of the population which were outside the formal financial sector (the Jan Dhan Yojna) were an innovative policy.[32]

---

[30] The statistics are taken from the *Economist Intelligence Unit* country report on India (April 2008), 11.

[31] Similar to China and the US, the Pradhan Mantri Fasal Bima Yojna has an 80 per cent contribution by the government in favour of farmers. Maharashtra has already implemented the scheme from 1 April 2016. See Vinod Rai, 'The Pradhan Mantri Fasal Bima Yojana: India's New Safety Net for Farmers', ISAS Brief No. 432 (June 2006).

[32] http://timesofindia.indiatimes.com/budget-2016/union-budget-2016.

STILL SEEKING BALANCE

India's experience with the political economy of development helps us respond to the paradox that Barrington Moore pointed out. Towards the end of his magisterial study of paths to economic growth and modernization, he drew on the case of India to emphasize the dilemma of development in transitional societies that choose the democratic path. 'A strong element of coercion remains necessary if a change is to be made.' Since democracies do not permit the kind of coercion and economic squeeze that the extraction of surplus requires, the result could only be a 'peaceful paralysis'. He said, 'Barring some technical miracle that will enable every Indian peasant to grow abundant food in a glass of water or a bowl of sand, labor will have to be applied much more effectively, technical advances introduced, and means found to get food to the dwellers of cities.' As he saw it, the choice was between painful reforms or economic stagnation as the 'price of peaceful change'.[33] This prediction, as we have seen in this chapter, has not come through in the Indian case.

The political context and the technological environment in which the initial design of India's political economy evolved have changed substantially over the course of the past decades. The dismantling of India's command economy and the revolution in the technology of communication, particularly the internet, have helped India jump into the ranks of the main players in this field. Harnessing these new technological inventions has been possible because of the innovative capacity of India's entrepreneurs, following liberalization of the economy and the steps taken by the government for a closer integration of India with the global market. New technologies of communication have helped India make a breakthrough into service industries.

With regard to agriculture, India, like other developing countries, has had access to the fortuitous invention of the HYV—the high-yielding variety 'miracle seed'—which made the breakthrough in food production possible in the 1960s. However, poverty still persists, and the dilemma between the need for rapid growth and the imperative of social justice still marks the process of development in India.

---

[33] All quotes in this paragraph are from Moore, *Social Origins of Dictatorship and Democracy*, 410.

The combined processes of electoral mobilization, positive discrimination, judicialization, and political movements have succeeded in providing the necessary economic space to those who have fallen out of the safety net of the welfare state in the face of the sustained assault of the policies of liberalization. Even the radical advocates of liberalization agree on the importance of the state as the careful observer and the site of political negotiation among competing groups, and most important of all, as the arbiter of the authoritative allocation of values. As a result, the state continues to be a key player in development in its capacity as regulator. Progress in the agrarian sector can be accelerated by transforming the popular mind-set about land as 'identity' to land as 'capital'. With this changed attitude towards land, a breakthrough in the agrarian sector is conceivable through skills development, investment in infrastructure, and incentives for innovation.

The contradictions between growth and distribution remain as deeply rooted as ever, if not more egregiously so, with the rise of families with great wealth. Going forward, we can expect a process of incremental change—with policies that fully satisfy neither advocates of growth nor redistribution—as Indian democracy and its large, poor, rural electorate continue to force its political leaders to seek balance and compromise.

3   Debating Land

The Indian Parliament and the Question of Land

Ronojoy Sen

Land is one of those rare issues that has animated Indian Parliament, and been intensely debated from the 1950s to contemporary times. One of the key elements of the very first amendment to the Indian Constitution, passed by the Provisional Parliament in 1951, was related to land reform and the abolition of zamindari or large landholdings. In response to court rulings that declared zamindari abolition laws unconstitutional, Jawaharlal Nehru and the Indian National Congress reacted by inserting article 31A in the Constitution, which stipulated that nothing in the fundamental rights could be used to strike down laws for the appropriation of property. The most important component of the First Amendment was, however, article 31B, which created the Ninth Schedule where legislation could be put and made immune from judicial review. Thirteen land reform acts were placed in the schedule.

This chapter analyses the parliamentary debates on land, beginning with a brief summary of the Constituent Assembly deliberations; an analysis of the First Amendment debates; and subsequent parliamentary interventions, including the Right to Fair Compensation and Transparency in Land Acquisition, Rehabilitation and Resettlement Act (LARR) passed in 2013, and continuing to the Bharatiya Janata

Party (BJP) government's attempt to amend the 2013 Act. The chapter examines three broad questions: How has the issue of land, landownership, land reform, land acquisition, and property been framed over time in parliament? How much have contemporary politics influenced the debate? What have been the recurrent themes as well as radical departures in the debates on land?

It is argued that three broad phases can be identified in the parliamentary interventions on land. In the first phase in the 1950s and 1960s, 'property' was a much-maligned word, and land reform was on top of Nehru's and the Congress' agenda. During the second phase, the courts were cast as the defenders of the right to property and compensation, and enemies of land reform and parliamentary supremacy, which eventually culminated in the state of emergency imposed by Prime Minister Indira Gandhi (1975–7). In the third phase, by the late 1980s, land reform had slipped off the radar. The state's power to acquire land had expanded greatly, and protests against big projects became common. Beginning in the 2000s, land and compensation were back on the agenda, and the government of the day felt the need to craft a new land policy. No one now was willing to challenge the current legislation for fear of appearing 'anti-farmer'. Though the BJP, after coming to power in 2014, was keen to amend parts of the 2013 legislation, it too was constrained by the fear of appearing to be anti-poor and anti-farmer.

THE CONSTITUENT ASSEMBLY

It is commonly accepted that the 1935 Government of India Act was the template for the Indian Constitution. Prior to the 1935 Act, the report of the Joint Committee on Indian Constitutional Reform had stated its opposition to including a section on fundamental rights. However, it recommended that 'some general provision should be inserted in the Constitution Act safeguarding private property against expropriation, in order to quiet doubts which have been aroused in recent years by certain Indian utterances'.[1] The 'Indian utterances'

---

[1] H.C.L. Merrilat, *Land and the Constitution of India* (Bombay: N.M. Tripathi, 1970), 41.

being referred to were the demands of the Congress, from the 1920s onwards, of abolition of zamindaris and large landholdings. These sentiments would come to the fore during the Constituent Assembly debates as well as during the debates on the First Amendment.

Clause 1 of section 299 of the 1935 Act stated: 'No person shall be deprived of his property in British India save by authority of law.' Clause 2 of the Act said:

> Neither the Federal nor a Provincial Legislature shall have the power to make any law authorizing the compulsory acquisition for public purposes of any land...unless the law provides for the payment of compensation for the property acquired and either fixes the amount of compensation, or specifies the principles on which, and the manner in which, it is to be determined.

Like many provisions of the 1935 Act, the first two clauses of section 299 were present in the Indian Constitution, adopted in 1950.

The provisions on property were fiercely debated in the Constituent Assembly, primarily because of the Congress' desire to abolish zamindaris and other intermediary tenures. Indeed, article 31 (originally article 24 of the draft Constitution), the key article on property, took two and a half years to sort out. The debate was over three things: amount of compensation to be given when the state took over property; whether zamindars should be treated as a special category; and the final authority to decide on compensation. Nehru was on record saying, 'I doubt if there are many other articles which have given rise to so much discussion and debate...'[2]

On 22 April 1947, when the Advisory Committee took up the Rights Sub-committee's draft clause on property, it was the question of 'just compensation' that exercised the members. On the occasion Patel said: 'If the word "just" is kept...every case will go the Federal Court. Therefore, "just" is dropped.'[3] The matter did not, however, end there and it took over two years for the issue to be settled. Granville Austin has documented how both Nehru and Patel wanted to abolish

---

[2] Constituent Assembly Debates (CAD) IX (New Delhi: Lok Sabha Secretariat, 1967), 1192.

[3] Granville Austin, *The Indian Constitution: Cornerstone of a Nation* (New Delhi: Oxford University Press, 2000), 88.

zamindaris, but differed on the question of compensation. It must also be kept in mind that the debates were taking place in the backdrop of bills to abolish zamindaris, which were pending in the United Provinces (later Uttar Pradesh), Bihar, and Madras.

When Nehru moved the adoption of the article on 10 September 1948, he called it a 'compromise' solution to the various approaches: 'It [the draft article] may not meet the wishes of every individual who may like to emphasize one part of it more than the other. But I think it is a just compromise and it does justice and equity not only to the individual but to the community.'[4] Nehru further made clear the distinction between land acquisition for 'public use' and measures of 'social reform':

> If property is required for public use it is a well-established law that it should be acquired by the State by compulsion if necessary, and compensation is paid and the law has laid down methods of judging that compensation…But more and more today the community has to deal with large schemes of social reform, social engineering, etc., which can hardly be considered from the point of view of that individual acquisition of a small bit of land or structure.[5]

Nehru also declared that the courts did not come into the picture in determining compensation: 'Naturally, the judiciary comes in to see if there has been a fraud on the Constitution or not. But normally speaking, one presumes that any Parliament representing the entire community of the nation will certainly not commit fraud on its own Constitution and will be very much concerned with doing justice to the individual as well as the community.'[6] Using language that would surface in the debates on the First Amendment, Nehru warned: 'It is obvious that no court, no system of Judiciary, can function in the nature of the Third House, as a kind of Third House of Correction.'[7]

Members such as Alladi Krishnaswami Ayyar and K.M. Munshi threw light on some of the technicalities of the draft clause. Ayyar pointed out, 'The expression "just" which finds a place in the American and in the Australian Constitutions is omitted in Section 299 of the

[4] CAD IX, 1193.
[5] CAD IX, 1192.
[6] CAD IX,1193.
[7] CAD IX,1195.

Government of India Act 1935 and in Article [31].[8] Munshi clarified, 'The Parliament is to judge in each case as to what is fair and equitable and whether the principles laid down are calculated to yield compensation, fair and equitable…'[9]

The principal clause of article 31 (or article 24 in the draft Constitution), as it was adopted by the Constituent Assembly, was very similar to section 299 of the 1935 Act. One major difference in clause 2 was that it now applied to property 'taken possession of or acquired for public purposes' and was no longer limited to 'compulsory acquisition'. Clauses 4 and 6 also protected any state legislation on abolition of zamindaris from judicial intervention. Keeping in mind the legislation in the United Provinces, Bihar, and Madras, article 31(4) said that a bill pending in a state legislature 'shall not be called in question in any court on the ground that it contravenes the provisions of clause (2)'.

While the question of compensation and who should determine it greatly exercised the framers, the provision in article 19 (1)(f), which gave citizens the right to 'acquire, hold and dispose of property,' was approved without much discussion as was assigning of land as a state subject. These would prove to be contentious in future.

THE EARLY AMENDMENTS

Soon after the Constitution was adopted, the zamindari abolition laws were challenged in court. One of the first challenges came from Kameshwar Singh, maharaja of Darbhanga, who during the Constituent Assembly debates, had denounced article 31 as a 'vicious principle' because it allowed 'virtual expropriation of private property'.[10] Even as the Patna High Court held the Bihar Land Reforms Act, 1950 invalid on the ground of violating article 14, which guarantees equality before the law, the Congress and Nehru introduced the First Amendment Bill to 'take away the question of zamindari and land reform from the purview of the courts'.[11] Incidentally, the

---

[8] CAD IX, 1272.
[9] CAD IX, 1299.
[10] CAD IX,1271.
[11] *Lok Sabha Debates*, 10 May 1951.

two other zamindari abolition laws were upheld in Uttar Pradesh and Madhya Pradesh. A new clause, 31A, was inserted to protect a 'law providing for acquisition by the State of any estate' from being deemed invalid on the ground that it violated a fundamental right. Further, a Ninth Schedule to the Constitution was created under article 31B to protect land reform laws from judicial intervention. The Bihar Land Reforms Act was one of the pieces of legislation listed in the Ninth Schedule.

The debate on the First Amendment, particularly with regard to land, pitted one of the finest parliamentarians from the opposition, Shyama Prasad Mookerjee of the Jan Sangh, against Nehru. Mookerjee pointed out some of the contradictions in the Congress' position:

> In article 31A you say that in future any law by any Legislature in re-spect of acquisition of estates will become good law notwithstanding the fact that it contravenes any provisions in the Constitution…you pass your Constitution, provide for certain safeguards and then say you can pass a law and even though that law is inconsistent with the provisions of the Constitution, still it will become good law.[12]

He added, 'If you feel today that zamindaris should be abolished with-out compensation, be straightforward and say so and amend article 31…You leave article 31 as it is and you include an article 31A and also an article 31B which are nothing but instances of "constitutional monstrosity".'[13]

In his reply, Nehru emphatically defended the amendments to article 31 on the grounds of the social revolution that the Congress was committed to:

> What do these Acts deal with and what is the purpose of Article 31?… Here is a proposition—a major proposition—the land problem with which we have been wrestling for years and years. We have come up against difficulties, legal difficulties and the rest. But nothing can be allowed to come in the way—I say nothing—in the way of effecting a solution to the land problem in India…If the courts come, we respect them. We obey them. But the Courts have to carry out the Constitu-tion and if the Constitution comes in the way, it is the Parliament and no other that can change the Constitution of India. Are we to

[12] *Lok Sabha Debates*, 30 May 1951, 9709.
[13] *Lok Sabha Debates*, 2 June 1951, 10086.

submit to things and wait till some great revolution comes to change things?[14]

In a rhetorical flourish, Nehru added, '[t]here is no other way, because millions wait and millions have been waiting for decades for this. Do you think that lawyers or petty legal arguments are going to come in the way of these millions?'[15]

Nehru also argued that the wording of article 31 might not have been clear enough, necessitating the amendment:

> The Constituent Assembly took great and considerable care to lay down that these changes should not be challenged in a court of law. In spite of this care, perhaps the language was not clear enough. That was our fault and so it has been challenged and these reforms have been in consequence delayed. Now, are we to wait for this delaying process to go on and for the process of challenge to go on month after month and year after year?[16]

When the First Amendment was challenged, the Supreme Court upheld it in *Shankari Prasad*.[17] Subsequently, when the *Kameshwar Singh* case[18] came up before the Supreme Court, it said that the zamindars had already 'lost the battle' when the Court had upheld the First Amendment. The Court though did find two provisions of the Act unconstitutional. However, the question of compensation was not yet settled as also what was covered by the definition of 'estate' in the First Amendment. In a series of cases, including *Bela Banerjee* where the West Bengal Land Development and Planning Act, 1948 was challenged, the Supreme Court said,

> While it is true that the legislature is given the discretionary power of laying down the principles which should govern the determination of the amount to be given to the owner for the property appropriated, such principles must ensure that what is determined as payable must be compensation, that is, a just equivalent of what the owner has been deprived of.[19]

[14] *Lok Sabha Debates*, 2 June 1951, 10095.

[15] *Lok Sabha Debates*, 2 June 1951, 10095–6.

[16] *Lok Sabha Debates*, 2 June 1951, 10099.

[17] Shankari Prasad v. Union of India, AIR 1951 SC 458.

[18] State of Bihar v. Kameshwar Singh, AIR 1952 SC 252.

[19] Bela Banerjee v. State of West Bengal, AIR 1954 SC 170.

In another case, *Sholapur Spinning and Weaving*,[20] the Court held that putting the company under government agents was 'deprivation' of property without compensation, and illegal.

The Fourth Amendment was a response to the Court's intervention. Article 31(2) was amended to prevent laws for acquisition of property for public purposes being 'called in question in any court on the ground that the compensation provided by the law is not adequate'. Article 31A was also amended to provide that no law for the acquisition of property 'shall be deemed to be void on the ground that it is inconsistent with, or takes away or abridges, any of the rights conferred by Article 14, Article 19, or Article 31'.

Moving the motion that the amendment be referred to a joint committee of both Houses, Nehru first made a general point that it is necessary from time to time to make changes in the Constitution to remove 'flaws'.[21] On the specific issue of land reform, Nehru said that the amendment was meant to overcome legal impediments, so that the decisions of the parliament were not challenged in courts. Nehru emphasized that compensation would be paid to individuals, but he made a distinction between individual compensation and acquisition for 'social reform' or 'social engineering': 'If we are aiming...at changes in the social structure, then, inevitably, you cannot think in terms of giving what is called full compensation.'[22]

While concluding his argument, Nehru also raised the important issue of the primacy of the directive principles, something that would become a leitmotif of judicial pronouncements at a later phase. He said, 'There is an inherent contradiction in the Constitution between the fundamental rights and the Directive Principles of State Policy. Therefore, again, it is up to this Parliament to remove the contradictions and make the fundamental rights subserve the Directive Principles of State Policy.'[23]

If Mookerjee was Nehru's most formidable opponent during debates on the First Amendment, in this instance it was another

---

[20] Dwarkadas Shrinivas v. Sholapur Spinning and Weaving, AIR 1954 SC 119.

[21] *Lok Sabha Debates*, 14 March 1955, 1945.

[22] *Lok Sabha Debates*, 14 March 1955, 1954.

[23] *Lok Sabha Debates*, 14 March 1955, 1956.

Bengali lawyer and Hindu nationalist, N.C. Chatterjee, who vocifer-ously opposed him. Indeed, Chatterjee had been the counsel for the West Bengal government in the *Bela Banerjee* case. First, Chatterjee strongly defended the Supreme Court: 'The judges recognize the need of social control. The judges cannot descend into the arena of public controversy and cannot defend themselves. It is entirely wrong to say that the Supreme Court did not recognize the necessity of social legislation or did not understand the implications of the Directive Principles.'[24] He pointed out that it was a misreading of the Court's position to say that it had 'stated that any curtailment of right to property would be struck down as ultra vires or repugnant to the Constitution unless and until compensation is paid'.[25] For Chatterjee, the real question was one of eminent domain: 'In no civilised country, which calls itself democratic, is there such a law...If the State must have the final voice, and if the State, by virtue of this sovereign power of eminent domain wants to take property, it can certainly do so but it shall have to pay compensation.'[26]

When the Fourth Amendment Bill was taken up for consider-ation after having been referred to a joint committee, Nehru made it a point to dwell on the minute of dissent by Chatterjee, who had been a member of the committee. Referring to Chatterjee's dissent, Nehru said, '[i]t is odd that words are thrown about confiscation of property, of expropriation when actually what the Constitution or amended Constitution, if you amend it, says is that there will be no such thing except by law and except on payment of compensation. Remember that. The quantum of compensation is to be determined by the legislature.'[27] Nehru also reiterated his commitment to land reform as central to his thinking: 'We talk about, many words, we use good words. Socialist pattern of society; we talk about industrialization, removing unemployment, higher standards...May I put it somewhat differently, that the thing that is really necessary is somehow to activise and dynamise the base of the Indian social structure.'[28]

[24] *Lok Sabha Debates*, 14 March 1955, 1964.
[25] *Lok Sabha Debates*, 14 March 1955, 1972–3.
[26] *Lok Sabha Debates*, 14 March 1955, 1977.
[27] *Lok Sabha Debates*, 11 April 1955, 4384.
[28] *Lok Sabha Debates*, 11 April 1955, 4846.

There were several members who, during the two-day debate, spoke up in support of the amendment. A.K. Gopalan of the Communist Party of India commended the government for taking a step in the right direction but felt that it was 'halting and half-hearted'.[29] Others like S.L. Saksena, who had been a member of the Constituent Assembly, believed that the amendment enabled India to do what China had achieved with redistribution of land.[30]

When it was the turn for Chatterjee to speak, he once again brought up the issue of compensation and turned around the question of who would be hurt the most:

> If you make compensation non-justiciable, my grouse against this Bill as it has emerged from the Joint Committee is this, that it is not progressive. It is putting the hand of the clock back. I am not fighting for the big bosses of capital. I am not fighting for the profiteers. I am fighting for millions and millions of poor people who will be left at the mercy of an executive that is neither efficient nor uncorrupt.[31]

None of Chatterjee's criticisms, however, had any impact on Nehru or the Congress. Before putting the amendment to vote, Nehru summed the government's position thus: 'It [the amendment] removes certain difficulties in our way; it makes it easier for us in future to proceed with our social plans, and at the same time, it does not injure really any interest; and certainly it does not injure the interest of the small producer or small owner.'[32]

The only other significant amendment during the Nehru era with regard to land was in early 1964, when the Seventeenth Amendment made changes to the definition of 'estate' in article 31A(1) to include land held under the ryotwari settlement. The amendment was partly in response to the Supreme Court's *Kunhikoman* judgment[33] where it ruled that the Kerala Agrarian Relations Act, 1958 violated article 14. The Supreme Court subsequently upheld the Seventeenth Amendment in its *Sajjan Singh* judgment.[34]

---

[29] *Lok Sabha Debates*, 11 April 1955, 4848.

[30] *Lok Sabha Debates*, 11 April 1955, 5113.

[31] *Lok Sabha Debates*, 11 April 1955, 4894.

[32] *Lok Sabha Debates*, 11 April 1955, 1524.

[33] K. Kunhikoman v. State of Kerala, AIR 1962 SC 723.

[34] *Sajjan Singh* v. *State of Rajasthan*, AIR 1965 SC 845.

THE INDIRA GANDHI YEARS

Indira Gandhi's tenure as prime minister saw significant amendments to the Constitution regarding the right to property and compensation. These amendments came once again in response to Supreme Court rulings. It was the momentous *Golak Nath* judgment,[35] where the Punjab Security of Land Tenures Act, 1953 was challenged, that was the initial trigger. An eleven–judge bench in a 6:5 decision in *Golak Nath* reversed earlier precedents. Significantly, in *Golak Nath*, speaking for the majority, CJI K. Subba Rao specified limitations on parliament's power to amend the Constitution. Subba Rao ruled that the fundamental rights were 'given a transcendental position under our Constitution and are kept beyond the reach of the Parliament'.[36] In effect, the judgment rendered the First, Fourth, and Seventeenth Amendments invalid. However, the majority ruling held that the decision would be prospective, thereby saving the earlier amendments.

Subsequently, the Supreme Court rejected two measures proposed by the Congress government, which were central to Indira Gandhi's socialist programme: nationalization of banks and abolition of the privy purses of the former princes. This would first lead to the Twenty-fourth Amendment which empowered Parliament to make laws infringing on the fundamental rights. Immediately afterwards, parliament passed the Twenty-fifth amendment, which barred the court from questioning the amount of compensation for land acquisition, as well as inserted article 31C, which said that no law aimed at fulfilling articles 39(b) and (c)[37] of the directive principles of the Constitution could be challenged in court.

---

[35] *I.C. Golak Nath v. State of Punjab*, AIR 1967 SC 1643. Here the Punjab Security and Land Tenures Act was challenged on the ground that it denied constitutional rights to acquire and hold property and practice any profession.

[36] *Golak Nath*, at 1656.

[37] Article 39 says: The State shall, in particular, direct its policy towards securing—(b) that the ownership and control of the material resources of the community are so distributed as best to subserve the common good;

(c) that the operation of the economic system does not result in the concentration of wealth and means of production to the common detriment.

Moving the amendment for consideration, the law minister H.R. Gokhale, considered an 'excellent draughtsman',[38] began by saying that the Twenty-fourth Amendment had overruled the *Golaknath* ruling. 'Having asserted the supremacy of Parliament,' he said, 'it is now open to amend any provision and the decks are now cleared for the passage of the Constitution (Twenty-fifth Amendment) Bill'.[39] Gokhale specifically referred to the Bank Nationalization case as necessitating the Twenty-fifth amendment:

> After the Fourth Amendment was passed by Parliament, there have been many judicial somersaults on the interpretation of the Fourth Amendment, but in the last case, the Bank Nationalisation, the continued use of the word 'compensation' led to the interpretation that the money equivalent of the property acquired must be given for any property taken by the State for a public purpose. This interpretation given by the Supreme Court completely renders nugatory the provisions of the Fourth Amendment which made the adequacy of compensation fully non–justiciable.[40]

Gokhale laid out two main features of the amendment. One, it substituted the word 'amount' for 'compensation'. Two, it provided that laws fixing the amount of compensation could not be challenged in court. He justified the amendment by saying, '[i]t is obvious that it should not be possible for the court to block measures of social change by compelling payment of compensation of such a high quantum as to make it impossible to implement the socio-economic measures'.[41]

Gokhale termed article 31C a 'landmark in the constitutional history of India' for giving primacy to the directive principles: 'This article, for the first time, gives to the directive principles of State policy…a place of primacy and predominance…Though the directive principles are not in terms enforceable by any court, the proposed amendment makes the enforcement of the directive principles possible.'[42] Though opposition members, such as Piloo Mody of the Swatantra Party,

---

[38] Granville Austin, *Working a Democratic Constitution: A History of the Indian Experience* (New Delhi: Oxford University Press, 2003), 375.

[39] *Lok Sabha Debates*, 30 November 1971, 220.

[40] *Lok Sabha Debates*, 30 November 1971, 220–1.

[41] *Lok Sabha Debates*, 30 November 1971, 222.

[42] *Lok Sabha Debates*, 30 November 1971, 226.

criticized the amendment as an 'arbitrary exercise of naked power,' Congress stalwarts strongly defended it in parliament.

Minister of steel and mines and proponent of the idea of a 'committed' judiciary, Mohan Kumaramangalam, said, 'We have been appointed as members of Parliament because of our political philosophy. That is why it is wrong to give the power to the judges. It would mean compelling them to take political decisions, though some of them unfortunately have been eager to do so in the past. I hope they would not do so in the future.'[43] Yet another Congress leader, Siddhartha Shankar Ray, quoted Harold Laski at length to argue that when 'public purpose and the right to property are in conflict, obviously public purpose must have way.'[44]

When it was the turn of Indira Gandhi to speak, in her short speech, she pointed out that 'amendments to the Constitution became necessary because the courts have made it difficult for Parliament to implement programmes of social justice'.[45] She further reiterated that the amendment was 'an effort to safeguard the intent of the Constitution. The Constitution-framers did not envisage any unregulated right to private property nor did they want property rights to come in the way of socio-economic progress.'[46]

The back and forth between the Indira Gandhi government and the courts would continue on the question of fundamental rights, and the issue of land remained the trigger. The landmark *Kesavananda* judgment, which involved a challenge by the head of a Kerala *math* (monastery) to two land reform acts, introduced the 'basic structure' doctrine.[47] The hearings, which went on for five months, involved some of the best legal brains in the country, and were marked by plenty of backroom intrigue. On 24 April 1973, 13 judges delivered 11 separate opinions with nine of them putting their signature on a statement which is regarded as the majority decision. In a nutshell this said that article 368[48] did not give

[43] *Lok Sabha Debates*, 30 November 1971, 317.

[44] *Lok Sabha Debates*, 1 December 1971, 307.

[45] *Lok Sabha Debates*, 1 December 1971, 343.

[46] *Lok Sabha Debates*, 1 December 1971, 346.

[47] Kesavananda Bharati v. State of Kerala, AIR 1973 SC 1461.

[48] The original article 368 stated: 'An amendment of this Constitution may be initiated only by the introduction of a Bill for the purpose in either

Parliament the mandate to 'alter the basic structure or framework of the Constitution'.

The *Kesavananda* judgment prompted the infamous Forty-second amendment, masterminded by S.S. Ray, D.K. Barooah, and Rajni Patel, and moved for consideration on 25 October 1976, during the height of the Emergency. On the occasion, Gokhale said, the government was taking a 'big step forward':

> We are saying: it is not only articles 39-B and C, but all the Directive Principles; and that if they are to be implemented by legislation then Fundamental Rights mentioned in articles 14, 19 and 31…will not come in the way of making any legislation which will give effect to any or all of the Directive Principles of the Constitution.[49]

When it was the turn of Indira Gandhi to speak, she said the Bill was a 'vital step in curing our political system of some of the ills to which it is subject'.[50] She also referred to the property clause in the Constitution:

> Many have pressed for the deletion of the property clause. Today our thrust is not merely on directions or intentions, but on actual action. Hon. Members will remember a time when the Congress party passed a resolution regarding co-operative farming. There was nothing in it about people having to give up their land, there was nothing in it about collective farming, yet such a tremendous campaign of propaganda was launched that even that very moderate programme could not get off the ground. You all know how easy it is to spread misunderstanding, especially amongst those who have little property.

Aiming a jibe at the propertied classes, she added, 'Perhaps it is those who have more, who spread misunderstanding but, whatever it is, the result is that even the man who has a small piece of property gets upset that his little bit will be touched. Hence our caution not to be pushed

---

House of parliament, and when the Bill is passed in each House by a majority of the total membership of that House and by a majority of not less than two-thirds of the members of that House present and voting, it shall be presented to the President for his assent and upon such assent being given to the Bill the Constitution shall stand amended in accordance with the Bill…'

[49] *Lok Sabha Debates,* 25 October 1976, 57.

[50] *Lok Sabha Debates,* 27 October 1976, 135.

into any position which would make it more difficult to implement our programmes.'[51]

Once Indira Gandhi was voted out in 1977, the Janata government introduced the Forty-fourth amendment to 'restore the Constitution to its condition before the Emergency amendments and to add safe-guards to restrict the executive's emergency and analogous powers'.[52] Among the many objectives of the amendment was the 'deletion of the right to property' that Indira Gandhi had talked about. It is worth quoting at length the law minister, Shanti Bhushan, when he moved the amendment for consideration, on removing the fundamental right to property:

> It was felt that in regard to the right to property which was conceived as a fundamental right in the context of India which consist (sic) of vast majority of poor people where there are only a few people who really can claim to possess extensive properties, to equate the right to freedom of speech, the right to liberty, the right to move freely, the right to form associations and so on…to equate them and put them on the same footing had produced this result that both important rights and not so important rights, namely, the right to property, being in the same cat-egory of fundamental rights…While recognizing the right to property, while there will be sanctity attached to the right of property, while there will have to be a law to justify deprivation of property, etc. at the same time it will not have the status of a fundamental right so that a case for imposing any restriction for curbing other more fundamental rights in which the Indian humanity (sic) is interested may not arise. That is the reason for removing article 19(1)(f) and article 31 from the Chapter of Fundamental Rights and introducing a new article which would be a constitutional right, which would be a legal right, but not having the status of a fundamental right.[53]

Article 300A was added to the Constitution which, echoing the colonial-era 1935 Act, merely stated: 'No person shall be deprived of his property save by authority of law.'

The issue of the basic structure doctrine and parliamentary suprem-acy returned during Indira Gandhi's tenure after she was returned to power in 1980. But this time around, land was only tangentially related

---

[51] *Lok Sabha Debates*, 27 October 1976, 139.

[52] Austin, Working a Democratic Constitution, 425.

[53] *Lok Sabha Debates*, 7 August 1978, 307.

to the case. In the *Minerva Mills* case, the nationalization of a privately owned mill had been challenged. The case had come to the Supreme Court in 1979, but was decided in 1980 by when Indira was again prime minister. The counsel for the mill owners, N.A. Palkhivala, made the Forty-second amendment and article 31C, which the Forty-fourth amendment had failed to remove, the centrepiece of his arguments. The *Minerva Mills* judgment upheld the basic structure doctrine, and Indira in her second tenure decided not to challenge it.

POST-1980S

Through the 1980s and 1990s, there was no serious challenge to the government's policy on acquisition of land. Land did not figure prominently in parliament or the courts. Indeed, in *Jilubhai Khachar v. State of Gujarat*,[54] the Supreme Court refused to go into the question of adequacy of compensation. Again in *Rajiv Sarin v. State of Uttarakhand*, a Constitution Bench's observations reflected the settled nature of the question of land acquisition:

> The incident of deprivation of property within the meaning of Article 300A of the Constitution normally occurred mostly in the context of public purpose. Clearly, any law, which deprives a person of his private property for private interest, will be amenable to judicial review. In last sixty years, though the concept of public purpose has been given a wide interpretation, nevertheless, the 'public purpose' remains the most important condition in order to invoke Article 300A of the Constitution.[55]

This status quo would be shattered from the late 1990s, when protests against land acquisition for government and private projects became common. It was no longer the right to property or land reform that was the issue, but land acquisition and the British-era legislation that governed compensation.[56] This would lead the Congress-led United Progressive Alliance (UPA) to draft LARR.

---

[54] (1995) Supp (1) SCC 596.

[55] (2011) 8 SCC 708.

[56] See Sanjoy Chakravorty, *The Price of Land: Acquisition, Conflict, Consequence* (New Delhi: Oxford University Press, 2013).

The 2013 LARR and its implications have been widely discussed and debated. For our purposes some of the key features are worth mentioning. Some of the elements of the LARR Bill, which was introduced in the Lok Sabha in September 2011, were: the process for land acquisition would involve a social impact assessment survey; compensation for the owners of the acquired land would be four times the market value in case of rural areas and twice in case of urban areas; and in case of acquisition of land for use by private companies or public–private partnerships (PPPs), consent of 80 per cent of the displaced people would be required.[57] The Bill was referred to the standing committee on rural development, headed by Sumitra Mahajan, in May 2012. Among the recommendations of the standing committee were: land may not be acquired for use by private companies and PPPs; including 'infrastructure projects' within the definition of public purpose; the wide discretion to the government in notifying any project as an infrastructure project should be deleted; and no exemptions made for a Central act from the provisions of this Bill. Most of these recommendations were taken on board.

When the LARR Bill was put before parliament in 2013,[58] there was none of the ideological divide that accompanied earlier debates on land in the 1950s and 1970s. The members were all agreed on the need for a more humane land acquisition where those who gave up their land were adequately compensated. The hair-splitting was on the details rather than the intent of the legislation. The opposition BJP MP, Rajnath Singh, set the tone when he talked about the 'spiritual' connection between the farmer and his land. From Communist MPs to those from the BJP, all were agreed on the need for a legislation governing acquisition and compensation, but sparred over issues such as the definition of 'public purpose' and evaluation of the value of land. The Lok Sabha passed the Bill with an overwhelming majority of 216:19, while the Rajya Sabha passed it by a vote of 131:10.

After the Narendra Modi government came to power, it sought to undo some of the provisions of the 2013 Act as part of its reforms.

---

[57] For more details, see Jairam Ramesh and Muhammad Ali Khan, *The Making of the 2013 Land Acquisition Law* (New Delhi: Oxford University Press, 2015).

[58] http://www.prsindia.org/billtrack/the-land-acquisition-rehabilitation-and-resettlement-bill-2011-1978/.

The Union Cabinet on 28 December 2014 approved an ordinance to amend the 2013 Act. The ordinance, promulgated on 31 December 2014, exempted five categories of projects from certain provisions of the 2013 Act. These were defence, rural infrastructure, affordable housing and housing projects for the poor, industrial corridors, and infrastructure or social infrastructure projects, including public–private projects in which ownership of land would remain with the government. The ordinance waived the critical consent clause, which required consent of 80 per cent of the landowners for private projects and 70 per cent for PPP projects, for these five categories. The ordinance exempted the five categories from two other crucial provisions of the 2013 Act: a social impact assessment of affected families; and restriction on the acquisition of irrigated multi-crop and other agricultural land. The ordinance also removed the restriction on acquisition of land for private hospitals and educational institutions. Among the other changes were bringing the compensation, resettlement, and rehabilitation of 13 exempted laws, such as the National Highways Act, 1956, in consonance with the land Act; and changing the period after which acquired but unutilized land would have to be returned to the original owners from five years to 'five years, or any period specified at the time of setting up the project, whichever is later'.[59]

Before the 2015 parliamentary budget session began, however, there was acute pressure on the government to roll back some of the amendments. The Congress publicly said it would oppose the ordinance in parliament. Most of the other political parties saw sense in opposing a measure that could be construed as anti-farmer and anti-poor, two constituencies that no one was willing to alienate. There was public pressure too on the government with anti-corruption activist Anna Hazare, who had virtually disappeared from the national scene, making a comeback of sorts by participating in a two-day sit-in in Delhi against the ordinance. In face of concerted opposition, the BJP's then parliamentary affairs minister Venkaiah Naidu admitted that land acquisition was an 'emotive' issue.[60] This was the backdrop against which a new

---

[59] Clause 9 of the ordinance, https://www.prsindia.org/sites/default/files/bill_files/RTFCTLARR_Ordinance_2014_1.pdf.

[60] Pradeep Kaushal and Liz Matthew, 'Land Law: Oppn Staring Down, Govt May Blink', *The Indian Express*, 23 February 2015.

bill amending the 2013 Act was introduced in the 2015 budget session of the Lok Sabha.

THE DEBATE ON THE LARR AMENDMENT BILL

When the LARR amendment Bill was introduced in the Lok Sabha, the opposition made common cause against it. Taking the lead were the Congress, the Trinamool Congress (TMC), and the Janata Dal (United). But what pushed the BJP into a corner was that its regional allies, including the Shiv Sena, Akali Dal, Lok Janshakti Party, and the Swabhimani Pakhsa, raised their voices against it.[61] Even within the Sangh Parivar there were rumblings, with the Bharatiya Kisan Sangh, the farmers' wing of the Rashtriya Swayamsevak Sangh (RSS), coming out against the amendments.[62]

The aggressive stand of the opposition, and the misgivings of its allies on the land legislation, forced the BJP and Modi to rethink their strategy in parliament. Union minister for road transport and highways Nitin Gadkari said that the government was 'open to suggestions' on the social impact assessment and consent clauses.[63]

The LARR amendment Bill was debated in the Lok Sabha for eight hours over two days on 9–10 March 2015. The government made nine amendments to the 2013 Act, all of which were adopted.[64] The Congress and the Biju Janata Dal (BJD) walked out before the voting began. The government yielded to the opposition on certain points, but no concessions were made on the critical consent and social impact assessment clauses. Some of the points on which the government gave in were concessions made in the ordinance to the private

---

[61] Liz Mathew, Pradeep Kaushal, and Maneesh Chhibber, 'Allies Akali Dal, Sena Join Opp to Push BJP in a Corner over Land Law', *The Indian Express*, 25 February 2015.

[62] Shyamlal Yadav, 'There's Pressure from Within Too: Red Flag from RSS Farm Chief', *The Indian Express*, 23 February 2015.

[63] *The Indian Express*, 26 February 2015.

[64] For the list of amendments, see http://www.prsindia.org/uploads/media/Land%20and%20R%20and%20R/Notice%20of%20amendments-LARR.pdf. For the full text of the bill as passed by the Lok Sabha, see http://www.prsindia.org/uploads/media/Land%20and%20R%20and%20R/LARR,%202015%20as%20passed%20by%20LS.pdf.

sector. This included clauses in the ordinance which were open ended regarding acquisition of land for industrial corridors, irrespective of whether they were being developed by the government or the private sector; and expanding the scope of social infrastructure projects to include private schools and hospitals. The government also included a clause providing for employment to one member each of 'affected families of farm labourers'.[65]

In the debate on the legislation, the first opposition speaker was the Congress's Jyotiraditya Scindia. He began by questioning the rationale of the BJP in amending a legislation to which they were a party in 2013. He pointed out that the 2013 Act was the result of two years of discussion; furthermore, a parliamentary standing committee, headed by BJP leader and current speaker Sumitra Mahajan, had debated it for a year. The final legislation, according to him, took the inputs and suggestions of 14 political parties, including the BJP. He demanded that if further amendments were to be made to the legislation, it should be referred once again to a standing committee. The leader of the Congress in the Lok Sabha, Mallikarjun Kharge, too, articulated this demand later.[66]

Several speakers, including Tathagata Satpathy of the BJD, a party which was sympathetic to the BJP, argued against the new law. He said that his party strongly opposed the 'elimination of the social impact assessment clause'. He also wondered if the new law was only meant for corporate groups, and to 'appease the super rich'.[67] Later, the leader of the BJD in the House, Bhartruhari Mahtab, before asking his party to walk out, said his party disagreed with scrapping of the consent clause for PPPs and rural infrastructure.[68]

The government's stand was spelled out in some detail by Venkaiah Naidu. He explained, repeating what Modi had said earlier in a speech in the Lok Sabha, that the reason why the government was amending the land legislation was requests by a majority of state chief ministers to have a relook at the 2013 Act. The ace up his sleeve was a letter

---

[65] Ruhi Tewari, 'Land Bill Clears LS: Consent Clause Stays, Govt Yields on Private Parties', *The Indian Express*, 11 March 2015.

[66] Tewari, 'Land Bill Clears LS'.

[67] *Lok Sabha Debates*, 9 March 2015.

[68] Tewari, 'Land Bill Clears LS'.

written by the commerce minister under the UPA, Anand Sharma, to the then prime minister where he had said, 'The instance of consent of 80 per cent of affected families will seriously delay acquisition and, in many cases, halt essential infrastructure projects...A legislation of this nature...will render key infrastructure projects unviable and slow down the process of urbanization considerably.'[69]

Naidu stressed that exemption clauses in the amended Bill related only to defence and security, infrastructure, affordable housing, and industrial corridors. He was at pains to point out that the government would not use the provisions of the Act for the 'sake of private people. It will use it for the public interest. For the common man of the country.' Echoing Modi, he said the government was making the Act 'more pro-poor, pro-people and pro-farmer'.[70] Replying to the debate, rural development minister Birender Singh did not make too many substantial points except enumerating the changes that the government was putting in place in the legislation. Subsequently, when voting took place on the statutory resolution, it was negative, while all the amendments moved by the government were passed.

After the budget session resumed, the amended Bill was reintroduced on 11 May 2015 amid protests and a walkout by several opposition members, including the Congress, the TMC, and the Left. The next day in parliament, Rahul Gandhi accused the government of wanting to take land from farmers and give it to their 'industrialist friends'. He said, 'Land prices are increasing and its benefit should go to the farmers and labourers. But you want only your friends to benefit.'[71] The same day the government referred the land bill to a 30-member joint committee, headed by the BJP's S.S. Ahluwalia and comprising members of both houses, with a mandate to submit its recommendations by the first day of the monsoon session of parliament, beginning on 21 July. The move was a strategic one which divided the Congress. While one section argued that the party should not take part in the panel since its stand was that the 2013 legislation should remain unchanged, another

---

[69] Tewari, 'Land Bill Clears LS'.

[70] Tewari, 'Land Bill Clears LS'.

[71] Lok Sabha Debates (uncorrected), 11 May 2015. See http://164. 100.47.132/newdebate/16/4/12052015/Fullday.pdf. Also see *The Indian Express*, 13 May 2015.

section felt that the party should participate and give dissent notes.[72] Even as the committee was deliberating, the government repromulgated the land ordinance for the third time. This again set off a debate on whether it made any sense for the Congress and other opposition parties to participate since the BJP was in a majority on the panel.

Subsequently, the enthusiasm for amending LARR has died down. At the time of writing, the joint committee was still in existence but its meetings had increasingly become infrequent. According to one report, the committee has met only twice in 2016 and four times in 2017 compared to 19 times in 2015. A meeting scheduled for 27 February 2018 had to be cancelled due to a lack of quorum.[73]

★★★

This chapter has traced the long arc of the debate on land beginning with the Constituent Assembly to the amendments proposed by the Modi government to LARR. In post-independence India, Nehru and the Congress were intent on land reform and land redistribution, and in the process whittled down the right to property. This resulted in the eventual removal of the right to property from the fundamental rights and a concomitant expansion in the powers of the state to acquire land for public purposes. However, over the past two decades or so due to protests over land acquisition and inadequate compensation, the pendulum has swung the other way. The recent judicial pronouncements have been interpreted by some as an attempt at reinstating the fundamental right to property.[74] But unlike earlier, the Court has not instigated the changes. The 2013 LARR and the Modi government's inability to amend it were a demonstration of the political passions generated by land acquisition, and a pushback by farmers against the

[72] Manoj C.G., 'Land Bill Sent to Joint Panel, Cong Split on Move', *The Indian Express*, 13 May 2015.

[73] https://timesofindia.indiatimes.com/india/joint-parliamentary-committee-meeting-on-land-acquisition-bill-not-held-due-to-less-member-turnout/articleshow/63101188.cms.

[74] Namita Wahi, 'Property', in *The Oxford Handbook of the Indian Constitution*, eds Sujit Choudhry, Madhav Khosla, and Pratap Bhanu Mehta (Oxford: Oxford University Press, 2016), 963.

state's powers to acquire land. The expansion of the powers of the state with regard to land that Nehru and Indira so strenuously pushed for from the 1950s to the 1970s was done in the name of the millions of poor and for social engineering and justice. Ironically, the curtailing of the state's power to acquire land along with institutionalization of safeguards on land ownership in recent years, have also been done in the name of farmers.

4   Land Acquisition in India

The Political Economy of Changing the Law

Sanjoy Chakravorty[1]

Land acquisition (or eminent domain) is one of the most contentious issues in India. It has been called India's 'biggest problem' by a range of politicians and policy-makers—a position that is itself revealing in a country with widespread poverty, corruption, deficits in human development indicators, and inequality. Whether or not it is India's biggest problem, there is no doubt that the issue affects every group in society: farmers and industrialists, home-buyers and slum-dwellers, the Left, the Right, and all ideological or opportunistic political agents in between. The issue is so contentious and large in political terms that at least one state government (in West Bengal) that had been in power for 34 continuous years was toppled by it, and more important, a national land acquisition law that had been used for over a hundred years (from 1894, in colonial India) was replaced by a new law in 2013, which the party that won the national election in 2014 almost immediately sought to replace—unsuccessfully, so far.

There are many important questions that arise out of the experience and evidence of almost 70 years of land acquisition in India, but

[1] This chapter originally appeared in the journal *Area Development and Policy* 1, no. 1 (2016): 48–62. I thank the journal and its publishers, The Regional Studies Association and Taylor and Francis, for permission to reprint.

in this chapter, the focus is on two central ones: (1) Why, despite very large-scale land acquisition, conversion, and displacement in the first six decades after independence, was there little resistance or political mobilization against it? (2) Why, despite the continuing deep precariousness of the Indian farmer, the large amounts of money to be made from acquisition now, and the relatively small scale of acquisition, is there so much political mobilization against it now?

This chapter is an attempt to answer these questions, and in the process a singular argument is presented. The first part of the argument—that the Indian state has seriously mishandled past land acquisitions—is well-established. The second part of the argument—that is less understood and much less agreed upon—is that the Indian state will continue to mishandle future land acquisitions. But the mistakes of the future will largely be in the opposite direction of the mistakes of the past. Before the mid-2000s, the state's approach to land acquisition was deeply regressive and created wipeouts for millions of households. The recently enacted legislation on land acquisition will reverse that process; it will create windfalls for owners whose land is acquired and thereby generate a tax on the rest of society. This effect will be felt most strongly in India's cities and their surrounding regions; so much so, that the new legislation is likely to lead to the end of the use of eminent domain in urban areas.

The material is presented in three parts. The first is a summary of the findings from over 60 years of land takings and conversions in independent India. The data include quantities of takings and affected populations and compensations, and show how regressive this process has been. The second is a presentation of some of the important details of the new land acquisition law, a demonstration of its economic challenges, and an outline of the events and discourse after the enactment of the new law—specifically, an attempt by a new regime to amend the new law that was less than a year old. The third and final section is focused on an explanation for these events and the core questions they raise—why did a regressive system last so long, and why did it die in the last decade—in terms of the increasing viability of 'wedge issue' politics in a polity marked by increasing political competition.

SIX DECADES OF LAND ACQUISITION

In 2013, the Indian parliament passed the Right to Fair Compensation and Transparency in Land Acquisition, Rehabilitation and Resettlement

Bill (LARR). The law was created by the United Progressive Alliance (UPA) led by the Congress party, and was supported by all the major political parties, including the main opposition, the Bharatiya Janata Party (BJP). The 2013 LARR replaced legislation that had been much-criticized for being a colonial-era law, the Land Acquisition Act of 1894 (LAA), that had been amended twice in independent India, in 1962 and 1984, both of which amendments had increased the state's taking powers.

Though the old land acquisition law had indeed been created by the colonial authorities, its real use (and abuse) took place in independent India. The postcolonial state under Prime Minister Nehru needed a law to enable land acquisition on a scale that had never been attempted before in India, because vast quantities of land were required to jump-start the developmental vision that guided policy in the new nation. The colonial state never had such an industrial vision for India; indeed, it was antithetical to the colonial enterprise. The newly independent Indian state, therefore, found it very convenient to have at hand a ready-made colonial law that solved two critical problems that made land acquisition preferable to purchase: it bypassed the significant transaction costs associated with negotiating with the millions of owners of the very fragmented holdings, and it wiped away all title disputes by fiat. Hence, the colonial law (the LAA) became critical to the postcolonial Indian state's transition to an industrial development model.

It is doubtful that land acquisition on such scale had ever been done anywhere other than in revolutionary communist states like the Soviet Union and China, where private property rights in land were abolished. On this newly acquired land in India were installed numerous dam and irrigation systems (like Bhakra Nangal and Hirakud, extending to more than 5,000 medium and large dams), industrial townships (like Durgapur, Rourkela, Bhilai, and so on), mines (for coal, iron ore, bauxite, and so on), and new and expanded roads, highways, train lines, airports, and so on. The economic geography of contemporary India was created by the LAA.

Measuring Acquisition and Displacement

There is no accepted account of how much land was taken or how many people were affected by the takings. The state has not kept track of the quantity of land taken or population displaced—neither the

Centre nor individual states (that, by constitutional authority, actually undertake acquisitions). Since there are no summary statistics available from the state, it is necessary to rely on estimates created by independent scholars. Despite the 'politics of counting' inherent in this situation, and the subjective assumptions built into any such accounting exercise, the recent methods used by independent scholars are quite robust.

A significant source of subjectivity arises from the fact that there is little agreement on who and what should be counted. Broadly, there are three categories of affected people: (1) Land-losers: who are the title-holders or owners of the acquired land, and are the directly displaced people. (2) Livelihood-losers: who are not landowners but are nonetheless displaced and deprived of their livelihoods—which are derived from lease contracts, or as farm labour, or as service-providers to the displaced communities; livelihood-losers can and frequently do outnumber land-losers. (3) Common Property Resource (CPR) users: who are the users, but not owners, of commonly or jointly held forest, fodder, and water resources; these are typically tribal communities that do not have traditions of private land ownership. In the literature, the first group is called displaced persons (DP), and the second, project affected people (PAP). Increasingly, CPR-users are counted among the PAP.

The state, in using the LAA, generally refused to count livelihood-losers as displaced people, and refused to compensate them. But perhaps the harshest treatment was reserved for the CPR-users. Because CPR land is not private land, the state did not even count it as acquired land. This creates a profound problem of accountability. India's poorest groups—typically tribal groups (or Adivasis) and scheduled castes (or Dalits, the most marginalized groups in India's caste hierarchy)—who have the least private property (especially land), are the most heavily dependent on community resources. The Indian state has alienated CPRs from their users by law over and over again. Various 'forest acts' have taken these lands from their using-communities for commercial or ecological reasons, for example, to harvest timber or to preserve forest land (creating a paradox of 'ecosystem people' being ousted to preserve the elite imagination of ecosystems).[2] When these CPRs are

[2] Madhav Gadgil and Ramchandra Guha, *Ecology and Equity: The Use and Abuse of Nature in Contemporary India* (New York and London: Routledge, 1995).

alienated, large numbers of people lose their livelihoods and sources of sustainability. How many? It is almost impossible to estimate these numbers with any accuracy.

The measurement of land acquisition and its impacts has become a small sub-field in Indian sociology, and Walter Fernandes is arguably its most important scholar. He estimated that at the national scale, 21.3 million DPs and PAPs were created in 1951–90. In 2004, he provided further details and updates.[3] His estimate for the total DPs/PAPs in 1947–2000 was 'probably around 50 million'. The total land acquisition in 1951–95 for all projects was estimated to be 50 million acres, including 17 million acres of forests, and 15 million acres of CPRs. More recently, he updated the estimates to more than 60 million DPs/PAPs in 1947–2000.[4] More details are available on dams (by Satyajit Singh), on mining (by Walter Fernandes), and on steel plants and dams (by S. Parasuraman).[5]

It is possible to draw three major conclusions from the data reported in Table 4.1 (compiled and partially updated by Lobo and Kumar from the work of Fernandes and others):[6]

1. *Fifty million people were adversely affected*: It is possible that upwards of 50 million acres of agricultural and non-agricultural land

[3] Walter Fernandes 'Development-induced Displacement in Eastern India', in *Antiquity to Modernity in Tribal India,* Vol. 1: *Continuity and Change among the Tribals,* ed. S.C. Dube (New Delhi: Inter-India Publications, 1998), 217–301; Walter Fernandes, 'Rehabilitation Policy for the Displaced', *Economic & Political Weekly* XXXIX, no. 12 (2004): 1191–3.

[4] Walter Fernandes, 'Displacement and Land Alienation from Common Property Resources', in *Displaced by Development: Confronting Marginalization and Gender Injustice*, ed. L. Mehta (New Delhi: Sage, 2008), 105–29.

[5] Satyajit Singh, *Taming the Waters: The Political Economy of Large Dams in India* (New Delhi: Oxford University Press, 1997); Walter Fernandes, 'Sixty Years of Development-induced Displacement in India; Scale, Impacts, and the Search for Alternatives', in *India Social Development Report 2008: Development and Displacement*, ed. H.M. Mathur (New Delhi: Oxford University Press, 2008), 89–102; S. Parasuraman, *The Development Dilemma: Displacement in India* (Basingstoke: Macmillan, 1999).

[6] Lancy Lobo and Shashikant Kumar, *Land Acquisition, Displacement and Resettlement in Gujarat 1947–2004* (New Delhi: Sage, 2009).

TABLE 4.1 Number of Displaced and Project-Affected Persons for Selected States and Major Categories

State	Period	Water	Transport	Welfare/ Administration	Environment	Industry	Mines	Other	Total
Andhra Pradesh	1951–95	1,865	47	38	136	540	101	490	3,216
Assam	1947–2004	449	169	746	265	58	41	191	1,919
Goa	1965–95	6	43	7	0	1	0	3	61
Gujarat	1965–95	2,379	1,356	45	26	141	4	124	4,075
Jharkhand	1951–95	233	0	0	510	88	403	314	1,548
Kerala	1947–2000	134	152	17	15	223	0	12	552
Odisha	1947–2000	800	0	0	108	158	300	100	1,466
West Bengal	1947–2004	1,724	1,164	1,674	785	404	418	775	6,944
TOTAL		7,590	2,931	2,526	1,845	1,613	1,267	2,009	19,781
Share (%)		38.4	14.8	12.8	9.3	8.2	6.4	10.2	100.0

Source: Lancy Lobo and Shashikant Kumar, *Land Acquisition, Displacement and Resettlement in Gujarat 1947–2004* (New Delhi: Sage, 2009).
Notes: All figures are in thousands. Significant categories not detailed here include urban projects, defence, and power (all are included in the category 'Other').

(including forests)—somewhere around 10 per cent of the nation's usable land—were converted to different uses in independent India. As a result of these land-use conversions, upwards of 50 million people, possibly as many as 60 million people were affected. Land-losers alone number far less than these upper bounds. They are still unacceptably large. But the true impact—that includes livelihood-losers and CPR-losers—is staggering.

2. *Ninety per cent were displaced for state projects*: The state was directly responsible for the vast majority of this impact. The really large categories of displacement-impact in Table 4.1 are all entirely in the domain of the state—water (over 38 per cent), transportation (almost 15 per cent), welfare and administration (almost 13 per cent), and environment (over 9 per cent) are the top categories. The two categories where the private sector had a significant but not exclusive or even dominant role (in a nation where the state occupied the 'commanding heights of the economy') are industry and mines, which together account for less than 15 per cent of the total impact. Therefore, it is reasonable to argue that the private sector was responsible for 10 per cent or less of the total impact; the state was responsible for 90 per cent or more.

3. *Adivasis were the most severely affected*: A disproportionate burden of this displacement fell on India's Adivasi (tribal) population; also disproportionately burdened, but possibly not as heavily as the Adivasis, were Dalits and other socially marginalized groups. The former were impacted primarily as a result of the conversion of CPRs. The latter were affected less as land-losers (since they owned little land), but more as livelihood-losers on taken lands. Both groups received little or no compensation because they were generally not the owners of the acquired or converted land.

Compensation, Resettlement, and Rehabilitation

There is little systematic data on compensation for land acquisition. There are several reasons for this, including significant variation in acquisition policies from state-to-state and project-to-project, and even within projects. There is variation in who gets counted, whether the payment is in land or cash or both, whether the type of project or location or fertility of land makes a difference, and whether any resettlement/rehabilitation is made available. Moreover, since the compensation information is both valuable and potentially explosive, all governments have developed a culture of secrecy over it. Nonetheless, there are scattered data available on compensation for land acquisition (especially from litigated acquisitions).

Some projects have been studied in depth, including the Bhakra Nangal dam that Nehru called a 'new temple of resurgent India,' and the Hirakud dam that submerged about 240 villages and took about 170,000 acres from about 22,000 families in the 1950s; the payment per acre ranged between INR 50 and INR 200 (in current values these figures are approximately INR 1,500–6,000 per acre).[7] There are comprehensive data available in Lobo and Kumar's work on Gujarat. Their analysis shows that water projects, which use the most land, pay the least (around INR 0.15 million/acre in the 2000s); and transportation and urban development projects pay the most—on average, in 2001–6, about INR 0.3 million/acre for transportation, and close to INR 1.5 million/acre for urban development.[8]

The source of the most accessible and detailed (but unorganized) information on land acquisition—including the specifics of compensation and location—is the archive of court judgments on land acquisition cases. My own work has a compendium of such cases.[9] There are three patterns that run through most litigation on land acquisition. First, the land acquisition officer sets a low compensation level. Second, courts set the compensation at higher levels, often at much higher levels. Third, the final judgment comes many years, even decades, after the land was acquired.

The land acquisition officer, arguably the most important figure (operating at the ground or district level), tends to set the acquisition price at a low level. This level was as low as INR 12,000 per acre as

---

[7] Manthan Adhyayan Kendra, 'The First Development-caused Displacements in India: The Forgotten People of Bhakra Nangal', in *Beyond Relocation: The Imperative of Sustainable Resettlement*, ed. R. Modi (New Delhi: Sage, 2009).

[8] Lobo and Kumar, 'Land Acquisition, Displacement and Resettlement in Gujarat'.

[9] Sanjoy Chakravorty, *The Price of Land: Acquisition, Conflict, Consequence* (New Delhi: Oxford University Press, 2013). Interested readers can look up the cases at www.indiankanoon.org.

recently as the mid-1980s in a region as well-located as Saidapet in Tamil Nadu, for land on which the Madras Export Processing Zone was eventually established (where land probably costs more than INR 150 million/acre now). As recently as the late 1990s, the compensation rate was set well under INR 0.1 million/acre for an irrigation project in Karnataka. In the 1960s, the courts generally increased compensation by a factor of 1.5–2; by the 1980s and into the 2000s, the courts were increasing compensation by factors of 15–20 or even higher in many cases.[10]

The record of the state on resettlement and rehabilitation has ranged from unsatisfactory to unacceptable. Michael Cernea argued that 'because government agencies employ the weight of the state and the force of law to impose expropriation and displacement, it is incumbent upon the same government to also enable those displaced to get back on their feet and benefit from the development for the sake of which they are displaced'.[11] The large literature on resettlement and rehabilitation in India, including good reviews and analysis by Fernandes, Modi, and Parasuraman, leaves little doubt that the state in India has failed to meet this basic obligation.[12]

Giving and Taking, from Different People

The argument that as far as land is concerned, the Indian state was simultaneously a 'giving' state (that redistributed some land through measures like the abolition of the feudal zamindari system and various tenancy reform and land ceiling acts) and a 'taking' state, the bare outlines of which are sketched above, is detailed in my earlier work.[13] The redistributive 'giving' state largely failed in its professed objectives;

---

[10] See, in particular, Ram Singh's systematic analysis of land acquisition litigation and compensation in the courts of Delhi, Punjab, and Haryana; Ram Singh, 'Inefficiency and Abuse of Compulsory Land Acquisition: An Enquiry into the Way Forward', *Economic & Political Weekly* XLVII, no. 19 (2012): 46–53.

[11] Michael M. Cernea, ed., *The Economics of Involuntary Resettlement: Questions and Challenges* (Washington, DC: World Bank, 1999), 20.

[12] Fernandes, 'Sixty Years of Development-induced Displacement in India'; Renu Modi, ed., *Beyond Relocation: The Imperative of Sustainable Resettlement* (New Delhi: Sage, 2009); Parasuraman, *The Development Dilemma*.

[13] Chakravorty, *The Price of Land*.

at most 6 per cent of agricultural land was redistributed (more than one-third of which happened in two of the smaller states—Kerala and West Bengal—under communist governments), and the distribution of land was more unequal after 60 years of independence than it had been at independence or at the beginning of the twentieth century—a condition caused less by state failures than by the continuous fragmentation of agricultural land as the rural population almost tripled between 1951 and 2011.[14]

The prime objective of the 'taking' state was to enhance public welfare through irrigation, electrification, industrialization, conservation, transportation, and commerce by converting selected lands to developmental use. The problem was that the population that benefitted from the development projects was fundamentally different from the population that was displaced. This is not a version of the oft-repeated argument of 'accumulation by dispossession' (which could apply if the dispossession was for private sector use, which it largely was not); rather it is a phenomenon that is more aptly called 'development by dispossession' or 'spatial mismatch'. Accumulation by dispossession (enunciated by David Harvey) is an argument favoured by Marxist and Neomarxist critics of capitalist development (see Arundhati Roy for a populist take, Praful Bidwai for a journalistic treatment, and Swapna Banerjee-Guha and Michael Levien for academic approaches).[15] All these approaches, heartfelt as they are about the many injustices of land acquisition in India,

---

[14] Detailed data on the distribution of agricultural land are in Vikas Rawal, 'Ownership Holdings of Land in Rural India: Putting the Record Straight', *Economic & Political Weekly* XLIII, no. 10 (2008): 43–7; H.R. Sharma, 'Distribution of Landholdings in Rural India, 1953–54 to 1981–82: Implications for Land Reforms', *Economic & Political Weekly* XXIX, no. 13 (1994): A12–A25.

[15] David Harvey, *The New Imperialism* (Oxford: Oxford University Press, 2003); Arundhati Roy, 'Into the Inferno', *New Statesman*, 20 July 2011; Praful Bidwai, 'From Singur to Nandigram & Beyond: Development as Dispossession', http://www.prafulbidwai.org/index.php; Swapna Banerjee-Guha, ed., *Accumulation by Dispossession: Transformative Cities in the New Global Order* (New Delhi: Sage, 2010); Michael Levien, 'The Politics of Dispossession: Theorizing India's "Land Wars"', *Politics & Society* 41, no. 3 (2013): 351–94.

fail to understand the complexity of the political economy of the process, and are inadequate in analytical terms. The fact is this: the independent Indian state dispossessed many of its citizens for the benefit of many more of its other citizens, to undertake conventional state development projects, and that dispossession for private capital was miniscule in comparison (even if it increased in recent years).

The benefits of land takings generally flow to lands that have not been taken; in situations where the benefits of takings are generated on the taken land, the original people of the land are not present to take advantage. Land prices increase with better infrastructure and development, but these increases benefit people whose land has not been taken. Because there is a spatial mismatch between the costs and benefits of land-based development projects, the beneficiaries are effectively subsidized by the displaced. There are two subsidies: an indirect one that makes projects cheaper through poor compensation for the displaced, and a direct one whereby the beneficiaries of the projects get benefits (like water or electricity) for free or at a price that is well below its real cost. Land acquisition by the Indian state was a profoundly regressive process—it redistributed the benefits of land use from the poor to the less-poor and the non-poor.

ACQUISITION IN A BOOMING LAND MARKET

The new acquisition law (LARR), designed by rhetoric and intent to mitigate the problems of the previous law, and to quell the rising tide of resistance to acquisition, including several cases of extreme state violence, has five important elements: (1) Increased compensation for farmers—market prices are doubled in urban and quadrupled in rural areas. (2) Expanded coverage of compensation—non-owners facing livelihood-loss are compensated. (3) Rehabilitation and resettlement of people evicted from their lands is made compulsory. (4) Informed consent of land-losers is mandatory—but only when the acquisition has any private sector involvement (whereby there must be prior consent from at least 70–80 per cent of landowners depending on the extent of private capital involvement in specific projects). (5) Social impact assessments to determine a project's impact on people's livelihoods; more specifically, to identify all affected persons. The first three elements contribute to the direct price of acquisition (which are also the

direct benefits for land- and livelihood-losers); the latter two elements
contribute to the indirect price (transaction and opportunity costs).

How does one analyse the welfare consequences of this new law?
On the one hand, the benefits for the land- and livelihood-losers are
long overdue; on the other hand, the arbitrary multiplication of 'market
price' in India's booming land market is likely to generate a significant
social tax that will enrich just one particular class of landowner. The law
is a political solution (overpayment) to a problem of political economy
(development). At the heart of the problem is a failure to understand
India's land markets and the boom that has made land prices in much
of the nation arguably the highest in the world.

There are four types of land markets in India. Type A regions—all
of India's urban and peri-urban regions and several rural regions (for
example, in all of Punjab and Haryana and much of Tamil Nadu and
Kerala)—are those where the market price of land is several multiples
of the reservation price (which is the price below which a seller will
not sell unless forced to). Type B regions—in most settings that are close
to urban areas, not just the major cities, but also provincial towns and
district centres—are those in which there is little or no gap between
market and reservation price because of the rise in land prices. These
will soon become Type A regions. Type C regions are those with limited market activity and information, and a sizable but unknown gap
between reservation and market price. Many deep rural areas are in this
condition, especially the least urbanized regions of the poorer states,
and 'scheduled areas' (where laws have inhibited the formation of land
markets). Type D regions are those where the land is priceless because
community and cultural values place these lands outside the realm of
the market. These are often sacred lands and should remain off-market.

The LARR 2013 has been designed for the deep rural Type C
regions and may, with some modifications, indeed be appropriate for
them. But the 'one size fits all approach' in LARR is inappropriate for
the other three types of lands. The framers of this law clearly have not
thought through its consequences. These consequences are so large,
that where land is needed most, that is, where land use is most likely to
change—in peri-urban India—this law will simply end acquisition (see
Table 4.2 for a simple scheme on how LARR is likely to affect future
acquisitions). Most acquisitions—for public or private use—will no
longer be affordable. Not all of this increase will come from the new

TABLE 4.2   Acquisition Cost Scenarios after LARR

	Capital-intensive (power plants, manufacturing industry)	Land-intensive (water, transportation, housing, resource extraction, conservation)
Metropolitan Regions	Unaffordable	Unaffordable
Urban Periphery and Type A/B Rural Regions	Expensive	Very expensive to unaffordable
Type C (remote) Rural Regions	Affordable	Affordable to expensive

Source: Author.

An illustration with two projects:

(1) a 1,000 MW thermal power plant, with a capital cost of INR 60 billion that requires 1,000 acres of land.

(2) a four-lane highway that, per kilometre of length, requires 3.7 acres of land and costs INR 60 million to build.

At the edge of metropolises, the effective land acquisition cost for the power plant would be three times the cost of the plant and equipment (INR 200 billion for land, INR 60 billion for the plant). For the highway, the cost of land would be 12 times the other costs of the highway (for every kilometre: INR 740 million for land and INR 60 million for construction). At the other end of the price spectrum, in remote rural regions, the effective acquisition cost of land for the power plant (INR 2.5–5 billion) would be a small and easily affordable fraction of the capital cost (INR 60 billion). The highway too would be affordable; the land cost (INR 10–20 million) would be a substantial fraction of the remaining costs (INR 60 million), but not unaffordable. It follows that acquisition prices in the middle zone, around smaller urban settlements and in prosperous rural regions, will depend on the base or market price. Generally, land for capital-intensive projects will be expensive but a smaller and more affordable portion of the total cost than land for land-intensive projects, many of which may well become unaffordable.

law. A significant proportion will come from the very large increase in the price of land in all urban and many rural areas.

This is very important. The price of land in India has exploded in the last decade (for reasons that cannot be detailed here). It is now very likely the highest in the world. The most expensive land in the country (in south-central Mumbai) is almost as pricey as the most expensive land anywhere (including midtown Manhattan in New

York and Shibuya and Shinjuku in Tokyo). The average price of land in Bengaluru or Bhopal or Guwahati is several multiples higher than in comparable American cities (Atlanta or Austin or Tucson). The price of land on the urban fringe in India is twenty (or more) times higher than that of similar land in America or Europe—upwards of INR 100 million/acre around Mumbai and Delhi and no less than INR 20 million/acre near any significant city. The available evidence suggests that the current market price of remote, low-productivity rural land (Type C land from the schema above) is not less than INR 0.5 million/acre anywhere in the country; Rajshekhar's compilation of farmland prices from 26 villages in remote areas in seven states shows that, with one exception, prices are no less than INR 1 million/acre anywhere, going up to INR 6 million/acre in remote areas in Odisha and Uttar Pradesh.[16] Well-connected land (whether it is productive or not) costs at least INR 10 million/acre in states like Punjab and Haryana.

To put these prices in context: the average price of farmland in the United States (US) is INR 0.15 million/acre (USD 2,200). The lowest prices (less than INR 0.05 million/acre) are in barren states like New Mexico, and the highest (INR 0.7 million/acre) are in the urbanized states of New Jersey (sandwiched between New York City and Philadelphia) and Rhode Island (between New York City and Boston). Therefore, the price of farmland in India is completely unconnected to agricultural productivity; depending on location, it is roughly 5–100 times larger. The price multiplication formula in LARR is designed to make direct payments that are 20–400 times larger than the earnings that would be possible by keeping the land in agriculture in perpetuity. As a result, the distributional impact of acquisition has been reversed: from a deeply regressive one that frequently devastated land- and livelihood-losers to one that creates a windfall for land-losers (not livelihood-losers), and generates a tax on the rest of the population.[17]

---

[16] M. Rajshekhar, 'Great Rural Land Rush: 3 to 100-Fold Rise in Farm Land Prices May Not Bode Well', *The Economic Times*, 12 November 2013.

[17] See Chakravorty, *The Price of Land*; T.N. Ninan, 'The UPA's Worst Legacy', *Business Standard*, 21 March 2014; Maitreesh Ghatak and Parikshit Ghosh, 'Land Acquisition Act: Addressing Both Justice and Prosperity', Ideas for India, http://www.ideasforindia.in/article.aspx?article_id=1483.

Therefore, the multiplication of prices as a result of LARR will severely constrain urban development, the provision of public goods, and industrialization. The constraints will not be evenly spread between states, but will additionally disadvantage states that are land-poor, have fragmented land, and are more urbanized. There will be new windfall gainers, specifically landowners in many rural, and especially, peri-urban regions. The political problem of resistance to land acquisition will be much diminished—which is what the lawmakers want, no doubt—but an even bigger development challenge will be created.

Singur and Sanand

Consider the notorious case of Singur, about 30 kilometres from the outskirts of Kolkata, where the West Bengal government acquired about 1,000 acres of land for Tata Motors to build a factory to manufacture the Nano (the world's 'cheapest car') in 2006. This story is well-known not only to those who follow the news in India, but to ordinary citizens too—it was a turning point in the contemporary narrative of land acquisition in the nation. The state government paid about INR 1 million per acre, which was INR 0.2–0.3 million less than the market price for about 40 per cent of the land. The owners of this land resisted the acquisition, and came to be called the 'unwilling sellers'. Ms. Mamata Banerjee, a firebrand regional politician, used this dissent as a wedge to drive Tata Motors out of Singur, West Bengal to Sanand, Gujarat. Later, in 2011, Ms. Banerjee used this wedge issue to topple the communist government in the state that had been continuously in power for 34 years.

In Sanand, the state of Gujarat, led by Chief Minister Narendra Modi (who became Prime Minister of India in 2014), provided a package of government-owned and acquired land (paying acquisition prices of around INR 5 million per acre). Today, Sanand is an emerging 'global auto hub', and Singur a desolate landscape of desperate farmers.[18] If the same Singur acquisition is attempted with LARR rules now, the land-losers will be paid in excess of INR 5 million per

---

[18] S. Das, 'Sanand: The New Global Auto Hub', *Business Standard*, 23 March 2015, http://www.business-standard.com/article/companies/sanand-the-new-global-auto-hub-115032200818_1.html.

acre. The additional costs for livelihood-losers and resettlement and rehabilitation will total another INR 3.5 million per acre. Added to this, INR 8.5 million per acre (which is 50+ times the average price in the US) will be the costs of waiting for 4 to 5 years to complete the acquisition process.[19] Would the Singur landowners reject this windfall? It seems irrational and unlikely, but what if they did? What would a project developer do when it failed to get the land after 4 to 5 years? What are costs of waiting? Who pays these costs?

After LARR

These were surely among the questions that drove the BJP to propose an amendment to LARR in 2014–15. This is the same BJP that had voted for LARR when the law was passed in 2013; the same BJP that had achieved a massive victory in the parliamentary elections in 2014, led by Narendra Modi, the same Chief Minister of Gujarat who had managed to entice the Tata Nano factory from Singur to Sanand, and who preached a 'Gujarat model of development' for all of India. The BJP amendment sought to remove the 'informed consent' and 'social impact assessment' requirements in LARR for a range of projects, including those relating to defence and national security, rural infrastructure, affordable housing, industrial corridors, and infrastructure. These changes would probably reduce the acquisition time for these project types by several years, and thereby significantly lower the indirect costs of acquisition. It is likely that the BJP took this approach with the certainty that land-losers would not refuse their windfalls, especially in peri-urban regions, which is where most future acquisition will take place. Therefore, they implicitly argued (but never explicitly and openly, from the best available evidence) that there was no reason to raise opportunity costs for both land-acquirers and land-losers by waiting.

One assumes that they were aware, as were other political parties, of the condition of Indian agriculture revealed again in the National Sample Survey Organization (NSSO)'s 70th round on agriculture (covering 2012–13): that the average monthly family income (from

[19] M.R. Madhavan, 'Land Acquisition Process Can Take 50 Months' (2013), The PRS Blog, http://www.prsindia.org/theprsblog/?author=6.

farm and non-farm activities combined) for farming households was less than INR 6,500 (about USD 100); that over 75 per cent of farming households earned even less than this average; that in states like Bihar and West Bengal, this average was below INR 4,000. The Socio Economic and Caste Census of 2011 confirms these findings; the monthly income of the highest-earning member in almost 75 per cent of rural households was less than INR 5,000; for Dalit and Adivasi households, such a situation was seen in over 83 and 86 per cent of households, respectively. Amongst rural households, 30 per cent were landless, while another 20 per cent were engaged in manual casual labour to earn their primary income. This was known already, but perhaps a reminder is necessary: farming doesn't pay in India, mainly because there is too little land per household (less than 3 acres average in India versus hundreds in Europe and the Americas). It is the root cause of poverty in India.

But the BJP failed to get its amendment passed into law. Though it held an absolute majority in the lower house of parliament (the Lok Sabha, the directly-elected chamber), it did not control the upper house (the Rajya Sabha, the indirectly-elected chamber). The amendment ran into stiff opposition, led by the Congress party, which found in this issue the first opportunity to fight back after the devastating electoral loss of 2014, joined by almost all political parties. At the moment of writing, the BJP amendment is off the table (the party is attempting to make it a state-level law in states where it is in power), but the issue is far from being resolved. If LARR was a turn from the past of land acquisition, the BJP amendment was a twist in that turn, and no reasonable observer can conclude that all the twists and turns are over.

THE LONGEVITY AND DEMISE OF A REGRESSIVE SYSTEM

A critical question we must answer is this: How did the state manage to maintain the regressive system of land acquisition for such a long time (about six decades), and why did that system stop working? The first part of the question becomes even more urgent when we consider it in the context of the multiplicity of the 'state' in India's multiparty political system. The Congress party was a national hegemonic power in the first two decades after independence, but after the mid-1970s, the Central government has been run by coalitions. Thirty or more parties have seats in a typical parliament. The large states are generally governed by regional parties with regional agendas. Therefore, if so many people were adversely affected by land acquisition—and, as shown above, they were—why did the political process not produce a backlash or pushback or political parties to champion the rights of the displaced till the last few years?

These questions are probably less relevant for the first two decades after independence, during the Congress hegemony. A new nation was being built then. Land was a big subject on the political agenda, and land reforms of various types were being instituted. But the land reforms were not only largely ineffective, they petered out by the early 1970s. The Congress lost its dominant position. A vast system of national, regional, and local parties emerged, presumably to serve the interests of every identity group. Yet the acquisitions continued, without any organized political movement to oppose it.

The most direct explanation comes from electoral mathematics—that is, the 'winners' have consistently (and usually overwhelmingly) outnumbered the 'losers'. Some quick estimates show how true this is. The dams and irrigation sector is the largest for which land was acquired; almost two-fifth of the total acquisition. From data in *The Price of Land*, we see that roughly 100 million acres were brought under irrigation after independence by converting roughly 20 million acres (not all of it private land).[20] The 'winners' of irrigation projects outnumbered 'losers' by a factor of five. These calculations are more difficult for other sectors like power and transportation—where the beneficiaries are not geographically bounded, which means they are harder to count—but nonetheless they can be done. For instance, if a 1,000 MW power plant supplies electricity to 250,000 households and requires 3,000 acres of land for the plant, mines, and roads—the ratio of 'winners' to 'losers' is well over 100. This 100+ to 1 ratio is identical to the conclusion of the Wikipedia site for the impact of the Sardar Sarovar dam.[21]

Therefore, simple majoritarianism can explain the indifference to harsh land acquisition processes by all political parties (even if it does

---

[20] Chakravorty, *The Price of Land*, Tables 7 and 9.
[21] See https://en.wikipedia.org/wiki/Sardar_Sarovar_Dam.

not explain why these processes were so regressive; that is, why the poor had to subsidize the less-poor and non-poor). It is very likely that since the most disproportionate 'losers' of acquisition were also numerical minorities from India's most marginalized communities—Adivasis and Dalits—it was easier to use simple majoritarianism as a political principle.

Why Did This System Stop Working?

This regressive but developmental system began facing some resistance from civil society groups from the mid-1980s (initially isolated, and later, after the Narmada Bachao Andolan (NBA), in more organized and widespread form), and reached a breaking point around 2007, partly as a result of a new Special Economic Zones Act (2005) that created many new sites of acquisition, and partly as a result of several high-profile, violent cases. Not only was there more visible civil opposition, but in every case, sooner or later it was joined by some political party. Why was there an explosion of political opposition to land acquisition in the last decade? If majoritarianism was effective for 60 years after independence, why did it become less effective? Surely the electoral compulsion did not change. What did?

I have argued that there are two fundamental reasons for this change. One not considered in detail in this chapter is the radical change in India's information system that significantly weakened the information asymmetries of the past—asymmetries that had been the pillar propping up the old system of unjust and regressive land acquisition. There was an enabling technological change: the growth of the mass media first, and later the internet and social media. But the key player in weakening the information asymmetry was the non-governmental or civil society agent. These civil society agents helped spread and exchange information on land acquisition—within specific project-affected communities, between affected people in different projects and communities, and between affected people and the general citizenry and state institutions. Better information led to better organization and assertion of collective rights (which made some farmers realize that they could say 'no,' that they could negotiate or refuse acquisition). These collective resistance situations were frequently brought to public attention by the mass media.

But civil resistance can only go so far in challenging the state juggernaut. It is when a political party joins the civil resistance that it becomes a movement. A major political party brings organizational strength, numbers (of people and money), and visibility to a cause or event, especially in opposition. These interventions were transformative. Relatively low-intensity disputes turned into highly visible events; in the most extreme case, in West Bengal, it led to the toppling of a political coalition (of communists, no less, who had been, in the past, the most proactive redistributors of land). These highly visible events galvanized the creation of a new acquisition law.

But why would political parties take up the cause of acquisition now, after six decades of ignoring the issue? The logic underlying this support for minority groups may appear to be counterintuitive but there are many examples of such situations—which are called 'wedge issue' or 'hot button issue' politics. For example, in the US, sexuality, immigration, and crime are often used as wedge issues by both major parties. In India, analysts like Steven Wilkinson have understood much of the politics around minorities—Muslim or Dalit or other backward class (OBC)—in terms of wedge issue politics.[22]

How does a wedge issue work? It can create a wedge or split in the support base of a political opponent by highlighting an issue that has some support within the opposing party; peel off minorities from one party to another, or from both parties to a third party that is trying to create a political base; 'rebrand' a party and stimulate support for it, even from groups that are not the intended beneficiaries of the wedge issue. In general, the higher the level of political competition or political fragmentation, the more likely is the use of wedge issue

---

[22] On wedge issues in general, see D. Sunshine Hillygus and Todd G. Shields, *The Persuadable Voter: Wedge Issues in Presidential Campaigns* (Princeton, NJ: Princeton University Press, 2009). On the use of anti-Muslim violence as a wedge issue at the state level in India, see, for example, Steven Wilkinson, *Votes and Violence: Electoral Competition and Ethnic Riots in India* (Cambridge: Cambridge University Press, 2006); Peter Mayer, 'Are There Political Patterns in Communal Violence in India?', Biennial Conference of the Asian Studies Association, http://test.asaa.asn.au/ASAA2010/reviewed_papers/Mayer-Peter.pdf. The electoral success of the 'anti-Muslim' issue for the BJP is now well-established, and it may have moved from being a wedge issue to the primary plank.

political strategies that ostensibly favour only minorities. The electoral mathematics is relatively straightforward: if a wedge issue can attract 5–10 per cent of the electorate, when this is added to the base support of a significant party (20–5 per cent of the electorate), the combination can change defeat to victory in a 'first past the post' multiparty system.

Political mobilization against land acquisition is a tactical use of the wedge issue strategy. This is why the same party may be pro-acquisition in some settings, and anti-acquisition in others. At the extreme, the same political personality can be pro-acquisition when in power, and anti-acquisition when out. It is not surprising therefore, that land acquisition became a hot button issue in many parts of the country. As a result, the old acquisition system began to fail and a new acquisition system was created to replace it by the very same party (the Congress) that had been at the helm of the worst excesses of land acquisition. And, paradoxically, it is for that same reason—the electoral mathematics of increasing political competition—that another political party (the BJP), that had supported the new law when it was being enacted then turned around and tried to change it when it won power.

It would be a mistake, however, to view the intense partisan politics over land acquisition law through the narrow time frame of the immediate present or the sound-bites generated on TV shows. Land is arguably the most important subject in modern Indian history, and understanding it was possibly, at least till the 1980s, the most important subject of scholarly attention in India. This is because capturing the output of the land through taxes (which were as high as 75 per cent in colonial and precolonial regimes) or its value when it rises because of new uses has almost certainly been the most important exercise of state authority in all of recorded Indian history. What is unfolding now is merely the latest chapter of a living epic. Unlike what many appear to think, no single law is going to put an end to this story so that everyone can live happily ever after. Therefore, it is necessary to take the long view on land and the structural forces that stimulate the struggles over it, so as to understand precisely what is at stake.

PART II

A Variety of Land Markets

5 How the Market Mechanism Can Be Utilized in Land Acquisition

Case Studies in Foshan and Sanand

Yinghong Huang

The fundamental principle guiding the doctrine of eminent domain is that the state has to provide just compensation when it acquires private property for public use, where 'just compensation' is measured in accordance with the market value, which requires widespread and fully functional land markets. The English equivalent of this doctrine is 'compulsory purchase' where the term 'purchase' implies 'purchase in a free market'.[1] Therefore, just compensation must be applied in a free and prevailing land market, which is usually not found in developing societies.

Most of the current literature fails to discuss thoroughly the free land market which is in most cases either nonexistent or malfunctioning in developing countries. These countries are undergoing a transition from traditional or pre-modern to modern-era societies. The free movement of labour, land, and capital, the fundamental characteristics of a capitalist society, is still underdeveloped in these countries. For many parts of these societies, land has much more meaning than only as an

---

[1] Keith Davies, *Law of Compulsory Purchase and Compensation* (London: Butterworths, 1984).

economic resource. It may be deeply connected with people's social status, life security, religious sentiments, and so on. In some regions, people are unwilling to give up their land even at much higher prices. Land transition never or seldom happens, even though in some other more developed regions, a strong land market may exist and function well.

The land market in developing societies is uneven in this sense. As a consequence, legal doctrines like eminent domain may fail to function in strict terms in such societies. Without a fully developed land market, just compensation as a principle to balance public interests and private interests becomes an illusion, as the existing market prices do not reflect the true value of the land acquired. Confrontation arises due to the different evaluations of land value by different agents. In addition, the absence of a land market reflects the unwillingness of peasants to give up their land at any price in some extreme cases. All of these issues are inclined to cause conflicts between the peasants and the state in land acquisition, which makes land acquisition very difficult in developing societies.

Hence, the absence and the malfunctioning of the land market is one of the major hurdles in smooth land acquisition in developing societies. To overcome this difficulty, measures to build and strengthen land markets are inevitable and necessary in such societies. This chapter focuses on two typical and successful compulsory land acquisitions in India and China, including one in Foshan, Guangdong, China, and the other in Sanand, Gujarat, India. Both of them are in the most industrial and commercial regions in the two countries. The local authorities have respectively introduced measures to enhance the market mechanisms to smoothen the process of land acquisition, and contributed to a positive-sum game for all stakeholders in land acquisition for development. Through the analysis of the working of the land market in both cases, we will explore the necessity of local authorities' innovation in carrying out economic policy for development, which has been limited by national regimes, but can be improved by local endeavours.

The chapter is organized in five sections. In the first section we review the status of the land market in both countries, and the challenges it has induced. In the second section, the case of Sanand in Gujarat is discussed. The third section is focused on the case of Foshan New Town project in Guangdong province, China. In the fourth section we discuss the significance of land markets, while the role of local innovative practices and markets in improving the performance of land acquisition in developing societies like India and China is discussed in the final section.

LAND MARKETS IN CHINA AND INDIA

The Chinese Land Market

The legal land market system in China is complex and diverse. In terms of the ownership, urban land is owned by the state while rural land is collectively owned by the commune consisting of villages. As a result, there is no land market with private ownership in China. However, since the beginning of the reform and opening-up policy from the end of the 1970s, several private land property rights were formulated and admitted by the state, including the land-use right in urban regions, and contract and management right for agricultural land in rural areas. Land-use rights in urban regions are normally for development usage. This is a kind of arrangement where the government leases out the land legally for 70 years, 40 years, and 30 years for residential, commercial, and industrial purposes, respectively. It constitutes the primary urban land market. After acquiring the land with the right to use, companies and individuals are allowed to transfer the land in the secondary land market in the form of either developed or undeveloped land. In rural regions, developed land cannot be transferred except for the usage of the collective commune, but contract and management rights (that is, the lease of the member household from the commune) are permitted to be transferred, and consequently turn into the rural rental-land market (see Figure 5.1).

The land markets in China are different from their counterparts in more developed societies. With the adoption of a rigid agricultural land protection system, any agricultural land is not allowed to change to non-agricultural activities without the permission of the local government. Both individuals and communes are forbidden to sell such land for development purposes. However, if the transition of the land for industrial/commercial/residential activities is in line with urban or development planning, then such land can be acquired by the local government which represents the state, and thus becomes the owner of the land. By transferring the land acquired in the primary

Yinghong Huang

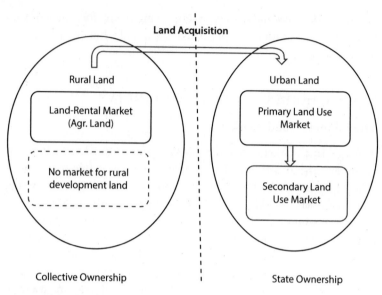

FIGURE 5.1 Land Market in China
Source: Author.

land market, the government, as the only provider of land, gets a large land-transferring fee in proportion to the transfer, which contributes around 40 per cent of the local revenue in China.[2]

This unified and strict usage control system leads to large land price gaps in various land markets. As for the suburb region, due to the limitations on the use of land, a plot of agricultural land cannot be transformed into development land unless the government acquires it under its eminent domain. The main flaw in this practice is that the actual value of the land before land acquisition is not known in advance. However, after the acquisition, it becomes land for urban/industrial development, and can be transferred in the primary land market. Here, land prices shoot up to 40 times the amount of the compensation paid to the owners (either to the commune or to the individual who has the contract and

[2] Shouying Liu, *Zhimian Zhongguo Tudi Wenti* (直面中国土地问题) [*Land Issue in Transitional China*] (Beijing: China Development Press, 2014).

TABLE 5.1 Criterion for Compensation of Land Acquired in Guangzhou, 2012

Administrative Districts	Arable Land	Field	Forest Land	Aquaculture Water Surface	Unutilized Land
Yuexiu District	12.0	9.24	4.2	10.8	3.72
Haizhu District	12.0	9.24	4.2	10.8	3.72
Liwan District	12.0	9.24	4.2	10.8	3.72
Tianhe District	12.0	9.24	4.2	10.8	3.72
Baiyun District I	12.0	9.24	4.2	10.8	3.72
Baiyun District II	10.0	7.70	3.5	9.0	3.10
Huangpu District	10.0	7.70	3.5	9.0	3.10
Huadu District I	8.0	6.16	2.8	7.2	2.48
Huadu District II	6.0	4.62	2.1	5.4	1.86
Panyu District	12.0	9.24	4.2	10.8	3.72
Nansha District	8.0	6.16	2.8	7.2	2.48
Luogang District I	10.0	7.70	3.5	9.0	3.10
Luogang District II	8.0	6.16	2.8	7.2	2.48

Source: Guangzhou Government, 'Yinfa Guangzhou Shi Zhengdi Buchang Baohu Biaozhun Zhidao Yijian (Shixing)de Tongzhi>'(印发《广州市征地补偿保护标准指导意见(试行)的通知》)['Circular on the Tentative Guidelines of the Criterion for Compensation for Land Acquired in Guangzhou'] (2012), http://www.gz.gov.cn/gzswjk/2.2.21/201201/42f8ed642461431d8970f1ecc36ed0de.shtml. In RMB 10,000/mu.[3]

management rights).[4] It contributes large amounts of financial resources to local governments, which enables them to provide civic amenities for the local population. However, it also gives rise to disputes and conflicts between the acquiring authorities and landowners.[5]

[3] One Chinese mu equals 666.7 square metres.

[4] YiBiao Lin, *Bei Zhengdi Nongmin Chayixing Shouchang Yiyuan Yanjiu* (被征地农民差异性受偿意愿研究) [*Studies on the Willingness of Peasants towards the Compensation in Land Acquisition in the Fujian Provinces*] (Fuzhou: Fujian People Publishing House, 2011), 36–8.

[5] Hui Wang and Ran Tao, *Zhongguo Tudi Zhidu Gaige: Nandian, Tupo Yu Zhengce Zuhe* (中国土地制度改革:难点, 突破与政策组合) [*Chinese Land Institution Reform: Issues, Advancement and Policy Package*] (Beijing: The Commercial Press, 2013) .

As a result, the compensation for agricultural land in China is not evaluated on the ground of market value because the change of usages is highly controlled, and the transfer of agricultural land into development land is banned. Land acquisition is the only legal alternative to develop agricultural land for urban purposes. The total amount of compensation is not allowed to exceed 30 times the average production value of the acquired land in the three years prior to acquisition. Normally this works out at around RMB 30,000 per Mu in many places. With the variation of location, in some coastal regions, such as in Guangdong province (see Table 5.1), the price may increase dramatically in accordance with the criterion set by the municipal government. For instance, arable land in Guangzhou which is to be acquired by the government may be compensated at an amount ranging between RMB 60,000/mu and RMB 200,000/mu due to the locations in different districts.[6] However, the land prices in each region are the same, and are not sensitive to their further value.

India's Land Market

Land markets in India function under a system different from that of China. The majority of the land is owned by private households, and there is no separate system regulated by the government. However, the development of land markets is varied in different regions. In some regions, such as Gujarat, Punjab, and Kerala, land markets exist and function very efficiently not only in urban or suburban areas but also in rural areas. But in some other regions, particularly in some underdeveloped rural areas, land markets are non-existent. In a field trip to Nandigram, West Bengal, the peasants argued that there was no land market.[7] People seldom sell lands. Those landowners who are willing

---

[6] 'Guangzhoushi Renmin Zhengfu Bangongting Guanyu Yinfa Guangzhoushi Nongmin Jiti Suoyou Tudi Zhengshou Buchang Shixing Banfa De Tongzhi'(广州市人民政府办公厅关于印发广州市农民集体所有土地征收补偿试行办法的通知) ['Circular on the Interim Measures for Land Expropriation of the Peasants' Collective-owned Land in Guangzhou by the Office of the Municipal Government of Guangzhou'], Guangzhou Government, 2017, http://www.gz.gov.cn/gzgov/s2812/201708/cb90a3dc-1c764b13bea3688fc9d66687.shtml.

[7] Fieldwork at Nandigram, West Bengal, 29 July, 2015.

to sell their land use private connections rather than going to an agent, who are absent in the region. The prices are set by the seller and the buyer through their mutual bargaining. No intermediary exists nor is it needed. Under such informal settlements, with the absence of an institutional framework, an effective land market cannot be developed, and it leads to the undercapitalization of land. This explains why the peasants do not want to sell their lands under the government's land acquisition policies as it is not easy to place a value on their land. It even leads to protests against the government or investors in development projects. So the lack of a land market is a major barrier in the government's efforts to acquire land for development activities in these parts of the country.

Even in the more advanced regions where land markets are by and large developed, the registered price is found to be much lower than the amount actually paid for buying the land to evade stamp duties to the government. In some research, it is argued that only 40 per cent of the actual market value is registered.[8] The compensation for the land is estimated by the average registered price of land in the region in the past three years; however, at even 130 per cent of this registered market value as the key part of the compensation set by the Land Acquisition Act, 1894 (LAA), it is still under-compensated, and only equals 50 per cent of the real market value theoretically. Therefore, due to the absence of or dysfunction of the land markets, the criterion of market value fails to fulfill the promise of just compensation to the land-losers. Even the compensation paid in accordance with the registered price is much less than the true value, and it consequently leads to disputes and conflicts between the landowners and acquiring authorities.

Last but not the least, the exchange of land is so rare in rural regions that families who lose their land to acquisition may fail to find other land to cultivate or invest in. Generally, many of them lose their livelihood, and become landless or marginal landowners, and fail to find an alternative livelihood. The challenges they encounter far exceed the compensation amount paid by the government.

In summary, compared with developed countries, the capitalization of land in developing societies like India and China generally lags far

---

[8] Walter Fernandes, 'Singur and the Displacement Scenario', *Economic & Political Weekly* XLII, no. 3 (2007): 203–6.

behind that of labour and goods. In China, highly state-controlled systems of land markets lead to a strong sense of deprivation among the landowners due to the prevailing high price gap.[9] In India, the imperfections of land markets, including the undervalued registered price, the non-availability of new land, and the absence of market price due to the rare instances of land transactions, render the market price criterion improper to give just and fair compensation to landowners. This generates a host of challenges in the entire process of land acquisition. Thus the lack of effective land markets is a hurdle for the governments to acquire lands under eminent domain in China or India.

In this context, some innovative measures taken at the local government levels towards developing land markets are significant for smooth land acquisition in these countries. Hereinafter, we will look into two cases which are apparently more successful than acquisitions in many other places in these countries. They are the Sanand Industrial Estate in Gujarat and the Foshan New Town project in Guangdong. From the analysis of these two cases, we will see how innovative measures can be taken to build and improve land markets which provide a fair price to the land-losers, and lead to smoother land acquisition.

SANAND INDUSTRIAL ESTATE IN GUJARAT

Sanand Industrial Estate is a subsidiary of the Gujarat Industrial Development Corporation (GIDC), which, as an agency of the government of Gujarat, is committed to provide the industrial backbone for the state. The GIDC was set up under the Gujarat Industrial Development Act, 1962, and currently has an inventory of 202 estates comprising over 63,000 units across the state. Sanand Industrial Estate is located at a distance of 35 kilometres from the business capital of Gujarat, Ahmedabad, on 2,055 hectares of land. It focuses on sectors like engineering, automobiles and ancillary units, engineering plastics, semiconductors, and electronics, among others.[10] The estate is known for introducing the Nano project from Singur, West Bengal to Sanand, Gujarat on 7 October 2008, after the West Bengal government faced

---

[9] Lin, *Bei Zhengdi Nongmin Chayixing Shouchang Yiyuan Yanjiu.*

[10] 'Sanand Industrial Estate', GIDC, https://gidc.gujarat.gov.in/pdf/gidc-presentation/GIDC_Sanand_Industrial_Estate.pdf.

furious protests from local communities resisting the acquisition of 997 acres of land in Singur. These protests incidentally turned out to be one of the key causes of the collapse of the 34-year-reign of the Communist Party of India (Marxist) (CPI(M)) in West Bengal.

Sanand Industrial Estate provides 1,100 acres of land to the Nano project. It has been acclaimed for creating numerous job and investment opportunities. At the inauguration of the first plant in 2010, just 14 months after the beginning of the relocation, it was announced that INR 20 billion would be invested with a capability of manufacturing 250,000 units annually, and generating 10,000 direct or indirect jobs in the state.[11] In a sharp contrast to the hurdles the Nano project encountered in land acquisition in West Bengal, the whole process was smooth and speedy in Gujarat. As a result of numerous factors like the business-friendly social–economic conditions and feasibility of high quality infrastructure, Gujarat became the most favourable state for investment according to a research report of the Deutsche Bank.[12] The state produces 30 per cent of India's chemicals and pharma products, and 38 per cent of its petroleum products. Ninety per cent of India's diamond processing takes place in Gujarat.[13] Even in a medium subsidiary like Sanand Industrial Estate, besides the Nano project, numerous world-class industries like Posco, Nivea, Coca Cola, Nestle, and so on have set up their units.

There are several factors contributing to the successful land diversion for developmental activities in Gujarat. Firstly, there are many other alternatives for land development in the state. In an interview with Mr B.B. Swain, the vice director of the GIDC, he referred to various ways of land development in Gujarat.[14] For example, private

---

[11] 'New Plant for Tata Nano at Sanand Inaugurated', Tata.com (2010), http://www.tata.com/article/inside/XFBpop5GFuM=/TLYVr3YPkMU.

[12] Eric Heymann and M. Vaeth, '450 Billion Reasons to Invest in India's Infrastructure', *Deutsche Bank Research Report*, Asia, Current Issues (28 November 2007).

[13] 'Industrial Park Development in the State of Gujarat', Gujarat Infrastructural Development Board, last modified 7 October 2013, http://www.igep.in/live/hrdpmp/hrdpmaster/igep/content/e48745/e49028/e56649/e57530/04_GIZintconf710_VR.pdf.

[14] Interview with B.B. Swain, 24 September 2015, at Sachivalaya, Gandhinagar.

industrial parks have been built and used in the state, such as Mascot Industrial Park near Ahmedabad, and Horizon Industrial Park and Nexus Industrial Park in Vadodara district, which are run by private companies. These private industrial parks are usually located near the estates of the GIDC, and provide high standard services and land plots to different enterprises. Land pooling is another alternative to develop land. Under the Town Planning and Urban Development head, local governments in Gujarat develop the acquired land into civil infrastructures, pool some proportion of the land into their land bank, and return the majority to the original owners. In three town planning schemes in Ahmedabad, 64–84 per cent of acquired lands were returned to the property owners, while 4–9 per cent were reserved for sale, and the remaining land was developed as infrastructure and public facilities, for example, roads, low-income houses, and so on.[15] Because an effective land market exists in Gujarat, companies in the state are able to buy land from the owners and develop their own warehouses. As an illustration, the first Ford plant set up its warehouses before it shifted to GIDC's estate in Sanand. Besides, even though GIDC is a non-profit government agency, it frequently purchases land from the property owners rather than indulging in compulsory acquisition. Land acquisition is adopted only as the last resort for land development in Gujarat.[16]

However, even when land transition in the state is efficient, in order to avoid the flaws of the national land acquisition regime which had been framed under the LAA, the state government has introduced several additional arrangements to improve land acquisition. The Gujarat state government released a new land acquisition policy formulated by the GIDC in 2010. It encompassed the following reforms which developed into an independent land acquisition regime:[17]

[15] Shishir Mathur, 'Use of Land Pooling and Reconstitution for Urban Development: Experiences from Gujarat, India', *Habitat International* 38 (2013): 199–206.

[16] Interview with B.B. Swain, 24 September 2015, at Sachivalaya, Gandhinagar.

[17] 'GIDC Land Policy 2010', https://gidc.gujarat.gov.in/pdf/Whats_New/Participative_Policy_Development_New_Estates.pdf.

- It is GIDC policy to acquire land for its estates normally by consent;
- The Centre for Environment Planning and Technology University (CEPT) will fix the prevailing market price for each plot of land;
- In addition to the payment for the land at market price, 10 per cent of the differential value between the raw land price and the developed land price, such as industrial, residential, or commercial land, shall be paid to the landowners. This amount shall be calculated annually based on a financial year, and shall be paid each June of the succeeding financial year;
- The original landowners are entitled to the allotment of a commercial plot to the extent of 1 per cent of their land acquired at a token rate of INR 1 per square metre;
- Any landowner whose total rural landholding has been acquired by the government shall be entitled to one-time financial assistance equivalent to 750 days of minimum agricultural wages for loss of livelihood, which amounts to INR 75,000. Likewise, any landowner who becomes a marginal farmer as a result of the land acquisition will be entitled to one-time financial assistance equivalent to 500 days of minimum agricultural wages;
- The GIDC will sponsor one person between the age of 18 and 45 from the landowner's family to study in ITI or a similar approved institution for a course for up to two-years duration;
- Special measures are taken for scheduled tribe (ST) landowners. For example, those who lose 50 per cent of their total landholding may be paid additional assistance equal to 500 days minimum agricultural wages, and those who are displaced due to land acquisition shall be resettled as close as possible to their natural habitat, and in a compact block in order to preserve their ethnic, linguistic, and cultural identity.

From my fieldwork in two villages in Sanand, the outcome of this policy seems quite positive. During fieldwork in Rasupa and Bod villages in August 2015, five families whose lands were acquired, were visited by random selection. The data regarding the total amount of land acquired, compensation, and the usage of the compensation were collected during the interview. As indicated by Table 5.2, several unique characteristics of the land acquisition in the region are highlighted as follows:

TABLE 5.2   Samples from Families Whose Land Was Acquired in Two
Villages of Sanand

No. of Interviewee	Land Acquired (bighas)	Total Compensation (INR million)	Average Land Price (compensated INR million/ bigha)	Use of the Compensation
1	4	12	3	Bought new land, built new house, other investment
2	30	85	2.83	Bought new land
3	18	55	3.05	Bought new land
4	12	21	1.75	Bought new land, opened a small store of mineral water
5	30	84	2.8	Bought new land, rebuilt houses, support relatives

Source: Interviews at Rasupa and Bod villages, Sanand, 20 September 2015.

Firstly, good compensations were provided. The average compensation ranged from INR 1.75 million/bigha to INR 3.05 million/bigha, which is dramatically higher than the standards set by the LAA. Peasants were happy with the compensation, and became *crorepati*s due to the land acquisition.

Secondly, as landowners narrated, their land was acquired through case-by-case bargaining. The price of land varied due to differential features of the land, such as the location, scale, and fertility. However, the location was far more significant in determining the final price than the rest, which is in consonance with the modern land economy.

Thirdly, most of the families whose land was acquired invested in more land elsewhere, and now possess an even greater amount of land than they used to have. Generally, the families whose land was acquired invested some part of the compensation in their homes, and the other part was deposited in banks. There were also some families who began to run stores to earn their livelihood. However, to buy land nearby or sometimes in neighbouring villages was a general practice for all families. Therefore, instead of losing their livelihood, they become larger landholders. Undoubtedly, not all such families improved their living standards. During the interviews, some peasants argued that some families failed to manage their compensation in a wise way; some even squandered their cash and became impoverished, as we can see in other cases like Gurgaon.[18]

On whole, the new land acquisition policy of the GIDC has been embraced by the local community. The landowning families improved their living standards not only by getting a fair compensation, but also by taking a share of the differential proceeds produced by the land development. Moreover, they actively participate in the land markets and invest more in land which makes their livelihood sustainable. During my fieldwork, much excitement and expectation for land acquisition was observed among the landowners.

The lack of effective land markets in the other parts of India appears to have been overcome in Gujarat. As discussed above, the successful stories of land acquisition/transition in Gujarat have multiple contributing factors, including the prevailing entrepreneurial culture, the huge migrant population, the state government's commitment to industrialization, and the diligent institutional design of the new policy. All these factors improve the functioning of land markets in Gujarat, and consequently contribute dramatically to the success of land acquisition and smooth industrialization/urbanization.

FOSHAN NEW TOWN

The Foshan New Town project is a city expansion project of establishing a new central business district (CBD) in Foshan city, which is

[18] Vishal Narain, 'Growing City, Shrinking Hinterland: Land Acquisition, Transition and Conflict in Peri-urban Gurgaon, India', *Environment and Urbanization* 21, no. 2 (2009): 501.

being targeted to bring an investment of RMB 22 billion, and expand the urban region geographically by 88 square kilometres since 2003. Around 66 square kilometres of the development land is located in the suburban region of Shunde District, Foshan, particularly in Lecong town, an industrial area known for manufacturing furniture and plastic products.[19] Several villages in Lecong consequently have witnessed large-scale reconstructions and relocations due to land acquisition for the development project.

From the year 2003 onwards, several rounds of land acquisition were undertaken in the local villages. The villages had become urban villages gradually with a hybrid of urban and rural landscapes. In these villages, only a small amount of land was really being used for agricultural activities. The majority of land was rented for industrial and commercial uses. More importantly, as the migrants coming from outside constitute half the population in these urban villages, a lot of land was rented to the migrants who managed small stores, factories, rental housing, and so on. Thus the landowners in these villagers had changed their lands to more profitable uses than agricultural cultivation. Besides, they took dividends from the communes as shareholders of the collectively owned land. Not surprisingly, the compensation paid according to the Land Administration Law, 1998 (LAL) in China certainly fails to make up for the losses incurred by the villagers who enjoy rights on the land.

The Guangdong Provincial government promulgated a policy to return at least 10 per cent of the acquired land as developed land to the villagers.[20] However, the scarcity of quotas for construction land;

---

[19] 'Foshan Xincheng Fazhan Licheng' (佛山新城发展历程) ['The Development Process of Foshan New Town'], Foshan New Town, 2016, http://www.fsnewcity.gov.cn/xwzx/rsdp/lsyg/201605/t20160506_5599133.html.

[20] This policy began in the early 1990s in Guangdong, and it has been ratified in the government ordinances thereafter in the province, see Guangdong Provincial Government, 'Guangdong Zhengdi Guanli Guiding' (1993) (广东征地管理规定) ['Regulations on Land Acquisition in Guangdong'], http://www.gd.gov.cn/govpub/dffg/200606/t20060616_1479.htm; Guangdong Provincial Government, 'Guangdong Renmin Zhengfu Bangongting Guanyu Zhuanfa Sheng Guotu Ziyuanting Guanyu Shenhua Zhengdi Zhidu Gaige

disputes over availability, the location, and the sale of the returned land, frequently lead to conflicts between the local government and communes.[21] Peasants expressed complaints on the delay of implementation of this policy during interviews. Consequently, the original compensation packages, including an amount of RMB 57,000 to 60,000 per mu set by the national regulations and 10 per cent of the land promised to be returned by the Guangdong provincial government, for many reasons, failed to satisfy the land-losing communes, and lead to confrontation between the government and peasants.

After the final decision of the municipal government to build a huge CBD in the region in 2012, negotiations between the local government represented by the Administrative Committee of Foshan New Town and the local communes, including the villages of Dadun (大墩村), Yuebu, and Xiaocong, among others, were conducted. The Administrative Committee was established by the municipal government. Several new policy innovations were adopted regarding the acquisitions. Under the Remake and Acquisition project of Dadun Village in 2015, for instance, the commune and the Administrative Committee reached an agreement called 'the Scheme of the Total Remake of Dadun Village, Lecong,' which includes following innovative arrangements regarding the land acquisition:

De Yijian De Tongzhi' (广东人民政府办公厅关于转发国土资源厅关于深化征地制度改革的意见的通知) ['Circular on the Opinion on Deepening the Land Expropriation Instituted by the Land and Resource Department', Issue No. 29] (2005).

[21] China has adopted a quota system to control the use change of its agricultural land since 1998. The quota is set by the Central Government in accordance with its five-yearly economic and social development plan. For example, in its thirteenth five-year plan for economic and social development, the overall scale of the quota for increase in land newly designated for construction (also called quota for construction land, *Jianshe Yongdi Zhibiao*) during 2000 to 2016 is less than 2.17 million hectares (see Central Compilation & Translation Press, Central Government of China, *The 13th Five-Year Plan for Economic and Social Development of the People's Republic of China* (2016), http://ghs.ndrc.gov.cn/ghwb/gjwngh/). The quota is distributed between the ministries and local governments, and only on this land is land-use change from agriculture to others legal.

Firstly, instead of compulsorily acquiring the land, the local government now takes several alternative measures to build a functional land market for the local commune. As stated previously, communes that collectively own rural land are banned from transferring their land directly to the developer even when a plot of land is planned to be developed under the master plan. It shall be acquired by the state, mostly represented by local governments, and then be transferred to the developers. In this regime, the peasants who will lose their land do not have the right to negotiate with developers. The compensation rate is standardized and fixed, and thus not sensitive to the potential market value. The market mechanism is absent totally in the first transition of forceful land acquisition, but it does exist when local governments transfer it to developers.

In the Dadun remake project, the local government would not acquire the land and subsequently transfer it to the private developer as it used to do. Rather, the land would be 'sold' in the primary land markets through direct negotiation between local communes and developers, and thus the land price would be fixed according to the market value. In order to legalize the purchase, the Foshan government still had to use parts of its quotas for construction land, which is precious and scarce to the local government in China for the limited amount they are granted. The title of the land would remain under the name of the government, and formally be transferred by the local government to the developers. However, the local government would return the land transferring fee back to the commune, and pool it as the funds for the whole project. In addition, the remake plan was discussed in the village, and several rounds of negotiation between the government and the commune proceeded. Finally, they came to a vote among all the adult villagers, with the result of 94 per cent of the peasants agreeing with the drafted plan.

Secondly, a lucrative compensation package was provided to the commune and all its members. It includes:

- A villager who holds stock in the collective economic group in the commune gets RMB 300,000 as a one-off dividend, and long-time annual dividend RMB 10,000 for the first five years, and RMB 20,000 annually since the sixth year. The stocks were distributed based on the criterion that an elderly person enjoys 3 shares, young and middle-aged get 2, and a child gets 1 share.

- A villager who may be relocated for losing his/her house will be compensated either by cash or with a new house according to his/her preference. Those who choose to get compensated with a new house will get it at a size 1.1 to 1.3 times the one they lost, and those who prefer cash may get around RMB 10,000 for each square metre, with adaption to the price changes.
- The developer will rebuild some real estate for the village, including the office of the village administration committee, a primary school, a kindergarten, stores, and so on. Historical or religious places, such as ancestral temples, religious temples, are also to be remade or shifted.

Thirdly, the sharing of developmental benefits has been included in the project. This is indicated in the distribution and the proposed usages of the land acquired for the remake project. As specified in Table 5.3, out of the 2,159 mu of land reconstructed, 1,051 mu (land no. 1-A) is provided for the relocation and resettlement of the villagers, and 63.7 mu (land no. 1-B) remains under their control as reserved land. For public

TABLE 5.3 Land Uses in the Remake Project

	Scale of Land (Mu)	Usage
Land No. 1-A being reconstructed for villagers	1051	For resettlement and relocation
Land No. 1-B reserved for village	64	Reserved land
Land No. 2 for infrastructures	353	For roads, green belts, river surge, etc.
Land No. 3 for financing	692	Land sold to real estate as financial source of the whole project
Total	2159	

Source: Urban Redevelopment Authority of Foshan New Town, the Dadun Village Committee, Dadun Village Economic Cooperative, 'Lecongzhen Daduncun Zhengcun Gaizao Shishifangan'(乐从镇大墩村整村改造实施方案) ['Implementation Plan of the Dadun Village Remake Project'] (2014).

infrastructure which is under the administration of the government, 353 mu land (land no. 2) is used. In order to finance all the expenses of the project, 692 mu land (land no. 3) is sold in the land market to real estate developers for residential and commercial development. Therefore, the distribution of land among the three stakeholders (the commune, local government, and developers) comes to the ratio of 51.6 per cent: 16.4 per cent: 32 per cent.

The sharing and exchange of the costs and benefits in the project are given in Table 5.4. The Dadun commune submits land no. 2 and land no. 3 to the local government and developers respectively, and gets the lucrative compensation package mentioned previously including 51.6 per cent of the land it originally holds. The local government supports the project with the urban renewal plan, quotas for construction land, and the land-use fees which constitute a major part of the land revenue, and in return, gets the land for public infrastructure and also collects a real estate development tax. More importantly, the success of the remake project changes the landscape of the city, and attracts a large amount of further investment. The ambitious development plan of the city is then accomplished. For real estate developers, the amount they paid for financing the land is utilized for compensation packages to the villagers. In return, all the construction works involved in the project will be delivered to them, which will increase their profits.

The total expenditure of the remake project was RMB 4.17 billion. In 2016, it was reported that two pieces of land of 195.7 mu were sold at a price of RMB 2 billion, or about 50 per cent of the whole expense of the project with only 28 per cent of the financing land. Undoubtedly the project does not have any financial difficulties. In an interview with local villagers, it was revealed that around RMB 158,000/share has been distributed to villagers, which is around

TABLE 5.4   Earning and Cost in the Dadun Remake Project

	Give	Get
Commune	Land 2 and 3/Tax	Compensation package, including land no. 1
Government	Plan/Quota/Revenue	Tax/Land no. 2
Developers	Compensation Package/Tax	Land no. 3/Development plan

52.7 per cent of the promised one-off dividend.[22] With the proceeds of the sale of the financing land, the compensation package will be delivered in the near future. This project is embraced by the local commune, especially the older generation that enjoys three shares with a dividend tantamount to RMB 900,000. With this amount they will never be dependent on their younger generation economically, and consequently will be more confident of their future. So they are eager for the quick implementation, and earnest supporters of the remake project. This contrasts sharply with other cases of land acquisition in China, where the older generation's livelihood relies far more on land than that of the younger ones, and makes them the core resistant group to the land acquisition exercise of the government.[23]

LAND MARKETS IN LAND ACQUISITION

As discussed above, the role of land markets is of extreme significance in land acquisition as compensations are normally paid in accordance with some proportion of the current or future potential market price. In the absence of a well-functioning land market, a reliable assessment of land prices cannot be made, and it thus creates a breeding ground for discontent of the landowners, and disputes between the state and the land-losers for their different views on the right price of the land acquired. The principle of fair compensation as a key element for smooth and just land acquisition is difficult to realize in such circumstances. This scenario is prevailing in developing societies like India and China due to the non-existence or weak functioning of land markets. Land acquisition efforts by the government have led to many cases of protest, and even violent conflicts between the landowners and acquiring authorities. However, the two cases discussed in this chapter, namely, Sanand, Gujarat and Foshan in Guangdong, present a contrasting picture. They demonstrate how innovative measures taken

[22] Interviews conducted at Dadun village, 28 April 2017.

[23] Yaoyun Feng, Chongtu de Chixuxing: S Cun Nongmin Yu Zhengfu Zhengdi Jiufen Wenti Yanjiu(冲突的持续性：S村农民与政府征地纠纷问题研究) [The Continuation of Conflict: A Study on Disputes on Land Expropriation between the Peasants and the Government in S Countryside] (PhD diss., Jilin University, 2013).

by the local governments to procure land could contribute to the development of a functioning land market. This land market, in turn, paves the way for smooth and hassle-free land acquisition by the local governments for developmental activities.

In Sanand, for instance, firstly the GIDC entrusted CEPT University with the mission of evaluating the market value of each piece of land, which determined the compensation in land acquisition. Hence it in fact forgoes the prevailing practice of fixing a price based on the last three years' transactions, which used to be much lower than the actual worth and failed to take into consideration many sensitive parameters, like location of the land, its accessibility to infrastructure, its annual output, and so on. A compensation calculated on its actual worth meets the standard of fair compensation as practiced in more developed societies where a sophisticated land market prevails. Secondly, the acquisition process was carried out through direct negotiations on a case-by-case basis where each household's concerns were respected, and instead of compulsory acquisition, land was procured through the consent of its owners and hence dramatically lessened their grievances. Thirdly, an effective land market also encourages land-losers to reinvest in new land, which enforces their economic strength as well as strengthens land markets. As shown in the Sanand case, the money received in compensation by the land-owners was spent on creating more capital either by investing in new land or developing new livelihood tools. Thus their living standards were improved.

As for the Foshan New Town project, as shown above, the core strategy is to 'bring the local commune into the land market'. This measure reverses the national land acquisition regime where the local commune is excluded from the land market. If the GIDC's practice in Sanand was aimed to improve the land market mechanism for the state to provide appropriate compensation (see Figure 5.2), what the local government in Foshan managed to achieve is to provide the local commune opportunities to become a real seller in the primary land markets.

Firstly, direct negotiations are allowed to take place between the local commune and the developers. The government has not interfered during the process of setting the land price. The final agreement is signed by both parties. This practice is unique, for in the rest of China,

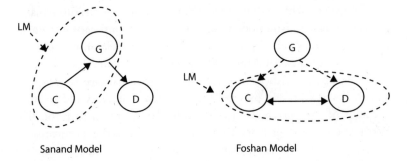

Sanand Model   Foshan Model

FIGURE 5.2 Innovation in Land Acquisition in Sanand and Foshan
Source: Author.
Note: C: local commune in China or household whose land is acquired in India; G: local government; D: developers; and LM: land market.

land is acquired by the government and subsequently transferred to developers in exchange for a large amount of land transferring fees. However, under the Foshan model, the structure of land acquisition and the primary land market in China are totally revised. The local commune becomes an active player in the primary land market, and reverses the legal monopoly of governments. This practice changes the very nature of land acquisition in China.

Secondly, in the Foshan project, the local government skilfully provides numerous forms of administrative support to avoid any legal violation of the current land acquisition regime. For instance, it gave quotas for construction land to the local commune, which is strictly required for a legal land-use change from agricultural land to other uses in China. Also, it nominally acquires the land and transfers it to developers as it generally happens all over China. But the price is actually negotiated by the commune, which collectively owns the land, and the developer. In addition, while the local government did receive the land transferring fee after rendering the financing land to developers, it returned 50 per cent of the land transferring fee to the local commune after charging some administrative fees and taxes. While the land acquisition is still in place formally in this case, numerous innovative measures have been adopted in the Foshan New Town project, which succeeded in overcoming the flaws of the current land acquisition regime.

Thirdly, a benefit-sharing mechanism was introduced in this remake project. Similar to land pooling in Gujarat,[24] the local commune gets the majority (around 52 per cent) of the developed land, and submits 16 per cent of their land for public infrastructure and 32 per cent to land developers. Furthermore, the compensation package is attractive and results in a smooth process. Without these deliberate and creative revisions of the current land acquisition regime, particularly on the reformation of the primary land market in China, this positive-sum game could not have been achieved.

THE MARKET MECHANISM AND INNOVATIONS OF LOCAL AUTHORITIES IN LAND ACQUISITION

Much of the land market in both India and China is weak or absent. It is partly due to the strict restrictions on land transitions such as land ceiling regulation, and partly because of the non-capitalization of land in both countries. As for China, the dual-track system separates the two levels of the land market, and consequently creates a large land value gap between agricultural and developed land. However, without the barometer of a land market, fair compensation, which is of great importance for just land acquisition, cannot materialize. Disputes and conflicts unavoidably occur as a result of the absence of consensus on a fair compensation.

On the other hand, with a workable land market, land transactions can be conducted smoothly. Many by-products arise in an efficient land market. For instance, landowners' livelihood no longer solely depends on land, they can invest, or more precisely speculate, rather than only cultivate. Land thus becomes a good or capital. Peasants are no more bound by land. The separation of land and its owners does not necessarily lead to the loss of livelihood or impoverishment of the latter. As in the case of Sanand, peasants end up possessing more land than they had earlier. In Dadun village of Foshan, villagers have given up agricultural activities and used their lands for non-agricultural purposes since the end of the 1990s. Half of the population living in this

[24] Mathur, 'Use of Land Pooling and Reconstitution for Urban Development'.

village are migrants from outside the village, who do not have any ownership of the land and work in factories or companies nearby. So the acquisition does not threaten any agricultural activities. Rather they have the rights either to get an equal size or even larger land in the ratio of 1.1:1 against the land acquired or to get cash compensation as per the real market price. In short, the existence of a land market enables peasants in both countries to get fair compensation, and to improve their situation by using the compensation.

However, to build and perfect the functioning of the land market in developing societies, the support of local governments with innovative policy instruments is of great relevance. In some regions of India and China, local governments make ingenious and creative arrangements. In Sanand, the GIDC introduced an independent and reputed agent (CEPT University) to determine the land price, and acquired land through direction negotiation with individual owners. In the Dadun remake project in Foshan, the local government deliberately revised the current national regime by providing opportunities for the local commune to enter the land market. There were several more innovations, as discussed above. All these measures have helped reverse the discrimination against rural communes in the current land regime in China, and against agricultural landowners in rural India.

However, the relationship between the current land regime and local creative innovations is complex and deserves more research. In both cases, the current land regimes have not been completely put aside by local governments. The basic structure of the current land regime is pro forma respected and adhered to. In Sanand, land was still acquired or bought by the representative agency of the local government, the GIDC. The compensation was paid according to the market value as mandated in the LAA. It is the GIDC rather than the local commune who built the industrial estate and leased land to private firms. The basic legal characteristics of acquisition remained untouched in Sanand. In the Dadun remake project, similar institutional conditions exist. The basic features of the national land acquisition regulation set by the LAL have been followed as in other regions. The difference lies only in the sense that the local government modified the current regime. Rather than changing the basic elements of the current regime, what the local government has done is to improve it with delicate provisions of new policy instruments.

***

The analysis of the two cases of Dadun and Sanand indicates that multiple factors contribute to the success of land acquisition by the government. These include local innovative measures, an entrepreneurial culture, a business-friendly policy environment, large proportion of immigrant population, and so on. However, local ingenuity in creatively implementing national regimes with adaptions to local conditions is of great significance. Without a careful and deliberate redesign of the land acquisition regime, the other factors may not be able to generate a smooth land acquisition. As we know, when new policy instruments were not adopted, land acquisition encountered resistance in other similar places when the local authorities were conservative with their policy.[25]

The innovative measures adopted by the local authorities in the two cases revolve around improving the market mechanism in land acquisition. As shown above, the market mechanism is generally inadequate during land acquisition in both countries. Compensation is not delivered according to the true market value. As a result, parting with a piece of land usually leads to the deprivation of livelihoods of some peasants. The landowners in India, or the land property right owners in case of China, are not only economically reliant on land, but are also socially and psychologically attached to it. All this contributes to their reluctance to give up land, and therefore leads to conflicts between them and the authorities.

Another noteworthy aspect is that the local authorities deliberately and cautiously introduce the innovative measures to keep them in line with the current national regimes, particularly to avoid any breach of

[25] For land acquisition cases in Kerala, see K.P. Chitra, Politics of Land Acquisition and Conversion: With Reference to Two Development Projects in Kerala (PhD diss., Tata Institute of Social Work, 2013); in Guandong, there is the well-known land acquisition case of Wukan, see Xuefei Ren, 'Land Acquisition, Rural Protests, and the Local State in China and India', *Environment and Planning* 35, no. 1 (2017): 25–41; for Gujarat, see Lancy Lobo and Shashikant Kumar, *Land Acquisition, Displacement and Resettlement in Gujarat 1947–2004* (New Delhi: Sage, 2009); for Fujian, read Lin, 'Bei Zhengdi Nongmin Chayixing Shouchang Yiyuan Yanjiu'.

the latter. The measures adopted are to supplement, rather than override the key features of the current regimes. It is a smart development approach, which avoids the possible accusation of violation of the current national regimes, and therefore legalizes their innovation and makes it more sustainable.

In sum, the secret of the success of the land acquisition in both cases lies in the local authorities' innovative measures to utilize the land market mechanism. The understanding of the importance of the market mechanism and its skilful introduction into the land acquisition process to supplement the institutional weakness of the current regimes results in smooth land acquisition, and brings about a win-win situation in these two cases. Nevertheless, this analysis does not provide any specific suggestions for institutional reform to current regimes; it instead stresses that local authorities can improve the regimes with a focus on using the market mechanism as per their own individual situations.

6 Land Making and Industry Making in Tamil Nadu

Sojin Shin[1]

Tamil Nadu is the most urbanized state in India with 48.45 per cent of its population living in urban areas.[2] The high level of urbanization is commensurate with the state's commitment to industrialization. The state's aggressive land acquisition for industrialization supports it. As of June 2017, Tamil Nadu has the largest number of 36 operational special

[1] I acknowledge that the original materials used and reproduced in this chapter with permission are from Sojin Shin, *The State, Society, and Foreign Capital in India* © Sojin Shin, 2018, published by Cambridge University Press. The earlier draft of this paper 'Land Management and Industrial Development in Tamil Nadu' was presented with Dr Rahul Mukherji at the 10th ISAS Annual International Conference on 'Politics & Economics of Land in Asia' in Singapore on 30 October 2015, and again discussed in the 19th Annual Conference of the Indian Political Economy Association at Goa University on 4 December 2015.

[2] The data is based on the ratio of population in urban areas to total population in Tamil Nadu measured for Census 2011. See Government of India, 'Selected Socio-economic Statistics', Ministry of Statistics and Programme Implementation (2011), http://mospi.nic.in/mospi_new/upload/sel_socio_eco_stats_ind_2001_28oct11.pdf. Tamil Nadu is followed by Kerala (47.72 per cent) and Maharashtra (45.23 per cent).

economic zones (SEZs) among the Indian states.[3] Building SEZs primarily aims at promoting growth through a massive flow of foreign and domestic investment in the SEZs, particularly in infrastructure and productive capacity.[4] It is also expected to generate additional economic activities like the creation of employment opportunities. Such aims are clearly stipulated in Tamil Nadu's Industrial Policy, 2007, which promotes manufacturing capacity to meet global manufacturing competence.[5]

As such, the higher level of land acquisition in Tamil Nadu poses a question of 'how,' particularly in its relation with socio-political facilitators, compared with other states that have struggled with land management for industrialization. How do socio-political factors explain a high level of land acquisition that is coupled with intensive industrialization in Tamil Nadu? This chapter attempts to answer the question by paying attention to the ideas of policy-makers on inclusive industrial schemes and societal structure promoting the upward mobility of low-caste groups in the state. It argues that the state's commitment to making industries by aggressively making industrial lands available has met the aspirations and needs of citizens favouring urbanization, thereby contributing to industrial development.

The chapter consists of two parts. The first part explores the political economy of Tamil Nadu in managing lands for industrialization by tracing the ideas of policy-makers towards lands, and analysing the societal structure of the state supporting the state-led industrialization. The second part discusses how the state and society in Tamil Nadu bargain over land conflicts where large-scale investment projects are involved. It deals with a case study conducted in the village of Thervoy Kandigai in the district of Thiruvallur, where a French tyre company

---

[3] See Government of India, 'State-wise Distribution of Approved SEZs', Ministry of Commerce and Industry (2017), http://www.sezindia.nic.in/writereaddata/pdf/StatewiseDistribution-SEZ.pdf. Telangana (29), Maharashtra (28), and Karnataka (26) follow Tamil Nadu.

[4] See the official website of SEZs in India run by the Government of India. It is available at http://sezindia.nic.in/about-introduction.asp.

[5] See Government of Tamil Nadu, 'The Industrial Policy 2007', Industries Department, http://www.tidco.com/images/industrialpolicy_e_2007.pdf.

proposed 3 million units of tyre production per annum within one of the SEZs. Data was collected from December 2011 to March 2012 during fieldwork, and a short revisit in August 2013.

THE POLITICAL ECONOMY OF MANAGING
LANDS FOR INDUSTRIALIZATION

Ideas for Industrialization and Land Management in the Bipartisan Leadership

In the 1970s, the Dravida Munnetra Kazhagam (DMK) government showed great initiative in transforming the economy by establishing state agencies for industrialization. For example, the Tamil Nadu Small Industries Development Corporation Limited (SIDCO) and the State Industries Promotion Corporation of Tamil Nadu (SIPCOT) were established to promote industrial development. These organizations, interestingly, later played important roles in supporting various foreign investment projects in the state, especially after the economic reforms of the Central Government in 1991. Incorporated in 1970, SIDCO has the specific objective of playing a catalytic role in the promotion and development of micro and small industries,[6] while SIPCOT was established in 1971 to encourage the participation of big businesses and the private sector.[7] The State Industries Promotion Corporation of Tamil Nadu has established, developed, maintained, and managed industrial complexes and SEZs in 12 districts of the state since then, by acquiring lands for domestic and foreign investors.[8] The Tamil Nadu Industrial Development Corporation (TIDCO) also began to operate actively in the 1970s, after it was founded in 1965. It has been supporting large and medium-scale industries by cooperating with the activities of SIPCOT.

The DMK government under Karunanidhi's leadership strongly supported the enhancement of the state agencies. In his budget speech

[6] See the official website of SIDCO, http://www.sidco.tn.nic.in/rti.pdf.

[7] Government of Tamil Nadu, 'Budget 1971–72 Speech of Thiru M Karunanidhi Chief Minister' (Madras, 1971).

[8] See the official website of SIPCOT, http://www.sipcot.com.

in 1975, Karunanidhi, the Chief Minister of Tamil Nadu at the time, appreciated their performance as follows:

> In the last four years, TIDCO has initiated 37 projects which are designed to cover the gaps in our industrial structure in petrochemicals, pharmaceuticals, chemicals, engineering and other industries....The SIDCO will take up a program for the construction of 100 industrial sheds at a total cost of 1 crore rupees in 1975–76. A provision of Rs. 20 lakhs as margin money has been made for this purpose in the Budget....The SIPCOT has sanctioned assistance to the tune of Rs. 9.8 crore under various schemes and has canalized a total investment of 73 crore rupees with direct employment potential for over 12,800 persons.[9]

As can be seen in Table 6.1, Tamil Nadu showed a dramatic increase in its growth rate from 1960 to 1980. The net state domestic product (NSDP) per capita in Tamil Nadu from 1970 to 1980 was 16 times more than that from 1960 to 1970. Table 6.1 presents the trends of growth rates from 1960 to 1980 in some select states like Karnataka and Delhi that performed well. Tamil Nadu's NSDP during the period is under India's average. However, it is remarkable that Tamil Nadu's

TABLE 6.1   Trends of Growth Rates in Selected States (1960–80)

States	Net State Domestic Product (NSDP)		Net State Domestic Product (NSDP) per Capita	
	1960–1 to 1969–70	1970–1 to 1979–80	1960–1 to 1969–70	1970–1 to 1979–80
Karnataka	3.4	4.3	1.2	1.8
Delhi	5.1	6.2	0.7	1.7
Tamil Nadu	2.1	3.4	0.1	1.6
All India	3.0	3.6	0.8	1.2

Source: Central Statistical Organization, cited in Government of India, *Report on Reforming Investment Approval & Implementation*: Part II: *Downstream Issues: Implementation and Operation* (New Delhi: Planning Commission, 2002), 35.

[9] Government of Tamil Nadu, 'Budget 1975–76 Speech of Thiru M. Karunanidhi Chief Minister' (Madras, 1975), 12–13.

NSDP per capita in the same period rose quickly. The rapid increase in the growth rate of the state, particularly in the 1970s, needs to be understood in the context of the industrialization that both the DMK and the All India Anna Dravida Munnetra Kazhagam (AIADMK) leaders pursued.[10]

The economic growth of Tamil Nadu has been substantially contributed to by private sector industry through a close tie with the state.[11] The state leaders' ideas on industrialization through close ties with the private sector have gradually evolved since 1967.

This argument challenges a perspective that the year 1967 was the initiation of the decline of economic growth in the industrial trajectory of Tamil Nadu. Aseema Sinha noted that Tamil Nadu in this period neglected growth-oriented industrial policies, and the DMK government merely asserted cultural populism by failing to connect welfare schemes with the state's economic growth until the Central Government's economic reforms in 1991.[12] As a significant factor that contributed to the failure of industrial growth, Sinha pointed to the political conflicts between the DMK and the Congress party. It is true that the election victory of the DMK under Annadurai's leadership in 1967 involved frequent political conflicts with the Congress party both at the union and the state levels. However, Sinha's analysis overlooks the ideas of DMK leaders on industrialization, and the detailed institutional arrangements that were implemented for industrial growth.

I, instead, would say that such political conflicts between the DMK and the Congress party extended to financial matters, and encouraged

[10] Leaders of the DMK initiated the public distribution system (PDS) after the 1967 election. The AIADMK government in the 1980s implemented massive welfare programmes for school children, villagers, and the weaker sections of society.

[11] It would be possible to say that Tamil Nadu is a developed state in this sense. For a discussion on the classification of Indian states, see Atul Kohli, *Poverty Amid Plenty in the New India* (Cambridge: Cambridge University Press, 2012). Kohli did not include the state of Tamil Nadu in the category of developed states. Instead, Kohli classified Gujarat and Maharashtra as developed states in India.

[12] Assema Sinha, *The Regional Roots of Developmental Politics in India: A Divided Leviathan* (Bloomington, IN: Indiana University Press, 2005).

the state leaders in Tamil Nadu to pursue industrialization by resorting to the private sector.[13] It is not obvious how much they depended on open market loans and commercial borrowings. However, the state not only utilized external financial aid from international organizations like the World Bank, but also encouraged exports to get out of its financial difficulties.

In the process of industrialization, the ideas of political leaders were reflected in inclusive industrial schemes. They include land distribution, employment, and enhancement of vocational education. For example, many parts of forest lands were distributed to the landless poor from 1967, while the state secured lands for industrialization.[14] Through the land distribution, urban landowners who lived in the city of Madras, in particular, had to pay increased taxes, while small landholders were exempted from the tax increase.[15]

Kosalram remarked on the revolutionary characteristics of the land reforms that were led by the DMK government at that time. Kosalram highlighted that the Land Ceiling Act, 1961 was modified in 1971, and amended five times after that. As he put it: 'the Government of Tamil Nadu shows the progress made in the assignment of surplus land. [It] has persuaded the landlords to offer concessions to the times.'[16]

A bureaucrat in the Land Reform Department of the Government of Tamil Nadu agreed with the perspective that the 1970s were a critical period for land reforms in the state. He said,

[13] V.R. Nedunchezhiyan, who served as the Finance Minister of Tamil Nadu from the AIADMK in the 1980s, pointed out that the substantial curtailing of financial assistance from the Central Government towards Tamil Nadu was not simply because of the Central Government's poor finances (see Government of Tamil Nadu, 'Budget 1980–81: Speech of Thiru V.R. Nedunchezhiyan, Minister of Finance', Ministry of Finance (Madras, 1980)). Nedunchezhiyan's remarks indicate that the political conflicts between the union government and Tamil Nadu led to a lack of financial security in the state.

[14] Government of Tamil Nadu, 'Budget 1971–72 Speech of Thiru M Karunanidhi', 20–1.

[15] Government of Tamil Nadu, 'Budget 1971–72 Speech of Thiru M Karunanidhi', 29.

[16] S.A. Kosalram, 'Political Economy of Agriculture in Tamil Nadu', *Social Scientist* 1, no. 12 (1973): 3–21, 13.

The land reform amendment in 1972 reflected the leaders' ideas on the utilization of lands for industrial purposes. Lots of surplus lands were not only assigned to the poor, but also commercialized with the purpose of selling to the private investors. Also, any public trust having aims to establish educational institutes or hospitals could easily purchase the land through the land reforms amendment.[17]

State's Commitment to Land Making and Upward Mobility Societal Structure

The ideas on industrialization were substantially materialized by making lands available for industrial purposes in Tamil Nadu after the Central Government's economic reforms in 1991. For example, the Tamil Nadu Land Reforms (Amendment) Act was enacted in 1991 aiming at retrieving *benami* (illegal) lands and distributing them to the landless poor.[18] The political leaders of the state thought that the speedy execution of land reforms was critical for securing more lands for industrialization and strengthening the economy. Indicating Jayalalithaa, who led the land reforms at that time, a member of parliament (MP) from the AIADMK mentioned, '*Purachi Thalaivi* [revolutionary leader] has taken this commendable step to retrieve benami lands from illegal holdings and to distribute them to the landless poor in the true spirit of land to the tiller'.[19]

The land reforms benefited citizens both in cities and rural areas. Lindberg also presented the positive effects of the land reforms in the rural areas of the state.[20] Through a case study of six villages in the Kaveri delta in Tiruchirappalli district in the state, they highlighted that

[17] Interview at the Government of Tamil Nadu in Chennai on 21 November 2012.

[18] Government of India, 'Demand for Creating of Tamil Nadu Land Reforms Measure', Rajya Sabha Secretariat (1994).

[19] Government of India, 'Demand for Creating of Tamil Nadu Land Reforms Measure', 375.

[20] Informal discussion with Lindberg in New Delhi on 14 December 2011. See also G. Djurfeldt, V. Athreya, N. Jayakumar, S. Lindberg, A. Rajagopal, and R. Vidyasagar, 'Agrarian Change and Social Mobility in Tamil Nadu', *Economic & Political Weekly* XLIII, no. 45 (2008): 50–61, for a study on villagers' mobility in the same villages in Tiruchirappalli.

the land reforms and industrialization have contributed to the increase in total income, and more equal distribution of assets and income in the villages.

The land reforms helped the state promote foreign investments. In the process of the reforms, the Tamil Nadu Urban Land Act was amended in 1992 to increase the tax on landowners in urban areas. The Acquisition of Lands for Industrial Purposes Act was also enacted in 1997 in the context of the revision of the Industrial Act in the same year that reflected the state leaders' ideas on the utilization of lands for industrial growth. These acts considerably helped the state enhance the role of SIPCOT to acquire lands for industrial purposes, especially in urban areas.[21] Supported by such institutional arrangements, SIPCOT was able to allocate lands actively to both domestic and foreign investors, who entered the market in the state. In an interview, C. Ponnaiyan, a former finance minister of the state, pointed to the aggressive and efficient role of SIPCOT. He said, 'I think our state does not need to worry about land acquisition for the next 15 years as we have already acquired enough lands for building various industrial complexes.'[22]

There has been close cooperation between SIPCOT and TIDCO, which is another state agency that attracts joint ventures, to establish various industrial complexes and SEZs in several districts of the state. An executive vice chairman of the Industrial Guidance and Export Promotion Bureau (GUIDANCE) in TIDCO, who has participated in promoting foreign direct investment (FDI) inflows for the past 22 years, pointed to the strong support from the state government and the coherent ideas of political leaders from different ruling parties as the most important factor that has boosted FDI inflows.[23] He said,

> Government support is very important to promote investments. The commitment of the government to creating relevant policies and incentives is necessary. In the system of democracy, the government (ruling party) keeps changing. An election keeps coming and after five years the government changes. But, an industrial development plan needs 40 or

[21] Interview with Jatindranath Swain, Principal Secretary of the Land Administration Department in the Government of Tamil Nadu on 21 November 2012.

[22] Interview in Chennai on 31 January 2012.

[23] Interview at TIDCO on 2 February 2012.

50 years, it does not respect this change of governments. The successful government should keep the promises of the previous government in pursuing such investment projects continuously. This is business, not politics. Both the DMK and the AIADMK governments consider investment projects as significant for industry, so the successive government has honoured such industrial promises of the previous government. In addition, both governments have tried not to create any social displacement while investment projects are embarked upon, through financial and infrastructural compensation.

He also mentioned that not only does a project facility committee in TIDCO hold regular weekly meetings to ensure the implementation of investment policies, but also a three-tier monitoring system efficiently operates to attract investment projects.

However, the process of land acquisition has sometimes been followed by agitations from society. The agitations, interestingly, which are mainly led by Left-wing political parties rather than non-governmental organizations (NGOs) in Tamil Nadu, as noted in articles in *The Hindu* on 21 August 2004 ('Centre Urged to Increase EPF Interest') and 5 December 2007 ('Call to Stop Outsourcing Jobs'), were not successful in mobilizing people in urban and rural areas of the state. This may be one of the reasons why conflicts between the state and the citizens have been quite muted in Tamil Nadu, compared to other states in India. It is possibly explained by the tendency of the state's inclusive industrial schemes that consider a broader strata of citizens in society.

In other words, the political leaders' ideas on industrialization include substantial concerns for the marginalized groups in society, providing vocational training programmes and employment. A study on human development in India by the Institute of Applied Manpower Research under the Planning Commission finds that Tamil Nadu has improved its human development status considerably. It is very intriguing to compare the development with that of Bihar and Uttar Pradesh that have a similar caste composition in society.[24] As Santosh Mehrotra,

[24] Institute of Applied Manpower Research, Planning Commission, Government of India, *India Human Development Report 2011: Towards Social Inclusion* (New Delhi: Oxford University Press, 2012), http://www.pratirodh.com/pdf/human_development_report2011.pdf.

the team leader of the research group on human development, put it, 'Tamil Nadu has shown the best performance especially in the areas of public health and education for the last ten years.'[25] It is plausible to say that the educated youth demanded that the state create employment, and has been quickly absorbed in the state's industry. This argument is strongly backed by the societal structure of the state, having a number of low-caste groups who have strong aspirations towards upward mobility.

The societal structure is associated with the low level of societal opposition to state-led industrialization in Tamil Nadu, which has a role in encouraging the state to pursue making lands available for industrialization. An interesting study conducted by Vijayabaskar sought answers in the state's strategies to curb resistance, to the puzzle of what combination of circumstances has produced the lack of resistance among farmers against the state's land acquisition for SEZs in Tamil Nadu. Vijayabaskar makes three arguments: First, Tamil Nadu's industrial evolution is in transition, moving away from the agriculture-oriented structure. The industrial transformation, interestingly, addresses the long-term crises of the agricultural sector, which includes the growing landlessness of marginal farmers, the backward castes thereby increasingly moving to non-farm employment. Second, the state's strategies are good enough to undercut resistance by using dexterous bureaucrats who know how to acquire lands efficiently. The author stressed that bureaucrats not only deploy stalling tactics for landowners who institute a legal claim, but also offer relatively generous compensation packages at the bargaining table. Third, the state can facilitate the negotiation process between landowners and private firms based on market mechanisms in a way with which both parties can agree. Based on fieldwork in several land conflict cases in selected districts, Vijayabaskar concluded that 'land acquisition in Tamil Nadu is accomplished more through consent than coercion'.[26] In fact,

---

[25] Seminar on India Human Development Report 2011 in New Delhi on 17 September 2012.

[26] M. Vijayabaskar, 'Tamil Nadu: The Politics of Silence', in *Power, Policy, and Protest: The Politics of India's Special Economic Zones*, eds Rob Jenkins, Loraine Kennedy, and Partha Mukhopadhyay (New Delhi: Oxford University Press, 2014), 326.

fieldwork findings collated from the tyre-manufacturing project are strongly supported by what Vijayabaskar argued. The next part of this chapter will discuss the findings and implications.

A CASE OF LAND CONFLICTS IN AN SEZ AT THIRUVALLUR

Field Notes

'M', a world-famous French tyre company, had proposed to build its manufacturing factory in the village of Thervoy Kandigai in Thiruvallur district at Tamil Nadu, which has more than 6,000 Dalit villagers. The factory is expected to produce 3 million units per annum at the initial stage, and extend its production capacity up to 20 million tyres every year. As the state has aggressively pro-moted FDI inflows in the automobile industry, key state leaders think that the tyre industry would be necessary to sustain the growth of the automobile sector. The state required M to promise to gener-ate a certain level of employment, when M proposed the project. The management of M promised that it would hire 1,500 domestic employees, and provide required training programmes to them.[27] The programmes include English language skills, computer skills, accounting, and vocational training.

The case of M highlighted that investors may encounter social opposition in the state, despite general observations about the weak level of social resistance against state-led large-scale investments in Tamil Nadu. An executive official from M mentioned that social agita-tion deployed by social activists and villagers acted as a barrier to the project, preparations for which were being made for seven to eight years.[28] Like many other cases found in other parts of India, for the agitation group, lands for M's project were problematic. The agitation against M, in fact, began in 2007 when the project, which has a budget of INR 4,000 crores, was reported to the public. On 30 January 2007, the gram panchayat of Thervoy Kandigai passed a resolution without

---

[27] Interview with HR manager at the company M in Tamil Nadu on 17 January 2012.

[28] Interview in Chennai on 24 January 2012.

any process of consent in the gram sabha (village council), stating that there was no objection to the land acquisition by SIPCOT.[29]

When I visited the factory site of M in the village of Thervoy Kandigai in January 2012, construction was in progress. The land was bulldozed and fenced following the boundary between the land development zone and the non-development zone that SIPCOT had set out. In fact, M's project site was part of an industrial complex that SIPCOT proposed to set up by allocating 800 acres of land. Construction work on making a new access road to the M factory was in progress in the development zone, but forests were being preserved in the non-development zone.

Activists and villagers insisted that the land for M which was in conflict is *meikal poromboke* (public grazing land), while the bureaucrats of SIPCOT and foreign investors of M were emphasizing it as dry and public land.[30] In fact, the dispute between a pro-M group and an anti-M group began with the use of this land rather than its ownership, since villagers were depending on the land for cultivating some crops even though it was categorized as public land. An employee in M had explained about the forest environment of the village before M began logging. According to him, the forest area was the main income source for Dalit villagers, leading them to organize large-scale protests against SIPCOT's land acquisition.

However, I did not feel any hostile atmosphere in the village, even though I was told by the activists that the villagers' opposition activities were still ongoing. The village seemed peaceful. Many villagers were kind enough to guide me to the M factory site when they were asked. The friendly atmosphere was the complete opposite of what I encountered in the state of Odisha while visiting several large-scale investment sites of other foreign companies. In Thervoy Kandigai, female farmers working in the fields were waving their hands when they saw me. It was quite surprising when M's employee told me that the female villagers and their children had participated in the anti-M protests.

[29] See the report issued by the Thervoy Youth and People's Struggle Committee, *Tale of a Village's Struggle for Survival* (14 July 2011), http://www.countercurrents.org/thervoy140711.htm.

[30] Interviews with social activists in Chennai on 4, 6, and 30 January, 2012; interviews with bureaucrats at SIPCOT in Chennai on 2 February 2012.

I found later that the state responded to the resistance with several strategies. It tried to persuade the anti-M group with a comprehensive compensation package. It was also regulating the anti-M group by using the coercive power of the police force, and by controlling the media.[31] It disabled communication about the resistance. At the same time, the strategies of foreign capital in bargaining with the agitation group were also supportive of the state strategies. M used both persuasion and discrimination strategies. It provided employment priority for those who supported the FDI project among villagers. Many job applicants who had engaged in the anti-M protest were excluded from the initial stage of recruitment. In the process of pacifying the agitation, officials in M utilized its support group to approach the anti-M group for conversation. Asked a question about how the state and M finally wrested consent from the anti-M group, an executive officer of M highlighted that they worked with NGOs that were supporting the investment project. The executive remarked, 'The NGOs tried to visit every household in the village. They met people and listened to them about what kind of problems they had with regard to our investment.' The Foundation for Rural Recovery and Development (FORRAD) was one of them.[32] The main objective of the NGOs' activities in the village was to persuade villagers by showing M's social concerns.

The state and M finally decided to provide a good compensation package for the villagers. The compensation included higher prices of land than market prices and a job offer for those who sell their private land, and substantial inclusionary packages such as the offer of shelter and substitute land for those who lose their livelihood even on public land. In the village, new houses for the displaced Dalit villagers were being built. In an interview, the villagers said that the state would provide alternative lands for their livelihood for free. Many villagers who initially opposed the investment project ultimately changed their mind towards supporting the project after the state and M negotiated with them.

[31] Interviews with activists in Chennai on 4, 6, and 30 January 2012.

[32] Interview with a member at FORRAD in New Delhi on 6 March 2012.

What Motivates Citizens to Support Investment Projects?

The discussion here addresses the puzzle of what motivates citizens to support FDI projects. The case of M demonstrated that the anti-M group was comparatively weaker than the pro-M group in many ways. It also presented why many citizens in Tamil Nadu negotiate or are being persuaded to agree to the investment projects. This may be associated with the low level of social opposition to the state-led industrialization in Tamil Nadu. Compared to other states in India, Tamil Nadu has reported very few cases of social opposition to investment projects.

It is worth noting that political parties in Tamil Nadu representing lower castes hardly participated in the anti-M group, though the majority of the residents in Thervoy Kandigai were Dalit.[33] This observation may challenge the prevailing perception of the active participation of Dalit parties in the state of Tamil Nadu for the improvement of the marginalized status of Dalits in political, economic, and societal relations with other caste groups.[34] Also, the communist parties in Tamil Nadu, except several individual activists from the parties, did not actively support the anti-M group. Unlike their active support to the activities of trade unions in foreign companies bargaining with the management for the better economic position of workers, their participation in mobilizing citizens for the anti-investment group was quite weak. Senthil Babu, a Communist Party of India (Marxist) (CPI(M)) activist, who has been devoted to labour movements in Tamil Nadu for more than 15 years, commented on this observation. He said, 'The

[33] Interviews with villagers on 6 January and 12 February 2012. I thank Dr. Ashik Bonofer in the University of Madras for accompanying me to Thervoy Kandigai and helping me to communicate with the villagers.

[34] For discussion on the rise of Dalit parties, see Brindavan C. Moses, 'Struggle for Panchama Lands: Dalit Assertion in Tamil Nadu', *Economic & Political Weekly* XXX, no. 5 (1995): 47–8; K.A. Manikumar, 'Caste Clashes in South Tamil Nadu', *Economic & Political Weekly* XXXII, no. 36 (1997): 2242–3; Pushpendra. 'Dalit Assertion through Electoral Politics', *Economic & Political Weekly* XXXIV, no. 36 (1999): 2609–18; and H. Gorringe, *Untouchable Citizens: Dalit Movements and Democratisation in Tamil Nadu* (Cultural Subordination and the Dalit Challenge) (New Delhi; Thousand Oaks, CA: Sage, 2005).

longer the lower-caste land workers stay in works that are connected with lands, the stronger they feel their low-caste identity. For them, one way to emancipate [themselves] from such feeling is to cut off themselves from the lands.'[35]

Babu's point of view implied that feudal societies witness increased bondage of lower-caste groups to lands in the process of production. For the lower-caste land workers, industrialization would be an opportunity to be liberated from the feudal bondage with lands. Upon considering that Tamil Nadu is one of the lower caste-dominated states in India, Babu's point of view seems strong in explaining why citizens in the state supported industrialization. Other observations also enhance this perspective.[36] The pattern of Tamil Nadu's changing economic structure shows the rapid growth of urban employment, with agricultural employment having the smallest share. That the 'benefits of growth regarding employment have largely gone to urbanized states in the years since liberalization,'[37] is borne out by the positive correlation between the level of urbanization and urban employment growth evolving from the early 1990s in Tamil Nadu. It means that a large number of workers in urban areas in the state have benefitted from the state's liberalization.

Here, especially the youth's aspirational shift favouring urban employment, perhaps promotes the movement. The employment opportunities have been offered by the private sector, including foreign investors, who have a great interest in establishing their production base in Tamil Nadu. As a state providing numerous technical education opportunities for citizens, having a strong tie with foreign investors must be a good strategy through which the skilled or semi-skilled workforce among the youth, in particular, can be quickly absorbed into industries where the investors provide employment. The narrative from the village of Thervoy Kandigai also coincides with the logic. The upward mobility of lower-caste groups in both political and economic spheres of Tamil Nadu challenges the conventional understanding of

[35] Interview in Chennai on 14 January 2012.

[36] See Ajay Gudavarthy, 'Can We De-Stigmatise Reservations in India?', *Economic & Political Weekly* XLVII, no. 6 (2012): 55–62.

[37] K.V. Ramaswamy, 'Regional Dimension of Growth and Employment', *Economic & Political Weekly* XLII, no. 49 (2007): 47–56, 49.

rural societies in India, where the rural landed class is influential in structuring and transforming society.

★★★

The primary aim of this chapter was to discuss the higher level of land acquisition, and the state's land management in Tamil Nadu. It underlined the idea that policy-makers have focused on inclusive industrial schemes that try to promote an inclusive societal structure, especially by supporting the upward mobility of low-caste groups in the state. It argued that the state remains aggressively committed to industrial development and urbanization by making industrial lands available, and in the process, tries to meet the aspirations and needs of citizens. The idea of the state leaders was to generate employment and export-promoting investment projects in the automobile sector, in particular. The state's capacities in facilitating educational institutes for citizens, the negotiation process for both citizens and investors, and regulating social opposition through strategies were addressed in the discussion.

7 Unpacking the Double Movement

Contentious Land Acquisition in India

Manjusha Nair

Acquisition of land privately or communally held by rural and tribal people for agricultural, industrial, infrastructural, and commercial development, termed critically as the 'global land grab',[1] has been a contentious topic in the global south, eliciting immense scholarly and activist response. The World Bank reported that in 2008 alone, transnational investors expressed interest in 56 million hectares of land worldwide.[2] Not surprisingly, these proposed and actual acquisitions have resulted in huge contentions from communities affected, with the support of transnational networks, non-governmental organizations (NGOs), social movements, and political parties. Quite often these contenders engaged with a political field that comprised of the provincial developmental states, multinational capitalists, local politics, and a prevailing growth ideology characterized by what has been termed

---

[1] Saturnino M. Borras Jr., Ruth Hall, Ian Scoones, Ben White, and Wendy Wolford, 'Towards a Better Understanding of Global Land Grabbing: An Editorial Introduction', *The Journal of Peasant Studies* 38, no. 2 (2011): doi: 10.1080/03066150.2011.559005

[2] Klaus Deininger, Derek Byerlee, Jonathan Lindsay, Andrew Norton, Harris Selod, and Mercedes Stickler, *Rising Global Interest in Farmland: Can It Yield Sustainable and Equitable Benefits?* (Washington, DC: World Bank, 2011).

as 'market fundamentalism'.[3] The responses to these contentions across the world have ranged from outright suppression by the state governments, and disregard by the powerholders, to a combination of making deals with the contenders such as offering a better compensation, and thus successfully evicting the landowners and continuing with the development projects. In India, many cases of land acquisition are embroiled in the legal system, halting the development projects,[4] and creating uncertainties in the lives of the protesting communities, where they fight court cases and continue to cultivate on contested land.

The Indian state held the right to acquire, distribute, and formulate laws on land according to a colonial law of 1894, and the state developmental agencies used it relentlessly to acquire cultivated land for the establishment of public, private, and joint ventures such as special economic zones (SEZs), agri-businesses, mining projects, expressways, sports cities, and real estate. Though no official tally of protests against land acquisition is available in India, a study by the Society for Promotion of Wastelands Development and Rights and Resources Initiative estimated that protests occurred in 130 of India's 602 districts, virtually in all regions, between 2011 and 2012.[5] A notable case was that of Singur in West Bengal, where farmers protested against the acquisition of land by the state to start the Tata Nano automobile factory. The irony of a Communist Party-run state that hitherto depended on the rural population for electoral support, eroding its mass base for the sake of private capital, revealed the persuasive power of market fundamentalism. Another notable case was that of Bhatta–Parsaul villages in Uttar Pradesh where farmers resisted the acquisition of land by the state for the construction of the Yamuna expressway, leading to circumstances in which violent clashes between the activists and the police resulted in deaths and destruction. These incidents and the general volatile political climate surrounding land acquisition persuaded the ruling United Progressive Alliance (UPA) to pass the new Right to Fair Compensation and Transparency in Land Acquisition, Rehabilitation

[3] Fred Block and Margaret R. Somers, *The Power of Market Fundamentalism: Karl Polanyi's Critique* (Cambridge, MA: Harvard University Press, 2014).

[4] Sanjoy Chakravorty, *The Price of Land: Acquisition, Conflict, Consequence* (New Delhi: Oxford University Press, 2013).

[5] Shankar Gopalakrishnan, *Control, Regulation and Expropriation of India's Forest and Common Lands* (Delhi: Rights and Resources Initiative, 2012).

and Resettlement Act (LARR) in 2013, which put in place legal safe-guards to protect the rural population, including the landless, from the negative effects of land acquisition. Under the Indian constitution, the right to govern land and derive revenue belongs to the states, and not the Central Government. Hence the question remains how the new Act will be interpreted and implemented in the states. New reports suggest that many states are forging ahead with land acquisition by amending LARR or twisting the rules, given the stalled attempt by the National Democratic Alliance (NDA)-run Central Government to amend the Act.

The land acquisition, the protests, and the protective measures instituted by the state are suggestive of a Polanyian double movement at work. According to Karl Polanyi, economic liberalism in the nine-teenth and twentieth centuries sought to establish a self-regulated mar-ket that was not embedded in society, requiring the commodification of previously non-commodified land, labour, money, and other social relations. This creation of 'fictitious commodities' de-stabilized society and displaced people to such a great extent that a countermovement to resist the market assault and re-embed markets in society began. These movements for and against the market, he termed as the double movement.[6] It has been argued that as against the contemporary neo-liberal globalization, a countermovement against commodification and marketization has been on the rise as well, demanding a re-embedding of the market in society.[7] Many scholars point to the emergence of a post-neoliberal state in this regard that has assumed a protective role of its citizens against the assault of the market, through welfare measures and social security provisions.[8]

---

[6] Karl Polanyi, The Great Transformation: The Political and Economic Origins of Our Time (Boston: Beacon Press 2001 [1944]).

[7] Nina Bandelj, Kristen Shorette, and Elizabeth Sowers, 'Work and Neoliberal Globalization: A Polanyian Synthesis', *Sociology Compass* 5, no. 9 (2011): doi:10.1111/j.1751-9020.2011.00408.x; Kurtuluş Gemici and Manjusha Nair, 'Globalization and its Countermovement: Marxian Contention or Polanyian Resistance?', *Sociology Compass* 10, no. 7 (2016): doi.org/10.1111/soc4.12389; Ronaldo Munck, 'Globalization, Labor, and the "Polanyi Problem"', *Labor History* 45, no. 3 (2004): doi: 10.1080/0023656042000257765.

[8] Jean Grugel and Pía Riggirozzi, 'Post-neoliberalism in Latin America: Rebuilding and Reclaiming the State after Crisis', *Development and Change*

In this chapter, I unpack the double movement surrounding land acquisition in India with the aim of presenting the multiplicity of interests and identities associated with land among the rural population. Polanyi himself has noted both the support and opposition of the farmers and peasantry to the market economy in twentieth-century Europe, and was ambivalent about their role in resisting the commodification of land. [9] He argued that the conflicts emerging from market interventions often created shifting constituencies of people that supported or opposed the expansion or constraining of the market.[10] I argue that in India, the contentions against the market that constitute the countermovement are often characterized by rural dwellers demanding assessment of land as a free commodity rather than de-commodification of land. Just as Tania Li has argued about how capitalism has incorporated rural folks into its fold in manifold ways,[11] I suggest that the market logic that permeates farmers' articulations derives from the longstanding interaction of Indian farmers with money, market, and the state. My findings will help unpack the complexity and heterogeneity that characterizes the double movement, which is usually thought about in monolithic terms.

Methodologically, I provide a state-level analysis of contentions around land acquisitions in India. In India, as in other parts of the world, the states have emerged as independent centres of power and direct negotiators with investors, often rewriting the rules to encourage a smooth functioning of the market.[12] As noted earlier, under

---

43, no. 1 (2012): doi: 10.1111/j.1467-7660.2011.01746.x; Loïc Wacquant, 'Crafting the Neoliberal State: Workfare, Prisonfare, and Social Insecurity', *Sociological Forum* 25, no. 2 (2010): doi: 10.1111/j.1573-7861.2010.01173.x; Shaoguang Wang, 'Double Movement in China', *Economic & Political Weekly* XLIII, no. 52 (2008): http://www.jstor.org/stable/40278334.

[9] Polanyi, *The Great Transformation*, 187–200.

[10] Block and Somers, *The Power of Market Fundamentalism*, 10.

[11] Tania M. Li, *Land's End: Capitalist Relations on an Indigenous Frontier* (Durham, NC: Duke University Press, 2014).

[12] Rob Jenkins, ed., *Regional Reflections: Comparing Politics across India's States* (New York: Oxford University Press, 2004); Aseema Sinha, 'Political Foundations of Market-enhancing Federalism: Theoretical Lessons from India and China', *Comparative Politics* 37, no. 3 (2005): doi:10.2307/20072893.

the Indian constitution, the right to govern land and derive revenue belongs to the states, and not the Central Government, making them an essential analytical focus for examining land acquisition.[13] Regional variations in policies pertaining to land and the market, and regional characteristics of politics, state-society relations, and social movement mobilizations further highlight the significance of a regional analysis. However, I also point out the commonalities across regions emerging from long-established national policies on agriculture. I highlight the continual power of the Central Government in India to introduce new legislation, and establish new national trends, that many states follow. Many regional civil society and social movement organizations look up to the Central Government for intervening on behalf of the citizens against the state governments.

This chapter is based on evidence gathered from field research in Uttar Pradesh and Chhattisgarh from 2013 to 2016. The collection of information included visiting villages where land acquisition was contested, and interviewing farmers from all social classes and officials involved in acquisition. Along with that, I analyse secondary literature and news reports for formulating my argument.

This chapter is structured as follows: In the next section, I examine the Polanyian conception of the double movement and its implications for understanding land acquisition. In the following section, I analyse the contestations against land acquisition in India to highlight the farmers' articulated grievances and the state responses. Then I outline some explanations that link the character of the protests to pre-existing ties with the market, state, and politics. The concluding section reiterates the findings and address the limitations of this chapter.

THE DOUBLE MOVEMENT

Polanyi conceptualized the double movement as the distinct action of two organizing principles of society, with specific aims and with the support of definite social forces and distinctive methods. In Polanyi's own words:

---

[13] Nikita Sud, 'Governing India's Land', *World Development* 60, no. 1 (2014): https://ora.ox.ac.uk/objects/uuid:bbd85621-4b2f-42f5-95b3-30256ecad1b4.

The one was the principle of economic liberalism, aiming at the establishment of a self-regulating market, relying on the support of the trading classes, and using largely laissez-faire and free trade as its methods; the other was the principle of social protection aiming at the conservation of man and nature as well as productive organization, relying on the varying support of those most immediately affected by the deleterious action of the market—primarily, but not exclusively, the working and the landed classes—and using protective legislation, restrictive associations, and other instruments of intervention as its methods.[14]

The Polanyian conception of double movement has been increasingly recognized to understand the current neoliberal globalization, where there is the ascent of the primacy of the market in economic ideology and societal organization since the 1980s, and a simultaneous rise of oppositional movements seeking to control the expansion of market forces.[15]

The contentions against land acquisition have been characterized directly and implicitly as a Polanyian countermovement that has been resisting the encroachment of market on society.[16] Compared to the historical countermovements that were focused on rights of labour and gender within the framework of nation-states, contemporary

[14] Polanyi, *The Great Transformation*, 139.

[15] Bandelj, Shorette, and Sowers, 'Work and Neoliberal Globalization'; Michael Burawoy, 'From Polanyi to Pollyanna: The False Optimism of Global Labor Studies', *Global Labour Journal* 1, no. 2 (2010): 301–13, doi: 10.15173/glj.v1i2.1079; Evans, 'Counter-Hegemonic Globalization'; John Harriss, 'Globalization(s) and Labour in China and India: Introductory Reflections', *Global Labor Journal* 1, no. 1 (2009): 3–11, doi: 10.15173/glj.v1i1.1062; Munck, 'Globalization, Labor, and the "Polanyi Problem"'; Beverly J. Silver and Giovanni Arrighi, 'Polanyi's "Double Movement": The Belle Époques of British and U.S. Hegemony Compared', *Politics and Society* 31, no. 2 (2003): doi: 10.1177/0032329203252274.

[16] Michael Levien, 'India's Double-movement: Polanyi and the National Alliance of People's Movements', *Berkeley Journal of Sociology* 51 (2007): 119–49, http://www.jstor.org/stable/41035623; Philip McMichael, 'Global Development and the Corporate Food Regime', in *New Directions in the Sociology of Global Development* (Research in Rural Sociology and Development, Vol. 11), eds Frederick H. Buttel and Philip McMichael (Bingley: Emerald Group Publishing Limited, 2005); Borras Jr. et al., 'Towards a Better Understanding of Global Land Grabbing'.

movements are transnational, oriented towards a civilizational goal of regulation of social life by ecological principles, and focus on more fundamental historical questions of living sustainably on Earth.[17] The Polanyian framework of protective movements to 're-embed' the market within society has been critically extended to examine the politics against land acquisition in India,[18] and to resist the 'exclusionary outcomes' of land-based rights and propose alternatives for re-defining access and property relations in South East Asia.[19]

Recent scholarship has, however, highlighted the variation in these resistances, demanding greater attention from scholars to their complexity.[20] In a recent article, editors of *The Journal of Peasant Studies*, the flagship journal of agrarian studies and rural development, recognized the diversity in the contentions against land acquisition. Beyond the local level, highly varied responses by societies and states at national levels, and in international multilateral forums and transnational movements also call for more detailed and critical assessment by social scientists.[21] For instance, in the Ukraine, peasants did not resist land acquisition of agri-businesses since large industrial farms reminded them of the Soviet collective and state farms, and expected employment in them to be a better alternative to uncertain futures.[22]

I propose that a nuanced understanding of Polanyi's double movement can be used to make sense of this market logic within the land

[17] Phillip McMichael, 'Rethinking Land Grab Ontology', *Rural Sociology* 79, no. 1 (2014): doi: 10.1111/ruso.12021.

[18] Levien, 'India's Double-movement'; Michael Levien, 'The Politics of Dispossession: Theorizing India's "Land Wars"', *Politics and Society* 41, no. 3 (2013): 351–94, doi:10.1177/0032329213493751.

[19] Borras Jr. et al., 'Towards a Better Understanding of Global Land Grabbing'.

[20] Ruth Hall, Marc Edelman, Saturnino M. Borras Jr., Ian Scoones, Ben White, and Wendy Wolford, 'Resistance, Acquiescence or Incorporation? An Introduction to Land Grabbing and Political Reactions "From Below"', *The Journal of Peasant Studies* 42, nos 3–4 (2015): doi: 10.1080/03066150.2015.1036746.

[21] Hall et al., 'Resistance, Acquiescence or Incorporation?'.

[22] Natalia Mamonova, 'Resistance or Adaptation? Ukrainian Peasants' Responses to Large-scale Land Acquisitions', *The Journal of Peasant Studies* 42, nos 3–4 (2015): doi:10.1080/03066150.2014.993320.

acquisition protests. Unlike Marx, who thought about the class conflict as crystallizing into two opposing classes comprised of the proletariat and the capitalist, Polanyi's double movement did not divide the participants into for and against the market. Polanyi had a more 'holistic' account of social conflicts rooted in their contexts.[23] He showed that while capitalists are likely to support the move for regulations that make a self-regulating market possible, there might be those among them who might participate in the countermovement. It is possible that some would find the restrictions due to environmental concerns desirable. It is also possible that some old industries who benefitted from earlier regulations might join the countermovement.[24] Block suggests that Polanyi, like Max Weber, recognized that in actual politics, classes divided along multiple lines, pitching the export-oriented capitalist against the domestic-market-oriented one, and unskilled worker of one ethnic group against the skilled worker of another ethnic group.[25]

Likewise, Polanyi was ambivalent about the historic role of peasants in resisting the commodification of land.[26] Polanyi pointed out that farmers and peasants of mid-twentieth century Europe defended the market system when the necessity arose. In Polanyi's own words, in that particular historical context, 'While the crisis of the inherently unstable [market] system was brought on by both wings of the protectionist movement, the social strata connected with the land were inclined to compromise with the market system, while the broad class of labor did not shrink from breaking its rules and challenging it outright'.[27] The peasants at that historical moment were in favour of the market because the agrarian policies of the European states made grain production profitable.

[23] Fred Block and Margaret R. Somers, 'Beyond the Economistic Fallacy: The Holistic Social Science of Karl Polanyi', in *Vision and Method in Historical Sociology*, ed. Theda Skocpol (Cambridge: Cambridge University Press, 1984).

[24] Fred Block, 'Polanyi's Double Movement and the Reconstruction of Critical Theory', *Revue Interventions Économiques* 38 (2008): 1–14, http://journals.openedition.org/interventionseconomiques/274.

[25] Block, 'Polanyi's Double Movement and the Reconstruction of Critical Theory'.

[26] Polanyi, *The Great Transformation*, 187–200.

[27] Polanyi, *The Great Transformation*, 200.

It is in the context of the above refutation of a simple resistance theory that I unpack the countermovement in India in this chapter. I seek to identify and explain the multiplicity of interests and demands surrounding land by the rural folk in the context of this in-depth understanding of the Polanyian conceptualization of the double movement. Specifically, I link the market logic that governs the rural residents to the postcolonial relationship of Indian agriculture with the market, state, and politics.

LAND ACQUISITION AND THE DOUBLE
MOVEMENT IN INDIA

There has been no official count of protests against land acquisition in India, and not all contestations are necessarily newsworthy in scale and scope. Sanjoy Chakravorty compiled a list of contestations between 2006 and 2011 based on newspaper reports, which I reproduce below in a succinct form in Table 7.1.[28]

The contentions occurred in 13 states against land acquisition for infrastructural, residential, and industrial projects. Of the 35 contestations mentioned in Table 7.1, in 22, the farmers clearly agitated for better compensation for their land. There were 12 agitations in which the rural residents did not want to give up their land; in four of them, the land was *well irrigated* and hence highly productive. Only very few wanted to hold on to land as a survival tool or due to ecological concerns. Thus while these protests contested the market interventions in rural lives, the protestors demanded an insertion of land into the market rather than holding on to it at all costs.

In many states, contestations were prevented from the onset of the lengthy land acquisition process by measures of accommodation of farmers' compensation within the neoliberal development schemes. The degree and variety of this accommodation depended on the historically embedded class structures and class relations. In the states of Haryana and Punjab, where the resistance to land acquisition has been relatively weak, the state successfully incorporated the farmers into its fold by offering them stakes in neoliberal development such

---

[28] Chakravorty, *The Price of Land.*

TABLE 7.1 Land Acquisition Contestations in India, 2006–11 (non-exhaustive list)

Location	Articulated Grievance/Demand	Date
AP*: Mahbubnagar district	Forcible acquisition; very low payment	April 2009
AP: Quila Mohammed Nagar	Absolute refusal based on livelihood and land dependency; poor compensation	March 2006
AP: Reddy district	Resistance and litigation based on livelihood and compensation	March 2006
AP:Vishakhapatnam	Unwilling to give up land	August 2010
AP:Vizianagaram district	Irregular acquisition process of tribal land	July 2010
Chandigarh: Manimajra	Insufficient compensation; unclear public purpose	April 2007
Chhattisgarh: Janjgir-Champa district	Poor compensation	February 2011
Chhattisgarh: Naya Raipur	Poor compensation	January 2008
Goa: Dabolim village	Legal challenge on ecological grounds	September 2010
Goa: Navelim	Destruction of lifestyle; poor compensation	October 2010
Goa: Navelim	Other (less productive) land available	January 2011
Goa: Panaji	Unwilling to give up land	December 2010
Gujarat: Bhavnagar district	Unwilling to give up livelihood; ecological concerns	March 2010
Gujarat (rural, south)	Poor compensation	November 2010
Haryana: Manesar	Unwilling to give up fertile land	January 2011
Haryana:Yamunanagar	Poor compensation	December 2009
Himachal Pradesh: Una district	Unwilling to give up newly irrigated land	December 2009
Jharkhand: Purbi Singhbhum	Poor compensation	May 2010

(*Cont'd*)

TABLE 7.1   *(Cont'd)*

Location	Articulated Grievance/Demand	Date
Karnataka: Bangalore–Mysore corridor	Insufficient compensation (price increased tenfold in a decade)	March 2010
Karnataka: Belgaum district	Unwilling to give up land; no livelihood alternative	December 2010
Karnataka: Mangalore	Poor compensation; destruction of livelihood	July 2009
Maharashtra: Lower Penganga valley	Absolute refusal based on livelihood and good soil	January 2009
Maharashtra: Nagpur district	Poor compensation; demand for rehabilitation	February 2008
Maharashtra: Nagpur district	Poor compensation	November 2010
Maharashtra: Nanded	Unwilling to give up fertile land; very low price	February 2011
Maharashtra: Pune–Ahmednagar highway	Refusal to give up irrigated land	August 2009
Maharashtra: Ratnagiri district	Absolute refusal based on livelihood and land dependency; very low price offered	July 2010
Tamil Nadu: Machilipatnam	Poor compensation	October 2010
Tamil Nadu: Peelamedu	Poor compensation	September 2010
UP★★: Unnao, Kanpur	Poor compensation; demand one job per family	November 2007
UP: Yamuna Expressway	Range from absolute refusal to price negotiation	August 2010
WB★★★: Burdwan district	Poor compensation; Successfully raised price	October 2008
WB: Burdwan district	Poor compensation	March 2010
WB: Burdwan district	Poor compensation; unpaid wages	January 2011
WB: Kolkata, Rajarhat	Forced acquisition and corruption allegations	November 2010

Source: Compiled from Chakravorty, *The Price of Land*.
Note: ★Andhra Pradesh; ★★Uttar Pradesh; ★★★West Bengal.

as residential plots, employment, and annuities.[29] In Haryana, the state government offered floor prices for land, and a 33-year annuity for landowners. The decisions favouring farmers were possible in Haryana because the landowning castes held a sway over politics.

In Tamil Nadu, the resistance to land acquisition has been weak because of the state tactics of accumulating land through land banks, and high compensation rates and market-based negotiations facilitated by the state.[30] Long-term crises in agriculture, growing landlessness of marginal farmers, the resulting shift towards non-farm employment, a relatively decentralized pattern of urbanization, and a degree of social mobility among the backward castes have all played a role in this phenomenon. The structural conditions of Tamil Nadu such as urbanization and agrarian stagnation facilitated the easy transformation of the rural dwellers to the state ideology of industrialization and business friendliness.[31] In all these cases, the rural folk, at least the landholding ones, had no qualms about commodification of land, once a compensation comparable to the market value was offered. In Rajasthan, farmers were offered 25 per cent of their original land as developed commercial and residential plots, thus inserting into the development deals as 'small entrepreneurs'.[32] In Uttar Pradesh, the Greater Noida Industrial Authority, an autonomous administrative body, entered into a contractual agreement, fixing the compensation and pegging it to the Consumer Price Index, and a return of 10 per cent of the total land, once it was developed, back to the farmers who had surrendered it.[33]

---

[29] Loraine Kennedy, 'Haryana: Beyond the Urban–Rural Divide', in *Power, Policy, and Protest: The Politics of India's Special Economic Zones*, eds Rob Jenkins, Loraine Kennedy, and Partha Mukhopadhyay (New Delhi: Oxford University Press, 2014); Heather Plumridge Bedi and Louise Tillin, 'Inter-state Competition, Land Conflicts and Resistance in India', *Oxford Development Studies* 43, no. 2 (2015): doi:10.1080/13600818.2015.1035246.

[30] M. Vijayabaskar, 'Tamil Nadu: The Politics of Silence', in *Power, Policy, and Protest: The Politics of India's Special Economic Zones*, eds Rob Jenkins, Loraine Kennedy, and Partha Mukhopadhyay (New Delhi: Oxford University Press, 2014).

[31] Sud, 'Governing India's Land'.

[32] Michael Levien, 'Special Economic Zones and Accumulation by Dispossession in India', *Journal of Agrarian Change* 11, no. 4 (2011): 454–83.

[33] Sudha Pai and Avinash Kumar, 'Uttar Pradesh: Contrasting Cases from the National Capital Region', in *Power, Policy, and Protest: The Politics of*

In the contentions against land acquisition in the instances where such accommodation of rural residents was not forthcoming, the latter not only demanded inclusion in the market logic, but started often disruptive agitations to persuade the state to grant such demands. Farmers in Bhatta and Parsaul villages in Gautam Budh Nagar district in Uttar Pradesh are continuing their agitation against the Yamuna Expressway Industrial Development Authority ('Authority'), an autonomous body within the local state, which acquired land in 2009 for the development projects associated with the construction of the Yamuna Expressway, a six-lane access controlled road connecting Delhi to Agra. Bhatta–Parsaul together comprised of 10,000 hectares of fertile land approximately, and around 800 families survived on it. Only less than 5 per cent of the population had employment outside the villages as servicemen or in other jobs in metropolitan Delhi. The bone of contention was not that the farmers were not willing to part with their farmland, but that the rates of compensation they were receiving were not sufficient to sustain their livelihoods that were entirely dependent on land. Farmers alleged that the land was being sold to a private construction company at INR 16,000 per square metre by the Authority, while the farmers were being offered only INR 600 per square metre. Once the farmers came to know of this discrepancy, they agitated for more compensation. The protests resulted in violence and police shooting, in which a few policemen and farmers were killed. Around 250 farmers were arrested and sent to jail accused of rioting, arson, and murder. In 2013, during my first field visit, 15 farmers were still languishing in jail, and about 40 cases were registered against them.

During my 2015 visit, I found that all the farmers were released from jail, and they were hoping to have a better resolution to their problems after talking to the rural development minister in the Central Government. In 2016, during my last field visit, the farmers were happy with LARR, their court cases demanding higher compensation were going on, and they had formed a new organization to continue their agitation. They were still continuing to cultivate on the 'acquired' land, since acquisition was suspended due to the court case filed by

---

India's Special Economic Zones, eds Rob Jenkins, Loraine Kennedy, and Partha Mukhopadhyay (New Delhi: Oxford University Press, 2014).

the farmers. An officer of the Authority said that it even agreed to give 64.7 per cent extra compensation per bigha (0.4 acre) to the farmers, but they were still not willing to withdraw their cases.

In the interviews held in Bhatta–Parsaul, farmers of all social and economic strata pointed out that their grievance was that the Authority manipulated them by withholding information about the market value of the land, and trying to buy the land at a cheaper price. The rate of compensation was decided by the Authority on its own, without any consultation with the farmers. Farmers were not consulted at any stage and were only informed that their lands would be acquired. Left with no choice and under financial strain, many farmers gave up their lands to the Authority. They were unaware about the process as well as the market rates of their lands. There were also instances of the Authority bribing farmers to take their compensations. It was only when the farmers realized that there is significant gap between the rate at which compensation has been given to them and the rate at which their lands have been sold to developers that protests began. A Dalit farmer who owned less than 3 bighas (1.2 acres) of land justified the agitation by emphasizing that farmers were not against development, they just wanted legitimate compensation:

> Farmers are not against giving up their lands. If industries are set up, it will contribute towards the progress and development of the nation. It will also help generate employment. But farmers want fair compensation for their land. You will not find any farmer in Gautam Budh Nagar who is against acquisition. But all farmers want the state to give them just and legitimate compensation.

> Q: *So what do you think is the main bone of contention: land acquisition or compensation?*

> Farmers are not opposed to acquisition. They only demand fair and just compensation for their lands, not just in terms of money but employment and rehabilitation and annual pension.

The farmers felt cheated that the Authority told them the land was acquired for residential schemes and not industrial development. Another small farmer holding 12 bighas of land suggested that the Authority and the state government should be eliminated as intermediaries, and the private companies should talk directly to farmers: 'Technically the government is taking away our share of the money.

Builders should be allowed to discuss the rate directly with us. But ultimately it does not matter who the builder buys from: government or us. But in both cases we should get the right price and the rate should be decided after consultation with us.' The government acted as a greedy real estate broker: It purchased the land for cheap from the farmers, and then sold it to the companies for a lot more. The farmers got nothing in the process. This farmer compared their compensation with that in the neighbouring Haryana. Each farmer was getting at least INR 2–2.5 crore per acre, and farmers were happy and prosperous there.

In Raigarh district in Chhattisgarh, where the land acquisition process for coal mining had resulted in social mobilizations organized by social movements, interviews showed a different intrusion of the market logic, where farmers wanted to start their own indigenous mining, and thus convert their land into an extractive resource. Social mobilizations started here around 1992 against acquisition of land for mining, and the main organization that led the protest movement was *Jan Chetna* (People's Consciousness) that was a civil society organization under the umbrella of broader organizations fighting for the rights of rural and tribal people of Chhattisgarh such as *Jan Hit*, *Ekta Parishad*, and *Chhattisgarh Bachao Andolan*. The main demand of this organization was to stop mining and restore land to the rural and tribal people; the latter's' rights were aligned with environmental protection. However, in the process of this movement, a local organization called *Mehnatkasht Mazdoor Kisan Ekta Samiti* (Workers and Peasants Organization) cropped up apart from these social movements, and organized a Coal *Satyagraha* (civil resistance) arguing that the land belonged to the locals, and demanding that locals should be able to sell coal mined from their villages. This organization registered a coal mining company in 2013, planned to mine coal sustainably, and use the money generated from the mining for the local development of the villages and people. The organizers leased about 700 acres of land from the farmers after forming an agreement for mining. Mining is yet to begin on these lands, but the organization has acquired permission from the government and built the mining infrastructure. In the meantime, around 2012, a Supreme Court of India judgement that ratified the use of local mineral resources found underground by locals, encouraged the organization further in the direction of local coal mining.

This above move by locals to mine coal created a rift in the main organization, *Jan Chetna*. Many were of the opinion that Chhattisgarh, which was already being exploited recklessly by the state and capital for its mineral riches,[34] did not need another mining operation. They argued that the local coal mining project was incompatible with the goals of environmental protection. In reply, the official stand of *Jan Chetna* was that if the locals were able to acquire the land for their own use from the government, this would prevent land acquisition by private industries. Since then a few organizations that had resisted land acquisition by locals moved away from *Jan Chetna* and became separate movements with distinct ideological bent. This split also divided the villagers, and the resistance movements were on the decline in 2015 during the last field visit. Undoubtedly this attempt by locals to start their own mining was a countermove to land acquisition by private firms for mining; but rather than a de-commodification of land, the rural dwellers demanded and used the right to use land as an extractive resource.

Certainly, there are instances where people held on to their land citing symbolic attachment to land, and environmental and livelihood concerns. A farmer in Singur village in West Bengal, where farmers' agitations stopped the construction of the Tata Nano automobile plant, summed up the loss of land and increasing vulnerability in unmistakable moral economy terms: 'Land is forever, but money is short-lived. Money does not spell security, but land does.'[35] In Goa, there are strong social movement organizations that span all social classes striving to protect land as a heritage, and embattling the state in multiple judicial encounters.[36] These instances that exemplify the Polanyian

---

[34] For instance, permission was granted to 42 coal-based thermal power plants, 85 sponge iron plants, seven cement plants, 26 captive power plants, five granite-cutting plants, three bauxite and lime plants, and one aluminium plant recently. Manjusha Nair, *Undervalued Dissent: Informal Workers' Politics in India* (Albany, NY: SUNY Press, 2016).

[35] Mahuya Pal and Mohan J. Dutta, '"Land Is Our Mother": Alternative Meanings of Development in Subaltern Organizing', *Journal of International and Intercultural Communication* 6, no. 3 (2013): 203–20, 214, doi:10.1080/175 13057.2013.765954.

[36] Heather Plumridge Bedi, 'Special Economic Zones: National Land Challenges, Localized Protest', *Contemporary South Asia* 21, no.1 (2013): doi/ abs/10.1080/09584935.2012.757582.

countermovement that demands de-commodification of land have to be understood in their specific political, social, and geographic contexts that make certain mobilizations possible.

A NEW MORAL ECONOMY?

In the previous section, we saw that farmers' protests against land acquisition did not always demand de-commodification of land, rather, many a time demanded a 'proper' commodification of land and a compensation to be provided at the market value without the intervention of intermediaries such as the state and the state's agents. Marc Edelman has argued that contemporary farmers were increasingly under pressure to provide an ever-higher level of consumption for the entire household, given that improved access to schooling, growing reliance on off-farm employment, and declining average fertility reduced the numbers of available family labourers, creating new moral economy demands on the markets and the state.[37] By moral economy, Edelman was referring to peasants' deeply rooted beliefs about the right to 'subsistence security',[38] and a generalized aversion to risks that might threaten this security.[39]

In Bhatta and Parsaul villages, farmers were angry at the state for not providing the right price for their crops, and making fertilizers expensive in the market. They claimed that they were debt ridden, and out of economic compulsion such as educating their children and maintaining a decent standard of living, were ready to give up their lands. The farmers sent their children, both girls and boys, to private English medium schools in the nearest town of Dankaur to which they commuted in their yellow school buses.[40] In the courtyard of

[37] Marc Edelman, 'Bringing the Moral Economy Back in…to the Study of 21st-Century Transnational Peasant Movements', *American Anthropologist* 107, no. 3 (2005): 336–7, doi:10.1525/aa.2005.107.3.331.

[38] James C. Scott, *The Moral Economy of the Peasant: Rebellion and Subsistence in Southeast Asia* (New Haven, CT: Yale University Press, 1976), 35.

[39] Scott, *The Moral Economy of the Peasant*, 101.

[40] Manjusha Nair, 'Land as a Transactional Asset: Moral Economy and Market Logic in Contested Land Acquisition in India', *Development and Change*, published online 22 February 2019: https://doi.org/10.1111/dech.12494.

the households, children spread their books and prepared for exams, when not helping their mothers with kitchen chores. A farmer leader commented: 'If the farmers are given the market rate as compensation for their plots of land, then I think they would be willing to give up their lands for the simple reason that the majority of farmers no longer want to continue in agriculture as it is not a profitable profession. It is for the government to think on this matter.'

Agriculture in India was integrated to the market much before the neoliberal policies, and farmers in many states were accustomed to making demands directly to the state. The structural changes initiated by the Green Revolution programme in rural India had already transformed the farmers to political entrepreneurs. The Green Revolution had embedded Indian rural society in the market, and commodified the social relations that were previously embedded in reciprocity and caste and class hierarchies.[41] The farmers produced for the market using new seeds, fertilizers, and machines.[42] The Indian state introduced the Green Revolution in the 1960s, and the idea behind it was to advance agricultural production in a selected few sites through intensive use of technology.[43] New technologies were implemented in 114 of the around 325 districts in India, where the state through its many agencies introduced new high-yielding varieties (HYV) of seeds, fertilizers, irrigation, credit, as well as knowledge and expertise. The farmers who benefitted from this subsidized capitalism[44] in states such as Maharashtra, Tamil Nadu, Karnataka, Punjab, Gujarat, and Uttar Pradesh mobilized based on interests, and made demands of further

[41] Manjusha Nair, 'State-embedded Villages: Rural Protests and Rights Awareness in India and China', in *Beyond Regimes: China and India Compared*, eds Prasenjit Duara and Elizabeth Perry (Cambridge, MA: Harvard University Press, 2018).

[42] John Harriss, 'Capitalism and Peasant Production: The Green Revolution in India', in *Peasants and Peasant Societies*, ed. Teodor Shanin (London: Penguin, 1987); Francine R. Frankel, *India's Green Revolution: Economic and Political Costs* (Princeton, NJ: Princeton University Press 1971).

[43] Frankel, *India's Green Revolution*.

[44] Christine Lutringer, 'A Movement of "Subsidized Capitalists"? The Multi-level Influence of the Bharatiya Kisan Union in India', *International Review of Sociology* 20, no. 3 (2010): doi: 10.1080/03906701.2010.511913.

protection from the market in the decade of the 1980s.[45] In Uttar Pradesh, middle-class farmers, beneficiaries of the Green Revolution, organized through the Bharatiya Kisan Union to persuade the state through often coercive politics to provide better procurement prices and regulate the market.[46] Their methods included refusal to pay electricity charges, blockade of roads and railway lines, and hostage taking of state officials.[47]

In sum, for many Indian farmers mentioned in this chapter, survival now included maintenance of a decent standard of living; private school education and preparations and aspirations for a non-farm job; the value of land derived precisely from its exchangeability for assured assets such as money, annuity, shares in developmental projects such as investment in farmhouses,[48] and employment. Hence the countermovement to the intrusion of market forces took the form of negotiations for a better deal within the domain of commodification rather than outside it. Of course, this was a double movement; farmers were demanding protection of their livelihoods, but they demanded a proper insertion into the market equation as compensation rather than de-commodification of their primary asset, land.

★★★

In this chapter, I examined the protests against land acquisition in the states of Chhattisgarh and Uttar Pradesh. The question that informed this chapter was how to understand these protests as a double movement, the resistance of society against the encroachment of the market,

---

[45] Tom Brass, *New Farmers' Movements in India* (Ilford, Essex; Portland, Oregon: Frank Cass, 1995); Ashutosh Varshney, *Democracy, Development, and the Countryside: Urban–Rural Struggles in India* (New York: Cambridge University Press, 1998).

[46] Lutringer, 'A Movement of "Subsidized Capitalists"?'.

[47] Lutringer, 'A Movement of "Subsidized Capitalists"?'; Akhil Gupta, *Postcolonial Developments: Agriculture in the Making of Modern India* (Durham, NC: Duke University Press, 1998).

[48] Farmhouses are suburban houses in Uttar Pradesh given on rent by owners to those residing in Delhi as vacation homes, wedding sites, retreat homes, and so forth. Interviewees in Bhatta and Parsaul mentioned this as a possible compensation for land acquisition.

pushing for a re-embedding of the markets in society. I argued that these demands made by rural dwellers on the state and market are connected to the new moral economy resulting from a rising living standard built on the advances of the Green Revolution, and new aspirations of social and geographical mobility, and employment. The marketization of agriculture and the politicization following the Green Revolution trained farmers in the market logic, and lobbying for benefits from the state. This chapter of course, has limitations: It does not discuss the particular moral economies at work where farmers and rural dwellers struggle to retain their land and resist commodification. It does not discuss the class and caste divisions in India, though it is highly likely that the landless and the Dalits are more in favour of the new developmental projects and employment provisions. The evidence in this chapter, however, does point to a divisive counter politics to the market, as Polanyi imagined.

8 Locational Politics of Land

Antagonistic Cooperation in Western Maharashtra

Sai Balakrishnan

LOCATIONAL LENS

In the past century, India has experienced two large rounds of new city building. The first began in the 1950s, shortly after Independence, when the country faced the imperative of nation-building in the aftermath of British colonial rule. State-directed urbanization posed an opportunity for enacting the Third World political project of import-substitution industrialization, and national decision-makers conceived of 'new towns' as key strategic entities in a national effort to reshape India into a modern, industrial society.[1] The Central Government financed the development of 120 new towns including steel town-ships, as well as 35 satellite towns. These satellite towns were located in or near newly erected borders with neighbouring countries, and they played an important role in integrating larger numbers of refugees from Pakistan. Rather than settle refugees in existing cities, the Central

---

[1] Rhodri Windsor Liscombe, 'In-dependence: Otto Koenigsberger and Modernist Urban Resettlement in India', *Journal of Planning Perspectives* 21, no. 2 (2006): 157–78; Srirupa Roy, *Beyond Belief: India and the Politics of Postcolonial Nationalism* (Durham and London: Duke University Press, 2007).

government intentionally directed the flow to these new towns, which were conceptualized as sites of national integration that could transcend the historically antagonistic divisions of religious and ethnic groups. Modernism in India had reached a zenith at this point, and the new towns were shaped by the belief that modernizing the built environment could allow for the making of liberal-democratic citizens. These capital-intensive new towns, particularly the steel towns, adhered to the non-alignment movement under the leadership of Nehru. But the condition of scarce capital to kick-start industrialization in a young democratic republic meant a heavy reliance on foreign aid, with strategic mobilization of aid from the Cold War powers, the United States (US) and the Union of Soviet Socialist Republics (USSR).[2]

Decades later, India now finds itself once again amidst a frenzy of 'new town' development, but the planning priorities have been fundamentally recalibrated. The 1991 economic liberalization reforms created a new paradigm for urbanization that focused on special economic zones (SEZs) and 'smart cities' as engines of economic growth. Proponents of the new paradigm assert that the combination of liberalization and electoral democracy puts India in a geopolitically idiosyncratic position—one which demands structurally adjusting the country for global competitiveness. Traditional ways of managing land, labour, tax, and other legal arrangements must be reformed to move India away from the inefficiencies of public sector reliance and the backwardness of an agrarian economy, they say. It is within this paradigm that new towns serve as pilot projects for dismantling the old regime and testing out new methods of liberalization, rather than transforming the national economy wholesale. Today's new towns permit policymakers, investors, and aspiring urbanites to escape the messy challenges of cities as they currently exist, and reimagine a technocrat's utopia of information technology, big data, and public–private-partnership (PPP) financing. In his 2014 election campaign, Prime Minister Narendra Modi promised to build 100 smart cities: 'Cities in the past were built

---

[2] K.C. Sivaramakrishnan, *New Towns in India: A Report on a Study of Selected New Towns in the Eastern Region* (A Homi Bhabha Fellowship Award Project with support from the Indian Institute of Management, Calcutta, 1976–7), http://www.cprindia.org/sites/default/files/books/NEW%20TOWNS%20 IN%20INDIA_1.pdf.

on river-banks. They are now built along highways. But in future, they will be built based on availability of optical fibre networks and next-generation infrastructure.'[3] Soon after assuming office, Modi allocated INR 70,600 million to the 2014 budget, and commenced talks with foreign ministers from Singapore and other private sector actors about bringing the dream of 100 smart cities into reality.

A fundamental difference between India's two waves of new town building is location. The public-sector-driven industrial steel towns in the 1950s and 1960s were all located in the 'economically backward regions' of states like Madhya Pradesh, Bihar, and Uttar Pradesh.[4] These settlements were conceived as strategic tools for rectifying economic imbalances established during colonial rule that had favoured investment in colonial port cities over the hinterland. The national plans envisioned that 'the steel plants and other industrial projects [would] provide the basis for the development of small and medium industries and programmes of education and training and other activities'.[5] In other words, the steel towns were expected to catalyze regional growth in parts of the country that had been disadvantaged by a colonial-era focus on port cities that were integral to imperial economic networks. Reversing this spatial unevenness became a top goal for national planners and decision-makers.

In contrast to the steel towns, the most recent development frenzy is occurring in some of the country's most prosperous regions. Prime Minister Modi's 100 smart cities initiative proposes development along the Delhi–Mumbai Industrial Corridor, for example, which connects the political capital of Delhi to the financial hub of Mumbai. The Delhi–Mumbai Industrial Corridor also passes through some of the country's most agriculturally productive regions. Research on the location of the 154 SEZs that have been approved by the Central Government show them to be located around already developed metropolitan areas

---

[3] Press Trust of India, 'Focus on "Skill, Scale and Speed" to Compete with China: PM', *The Hindu*, 8 June 2014.

[4] Amitabh Kundu, Girish Kumar Misra, and Rajkishor Meher, *Location of Public Enterprises and Regional Development* (New Delhi: Concept Publishing Company, 1986).

[5] Planning Commission reports, http://planningcommission.nic.in/plans/planrel/fiveyr/welcome.html.

of Delhi, Hyderabad, Bengaluru, and Chennai.[6] This spatial pattern reveals a break with earlier new towns' planning priority of balancing regional development. Instead, today's enclaves of liberalization heighten spatial inequities by concentrating around the valorized spaces of established economic nodes. What's more, these SEZs are typically accompanied by investments in high-visibility infrastructure projects, even though infrastructure from pre-liberalization investment may already exist. New economic corridors often run almost parallel to extant highways. For example, in the 1990s, the Maharashtra state government championed the Mumbai–Pune Expressway as a top priority, and today the Mumbai–Pune economic corridor tracks the old highway closely.

The reason for this locational divergence is that the contemporary geography of private capital is highly shaped by the past decisions of public investment. Rather than fundamentally reshaping patterns of capital flows, India's 1991 political and economic liberalization has reinforced the clustering of private capital in particular regions. Sanjoy Chakravorty's work[7] is one of the few that examines the locational politics of post-liberalization development. Using data from the Centre for Monitoring Indian Economy (CMIE) to map this geography, Chakravorty shows that 'the existence of any investment in the pre-reform era and the existence of new private investment in the neighboring districts in the post-reform era' are two essential factors for determining the locational attributes of private investment since 1991. Thus, in contrast to the efforts of the Nehruvian 'new towns' of the mid-twentieth century to reorient growth to economically lagging regions, post-liberalization private investments are centring on already economically prosperous regions, which has the effect of only amplifying spatial inequalities.

The clustering of private capital to regions with prior investment adheres to a basic tenet of economic geography, that firms cluster in

[6] Partha Mukhopadhyay and Kanhu Charan Pradhan, 'Location of SEZs and Policy Benefits: What Does the Data Say?', in Centre for Policy Research, *Special Economic Zones: Promise, Performance and Pending Issues* (New Delhi: Centre for Policy Research, 2009).

[7] Sanjoy Chakravorty, 'Capital Source and the Location of Industrial Investment: A Tale of Divergence from Post-reform India', *Journal of International Development* 15, no. 3 (2003): 365–83.

regions with prior market linkages. Unlike the nation-building and other imperatives of the state, there is little reason for private firms to locate in 'economically backward' regions. It was not only the steel and satellite towns that received prior public investment. Another geography of favoured public investment are the former Green Revolution regions. An agricultural modernization programme of the 1960s to 1980s, the Central and state governments concentrated generous state subsidies of water–seeds–fertilizers in strategic regions of the country that could emerge as surplus food-producing zones.[8] The Green Revolution programme not only helped develop prior market linkages that are now leveraged by private capital, but they also helped produce a new constituency of agrarian propertied classes. This then is at the crux of contemporary India's locational politics of new towns: Many of the desirable regions for post-liberalization private capital are the former Green Revolution regions, but the lands in these regions are also owned by an organized agrarian propertied class whose interests cannot be alienated without grave consequences at the ballot boxes. The desirability of former Green Revolution regions as sites for many of the new SEZs has resulted in land conflicts. Organized agrarian constituencies have responded to coercive land acquisition with such high-profile protests that the Central Government amended the Land Acquisition Act, 1894 (LAA) of the colonial regime, and issued the Right to Fair Compensation and Transparency in Land Acquisition, Rehabilitation and Resettlement Act, 2013 (LARR) in order to adjust to new demands. Conventional, coercive mechanisms like eminent domain for assembling fragmented parcels of land are increasingly becoming political nonstarters. In their place, public agencies are experimenting with different methods, like land pooling, for preparing agricultural land for the new 'new towns'. As public actors and private firms have reshuffled the responsibilities and norms of development, agrarian propertied capital has emerged as a key political player to contest the restructuring of their lands. This chapter takes an in-depth look at these locational politics by focusing on the Khed SEZ, located in the western region of Maharashtra.

---

[8] Francine Frankel, *India's Green Revolution: Economic Gains and Political Costs* (Bombay: Oxford University Press, 1971).

KHED SEZ: ANTAGONISTIC COOPERATION

The building of the SEZ in the Khed region in western Maharashtra exemplifies this locational politics of post-liberalization urbanization. Of the approved SEZs in Maharashtra as of 2017,[9] five are in the Mumbai city-district and in the two adjacent districts that make up the Mumbai Metropolitan Region (Thane and Raigad), 12 are in Pune and two in Satara district, and only one in the eastern-most district of Chandrapur. The SEZs in the Mumbai Metropolitan Region benefit from being in the agglomeration shadow of Mumbai. The SEZs in the Pune and Satara districts are of special interest to this chapter, because these districts were formerly arid regions that benefited from heavy doses of subsidized resources, including irrigation water, during the Green Revolution period. These districts have the highest concentration of irrigated, sugarcane-exporting zones in the country. The eastern-most region of Maharashtra has some of the 'most agriculturally distressed and backward districts' not just in the state, but in the country.[10] This is a stark illustration of the socio-spatial inequalities in the state, when one realizes that the western region has some of the most high-growth surplus-producing industrial, financial, and agrarian nodes in the country, and the eastern region is a neglected zone that is now the epicentre of Naxalism. Not surprisingly, there is only one SEZ in the eastern district of Chandrapur, and it is a power-producing SEZ.

The Khed taluka is located in Pune district, and in 2006, it became the site of the multi-product SEZ called Khed City. The Khed SEZ is a unique organizational innovation, in that it brings together historically antagonistic groups in a collective land experiment. A set of oppositional actors is the firm and landowners. The firm submits an SEZ petition, including a desired location, to the state government's 19-member single window SEZ agency, the SEZ Board of Approval. Once the application is approved, bureaucrats can start with land

---

[9] Source: https://di.maharashtra.gov.in/_layouts/15/doistaticsite/Marathi/pdf/SEZ.xls.

[10] Government of Maharashtra, *Report of Fact Finding Committee on Regional Imbalance in Maharashtra (under the chairmanship of V.M. Dandekar)* (1984); Government of Maharashtra, *Report of the High Level Committee on Balanced Regional Development Issues in Maharashtra* (October 2013).

acquisition. In 2006, the Maharashtra Board of Approval granted the private sector firm Bharat Forge the authorization to establish an SEZ in the Khed region. However, when the Maharashtra Industrial Development Corporation (MIDC) announced that it would acquire land in 17 villages, thousands of landowners, many of whom were part of the Maratha-Kunbi group of castes, responded with protests at the Khed Revenue Department, and called for an end to the planned SEZ. The bureaucrats knew the high political costs of alienating these organized agrarian propertied classes. Faced with a legitimacy crisis, the MIDC and Revenue Department bureaucrats, the agencies responsible for land acquisition and land assembly for SEZs, came up with an organizational innovation that would give the landowners shares in a new company called Khed Economic Infrastructure Private Limited (KEIPL). Bharat Forge and the MIDC would control 85 per cent of the shares; the remaining 15 per cent would be allocated to a farmers' cooperative, made up of landowners whose lands are acquired for the SEZ. Industrial and landed fractions of capital have antagonistic interests, as land rent and industrial profits work at cross-purposes with one another.[11] The KEIPL was a clever organizational solution that aligned otherwise conflicting interests of two powerful fractions of capital.

The other set of antagonistic groups is the dominant-caste and Adivasi landowners. In the wake of the protests, the bureaucrats commenced a one-year negotiation with the landowners. A key outcome of these negotiations was a change in the SEZ boundary. The Khed region is located at the foothills of the Western Ghats mountain range (see Figures 8.1, 8.2, and 8.3 for a visual sense of the region). It has a mixed landscape of irrigated fields that supply cabbage and other vegetables to Pune, Mumbai, and surrounding cities; these fields are interspersed with barren hillocks. Through a history of socio-spatial segregation, the more powerful Maratha-Kunbi and other backward classes (OBC) groups appropriated the cultivable lands in the plains, and the hillocks were relegated to an Adivasi group called the Thakkars. During the year-long negotiation, the dominant-caste landowners who had spearheaded the protest demanded that the SEZ boundaries be redrawn to include only the barren 'waste' lands. The bureaucrats

---

[11] Richard Fogelsong, *Planning the Capitalist City: The Colonial Era to the 1920s* (Princeton, NJ: Princeton University Press, 2014); David Harvey, *The Limits to Capital* (Oxford: Basil Blackwell, 1982).

acquiesced, and the final land acquisition details for the four villages for Phase 1 of the Khed SEZ are below (see Figure 8.1).

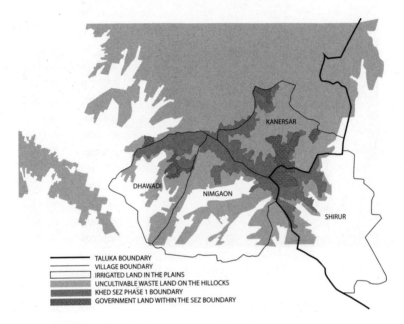

FIGURE 8.1   A Map of Khed City

Source: Author.

Note 1: Straddling the borders of four gram panchayats, the SEZ contains both uncultivable waste land in the hills, and arable land in the plains. The uncultivable waste land has public and private owners.

Note 2: This map is not to scale and is provided for illustrative purposes only. It does not represent any authentic national or international boundaries of India.

Notice that of the 4,066 acres, nearly 72 per cent of the land is categorized as privately owned 'waste' land, the remaining 28 per cent is government-owned land. Not a single acre of irrigated, multi-crop land in the plains was acquired for the SEZ. The Maratha-Kunbi land-owners own geographically dispersed plots of both fertile land in the plains and 'waste' land on the hillocks. Around 70 per cent of the 'waste' hillock lands acquired for the SEZ are owned by these dominant-caste landowners. The remaining 30 per cent are owned by Thakkars, who grow subsistence crops on their 'waste' land, and work as agricultural labourers on the vegetable-exporting fields of the dominant castes. Though the Thakkars were neither a part of the protests nor of the

FIGURE 8.2   Vegetable-Growing Arable Land in the Plains
Source: Author.

FIGURE 8.3   The New SEZ Boundary on the 'Waste' Land Hillock
Source: Author.

TABLE 8.1 Details of Land Acquired for the Khed SEZ

Village	Privately Owned 'Waste' Land, in Acres	Government-Owned Land, in Acres	Total Area for Khed SEZ, in Acres
Nimgaon	794	153	947
Kanersar	876	577	1,453
Dhawadi	747	0	747
Shirur	529	390	919
Total	2,946	1,120	4,066

Source: Author.

negotiations, because they own around 30 per cent of the acquired 'waste' land, they are now included as shareholders in the KEIPL company. The company then includes antagonistic agrarian groups of dominant-caste landowners and Adivasi labourers who have historically laboured on the lands of the propertied classes.

Why did these historically antagonistic groups come together in a shareholding land experiment? I borrow the term 'antagonistic cooperation' from Sanyal,[12] who argues that to understand institutional partnerships, we need to pay attention to 'simultaneous conflict and cooperation,' that is, why institutional actors who are critical of one another may decide, at a certain time and place, to cooperate with one another. I outline the clever timing of the KEIPL company, mediated by the Revenue Department, by focusing on the benefits of the Khed institutional arrangement for the private-sector firm Bharat Forge, the industrial parastatal MIDC, the dominant-caste landowners, and the marginalized tribal landowners.

The Firm, Bharat Forge

Firms and industrial parastatals have come under harsh public scrutiny recently as 'land grabbers' and 'real estate brokers'.[13] In the wake of the

[12] Bishwapriya Sanyal, 'Antagonistic Cooperation: A Case Study of Nongovernmental Organizations, Government and Donors' Relationships in Income-generating Projects in Bangladesh', *World Development* 19, no. 10 (1991): 1367–79.

[13] B.K. Lakshmikantha, 'KIADB Acts Like Real Estate Agent, Says Karnataka High Court', *DNA*, 11 December 2010; Abhishek Angad,

agrarian protests, both Bharat Forge and the MIDC recognized that negative publicity from these protests can hurt their image, and even terminate their projects.

The chairman and managing director (CMD) of Bharat Forge, Baba Kalyani, is the brother-in-law of the managing director of the private sector consortium, Nandi Infrastructure Corridor Enterprises (NICE). In 1994, the Karnataka state government selected the NICE consortium to build the Bangalore–Mysore Infrastructure Corridor—a six-lane private tolled expressway—along with five private townships along the corridor. According to the build–own–operate–transfer contract, the infrastructure corridor would be transferred to the government after 30 years, and the townships along the corridor would be sold to the private consortium. The NICE corridor and its five townships have been mired in litigation since 1994, with non-governmental organizations (NGOs) challenging the acquisition of agricultural lands for private township development. In October 2012, the Karnataka Lokayukta Court—an anti-corruption ombudsman organization—upheld the charges against the NICE consortium, and ordered it to return the INR 720,000,000 [USD 14,400,000] of toll collected to the state government.

Private firms have taken the NICE experience as a warning that acquiring land through coercion can indefinitely delay, and even end, projects. Given his close familial relationship to the debacle, it should come as no surprise that Baba Kalyani opted to take a far less coercive approach with the Khed SEZ.

The Industrial Parastatal, MIDC

The role of the industrial parastatal in contexts like Khed, which have fragmented land ownership, is crucial. India faces the endemic problem of poor land records and unclear land titles. Most agricultural lands have encumbrances, including mortgage claims and restrictions on the alienability of agricultural lands (instituted soon after Independence to protect agrarian landowners from speculative transactions on their land). The wide variety of encumbrances on agricultural land makes direct land transactions between the private sector firm and agrarian

---

'Lokayukta Verdict on BMIC "Land Grab" Case on October 4th', *Citizen Matters*, 2 October 2012.

landowners a risky proposition for the private sector firm. For instance, if, as in the Khed case, the industrial firm purchases 3,500 acres of land for an industrial development, and if even 2 acres of that land has encumbrances, the entire project will be stuck in court till the property dispute is settled. It is to the advantage of the private sector that the parastatal is involved in land acquisition.

The risk of project delays or termination due to encumbrance litigation is simply too much for most industrial firms in India, and they have been vocal in their insistence on state mediation. During Parliament's debate of LARR in the mid-2000s, one proposal involved shifting land acquisition and negotiations from the state to the private sector. The industrial lobby of India Inc. organized in opposition, putting an end to the proposal. To this day, private firms continue to rely on the state to acquire land for an SEZ, and to protect the owners of industrial capital from any uncertainties or liabilities related to land tenure. As a result, industrial parastatals like the MIDC play a fundamental role in ensuring the development of SEZs. Even the marketing materials for Khed City publicly advertise how the land will be delivered free of encumbrances: 'The land in Khed City has been acquired by MIDC under the MID [Maharashtra Industrial Development] Act and leased to KEIPL, the developer of Khed City. Therefore, you [potential industrial firms] have no worries about the title of the land. You are free from any concerns of future litigations on the title of the land.'[14]

The coercive acquisition of agricultural land means that the MIDC is in the cross-hairs of two organized fractions of capital: industrial firms that want state mediation to deliver encumbrance-free land, and dominant-caste agrarian landowners who face the threat of having their land acquired by the state.

Dominant-caste Agrarian Landowners

Land is a key source of agrarian power, and some of the most organized agrarian propertied classes in Maharashtra are the dominant-caste Maratha-Kunbi landowners. These dominant-caste landowners are powerful enough as local leaders to effectively block any urban developments that are not beneficial to them, and the Khed bureaucrats had to negotiate with them, placate them, and win their support

---

[14] https://www.khedcity.com/.

in order for the Khed project to continue. Due to structural changes in
the agrarian economy—including the shortage of agricultural labour
and the rising value of appropriately located agricultural land for
urban uses—dominant-caste landowners aspire to participate in India's
urban/industrial economy, but only with the requisite safety nets to
mitigate the risks of an uncertain transition.

AGRICULTURAL LABOUR SHORTAGE

One of the main push factors in agriculture is agricultural labour
shortages. A common refrain heard among dominant-caste landowners along the Pune highways is the phrase '*mazdoor nahi milte* [workers
cannot be found]'. The availability of alternative factory jobs has led to
intense labour shortages in these highway regions:

> Earlier, the villagers used to come for work—Thakkars, others. Once
> the land payment was made, people work less. Earlier, the Thakkars used
> to work from morning to night, now they do not. The nearby places—
> Chakan, Rajgurunagar, there is chota-mota [small] MIDC work there,
> people have gone to work there. Earlier, we used to pay INR 60, now
> no one comes for less than INR 100. And they come at 11 and leave at
> 5, take a break for lunch. This is everywhere. Here [in Khed], because of
> the land money [compensation for 85 per cent of the land], it is more.[15]

URBAN ASPIRATIONS

In addition to the agricultural labour shortage, a push factor towards
an urban/industrial economy is the agrarian aspiration to participate
in the 'India Shining' narrative. All the 20 Maratha-Kunbi landowners
I spoke to in Kanersar, the first village that had agreed to give up its
land for the Khed SEZ, were educating their children in private, rather
than government, schools, and all voiced a desire for their children to
move from agriculture to industry. Hence, the Maratha-Kunbi landowners highly valued that compensation from the Khed SEZ would
include the guaranteed admission of one family member to the Khed
Industrial Training Institute (ITI), a joint initiative for vocational education between the Government of India and Bharat Forge. The ITI

---

[15] Personal interview, 4 January 2011.

graduates will almost certainly be employed in the Khed industrial development. Not surprisingly, admission to the Khed ITI is coveted: 'We have an agreement now with the ITI. It is not difficult to get admission there. It is based on marks in the 10th standard. A person from every family gets admission to the ITI. The Thakkar families do not go there because they do not have education.'[16]

Of the 20 Kanersar landowners, 14 have some service/industrial business in addition to their agricultural fields. A smaller number of Nimgaon landowners—4 out of the 20 interviewed—have service businesses. The MIDC has targeted benefits for the Sarpanches of both Kanersar and Nimgaon—these political leaders have been guaranteed construction and earthmoving contracts for the new industrial development. Though they lack experience, a Bharat Forge employee acknowledged that these construction contracts played a vital role as 'confidence-building measures'.[17] Of the 14 interviewed Kanersar landowners with service/industrial businesses, 12 had transportation companies to transport agricultural produce from Khed and surrounding areas to Mumbai. The Maratha-Kunbis who were experiencing urbanization and industrialization without leaving their villages welcomed these developments with the view that 'we are becoming like Mumbai, like a city, with city life'.

MANAGING THE RISKS OF AN IN-SITU AGRARIAN TO URBAN TRANSITION

Despite its advantages, the transition from an agrarian to an urban/industrial economy is fraught with uncertainties and risks. The Khed case illustrates some of the uncertainties posed by land commodification. The Khed industrial development is being delayed by changes in political and bureaucratic administration. Both the district collector at the time of the negotiations and his mediating bureaucrats have been transferred to other administrative departments, and the Khed landowners have lost their main liaison with the MIDC and the Revenue Department. The lack of visible construction on the site, despite the land negotiations being completed in 2008, is a legitimate cause of anxiety for the dominant-caste landowners:

[16] Personal interview, 11 January 2011.
[17] Personal interview, 8 May 2011.

> We gave up our land four years back. I gave up 15 acres of land, but have not received the dividend on my 2.25 acres [15 per cent of the 15 acres that the landowner is the shareholder of]. For my 2.25 acres, I should have received INR 120,000 interest. But for four years now, I have not received anything. What assurance do we have that the SEZ will be completed? Will they give us jobs or not?[18]

Besides these delays, agrarian landowners face the typical market risks of real estate development of financial profitability. Changes in interest rates, in material costs, in demand for the industrial services provided by the SEZ, and more, can significantly impact project returns. Were the Khed SEZ to incur losses, the agrarian landowners would be forced to give up their landed assets.

It was in anticipation of these risks that the dominant-caste agrarian landowners protested against the initial Khed proposal in 2006. Following the protests, the Revenue Department and MIDC redrew the boundaries of the Khed SEZ: the earlier 2006 proposal included 'fertile' and 'waste' lands within the SEZ boundary, but the 2008 proposal moves away from a Cartesian rigidity to a more zig-zagged boundary that only encompasses the 'waste' lands on the hills, and leaves the fertile lands on the plains untouched. The dominant-caste landowners in the Khed region own multiple plots of land, sometimes in joint ownership with others, at several geographically dispersed sites.[19] Due to their anxieties over the status and performance of the Khed industrial development, the dominant-caste landowners continue farming on their fertile agricultural lands. If the Khed industrial development does not do well and undergoes losses, they still will have their fertile agricultural lands to fall back on. The land cooperative offered these landowners the possibility of making profits from 'waste' lands that were otherwise left unused.

Adivasi Owners of 'Waste' Land

Although the SEZ deal offers the Thakkars the opportunity to profit as shareholders in the new real estate entity, perhaps what is most

---

[18] Personal interview, 19 June 2011.

[19] Source: File with the details of landholdings for the SEZ project, compiled by the MIDC.

remarkable about the outcome of the negotiations is how the Thakkars have managed to win recognition as a legitimate party. I first visited the Kanersar Thakkar settlement in 2010, two years after the Khed negotiations had been completed. The Thakkars lived in spatially segregated settlements in the barren hillocks. Each Thakkar household owned less than 2 acres of 'waste' land. They depended on these lands for subsistence farming; the men had been working on the fields of the intermediate caste landowners for generations. During my first visit to the Kanersar Thakkar settlement, I reached the settlement by foot well after sundown, and was greeted by a cluster of rammed earth one-room homes that were cloaked in darkness. Goats and cows were tethered outside the homes, and cow dung was plastered on the walls. During the day, women trekked 45 minutes each way to reach the public taps located in the gaothan (main village settlement). Children also travelled these long distances on foot to reach the government schools, also located in the gaothan, where the rest of the caste groups lived.

The Khed Thakkars had not been a part of the negotiations with the bureaucrats. When the bureaucrats redrew the SEZ boundaries to include only the 'waste' land on the hillocks and to leave the 'fertile' land untouched, the Thakkars' lands became enclosed within the new enclave boundary. In May 2012, Bharat Forge completed its construction of the new Thakkar resettlement colony, located around 15 minutes from the main village settlement of Kanersar, where the non-Adivasi population lives. Eighty-five Thakkar households from the four gram panchayats were relocated to this new settlement, which is spatially segregated from the main village settlement, but is much closer to it compared to the locations of the previous Thakkar settlements. The new resettlement colony is a standardized row of 12' × 12' concrete blocks. Instead of livestock, it was bikes that were parked outside the Thakkars' new homes. The new colony is close to massive electricity distribution transformers, and each home has a Sintex plastic overhead tank on the roof. Of crucial importance to the Thakkars is the location of the new settlement. Though still spatially segregated from the gaothan, the resettlement colony is much closer to it, and is now less than a 15-minute walk to the public taps and government school in the gaothan.

The Khed City SEZ may only be the next chapter in a story of spatial segregation for the Thakkars, and this next iteration of sociospatial

FIGURE 8.4   The Kanersar Thakkar Settlement before the SEZ
Source: Author.

FIGURE 8.5   The New Resettlement Colony after the Redrawing of the
SEZ Boundary
Source: Author.

change is neither about complete dispossession nor complete emancipation, but of uneven social transformation. One sign of this is the unfulfilled promise of the ITI. The ITIs are vocational training institutes for industrial work, and they are a good stepping stone to coveted factory jobs. The compensation package for the SEZ land condemnees includes guaranteed enrolment to the Khed ITI. The ITI guaranteed enrolment was important to the Maratha-Kunbis. Most of the Thakkar residents, however, cannot avail of this benefit because they lack the requisite education (10th standard pass) to gain admission to the ITI. Even those who do meet the standard have not all been admitted to the ITI, as gram panchayat representatives have largely maintained the tradition of referring individuals through personal networks to the SEZ factories. Only four men of the 85 families in the new settlement have secured work, despite the fact that all members of the community have given up their lands in the deal.

The shifting labour practices of the Thakkars are a second sign that the SEZ deal has not produced wholesale benefits for their communities, but an ambiguous landscape of socio-economic relations in flux. '*Mazdoor nahi milte* (workers cannot be found)' has become a common saying among Maratha-Kunbi landowners in the Khed region, who have experienced a shortage of agricultural labour. Thakkars who had previously worked cultivating crops in the fields can now find alternative work—albeit informally—in construction and factory production. Many have opted for this route, even if precarious and risky, finding the emergent choice in employment a source of liberation from historical caste relations. The sense of assertiveness is particularly strong among the younger generation of Thakkars, in their twenties and thirties, who aspire to leave the agricultural economy for urban life, and are willing

TABLE 8.2   Literacy Levels of Thakkar Adults above 18 Years from 25 Households

	Men	Women
Primary school (1st–4th standard)	16	42
Middle school (5th–7th standard)	22	6
High school (8th–12th standard)	18	4
Diploma/ITI	3	2
College	–	–

Source: Author.

to embrace the uncertainty of an informal urban economy that lacks any obligations either on the part of the state or of employers to provide them with any basic benefits or safety nets.

Third, men and women have experienced the revaluation of their wastelands in diverging ways. Since the 1970s, dairy farming on village land collectively owned had been a common practice in the Khed region. As these lands are now enclosed for the new towns, the Thakkar dairy farmers are deprived of their common grazing lands (notice that almost 28 per cent of the acquired land for the Khed SEZ is government-owned land, which was previously open to the dairy farmers as grazing land). Thakkars have been forced to sell their livestock, and this has been experienced most harshly by women. Women have been unhappy with the disappearance of cows and goats from their lands, as the change has deprived them of both vital livelihood and a source of milk for their children. With market prices unaffordable, Thakkar women have been forced to remove milk from their children's diet.

These three vignettes of social change among the Thakkars demonstrate that the Khed City SEZ has neither uniformly advantaged nor uniformly disadvantaged members of their community; rather it is remaking an uneven geography of empowerment and disempowerment, only across different lines of lived experience. Hence, a new politics of recognition has emerged for the Thakkars, opening up not only new possibilities for social and economic equality, but also new risks. The urban informal economy, devoid of historical obligations on the part of either the state or the private sector, promises to realize socio-cultural aspirations just as it threatens to exploit, dispossess, and disenfranchise.

PART III

A Range of Land Policies

9 Land Market Distortions in India

K.P. Krishnan, Venkatesh Panchapagesan,
and Madalasa Venkataraman[*]

Land and real estate remain the most commonly held assets by households across the world. While they account for around 40 per cent of household wealth in developed economies such as the United States (US) and Germany, they represent a larger fraction in emerging economies—62 per cent in China and 77 per cent in India.[1] While land is needed for shelter, it is the ability to monetize its value that plays a crucial role in the economic growth and development of financial markets in these economies.[2]

[*] This chapter builds upon an earlier article of ours titled 'Distortions in Land Markets and their Implications for Credit Generation in India', *Economic & Political Weekly* LII, no. 35 (2017): 48–55. We thank Ajay Shah, Susan Thomas, N. Karthik, and participants of the Bankruptcy Law Reforms Committee Conference for their comments and suggestions. The views expressed in this chapter are those of the authors, and do not reflect the views of the institutions that they are affiliated to.

[1] Reserve Bank of India, *Indian Household Finance: Report of the Household Finance Committee* (Mumbai: Reserve Bank of India, 2017), https://rbidocs.rbi.org.in/rdocs/PublicationReport/Pdfs/HFCRA28D0415E2144A009112DD314ECF5C07.PDF.

[2] Lee Alston, Gary Libecap, and Robert Schneider, 'The Determinants and Impact of Property Rights: Land Titles on the Brazilian Frontier', *The Journal of Law, Economics, and Organization* 12, no. 1 (1996): doi:10.3386/w5405.

Secure tenure and property rights are the bedrock that enable individuals and firms to transact in land or to collateralize it. When secure property rights exist, landowners are more willing to invest in improvements in the land, enhancing its value further. Lenders find it less risky to provide credit against such land since their ability to ward off litigations is greatly enhanced. Moreover, the owners, and the economy at large, spend less in protective measures to defend property rights, and can repurpose such 'wasted' investment more productively.[3]

De Soto claims that poor property rights have 'restricted the ability of a vast majority of the global population to transform a "dead asset" like land into "live capital"'.[4] Roll and Talbott even provocatively argue that property rights are the single largest determinant of how much a country moves towards being a developed country from a 'developing country'.[5]

Despite being a country with high landownership, Indian land markets remain heavily constrained by legal, regulatory, institutional, and cultural factors, leading to a variety of distortions that hamper their effective functioning. Such distortions are reflected in the title, possession, usage, and pricing of land. Given that land remains largely a state subject in India, these distortions also vary considerably by state in their breadth and magnitude.

Land market distortions have both micro- and macro-level implications—they impact the ability to transfer property assets, estimate a reliable valuation for selling or mortgaging, provide compensation in case of eminent domain acquisitions, make reasonable estimates of land-based tax collections, and so on. A study by McKinsey Global Institute suggests that eliminating land market distortions alone could boost India's gross domestic product (GDP) growth by as much as 1.3 per cent annually.[6]

[3] Arun S. Malik and Robert M. Schwab, 'The Economics of Tax Amnesties', *Journal of Public Economics* 46, no. 1 (1991): doi:10.1016/0047-2727(91)90063-8.

[4] Hernando De Soto, *The Mystery of Capital: Why Capitalism Triumphs in the West and Fails Everywhere Else* (New York: Basic Books, 2000).

[5] Richard Roll and John Talbott, 'Political and Economic Freedoms and Prosperity, previously titled: Why Many Developing Nations Just Aren't' (eScholarship, University of California, 2001).

[6] McKinsey Global Institute, 'India: The Growth Imperative', last modified 2001, www.mckinsey.com/~/media/McKinsey/Global%20Themes/India/

A natural outcome of these distortions is that market participants adopt various sub-optimal coping mechanisms to deal with them. For example, lenders rationally respond to these structural issues through conservative lending policies. Loan-to-value (LTV) ratios in housing loans and loans against property are usually below acceptable regulatory norms to protect lenders from other distortionary costs. Murthi of Daksh indicates that given that 'two-thirds of all civil cases in Indian district courts relate to land and property matters,'[7] buyers undertake elaborate and costly searches to protect themselves against fraud. Expensive private valuations are sought by both lenders and buyers to determine land and property values in the absence of transparent valuation data. Furthermore, every state government creates its own estimate of market values to determine the base upon which stamp duty and registration charges (transactional taxes) are levied.

Several interventions have been introduced to overcome distortions in land markets over the years. Some are policy initiatives such as the land digitization pilot programmes that have tried to standardize the content capture and process across states using existing land records. However, these programmes are handicapped by the quality of existing records which, in the absence of a comprehensive official resurvey, will continue to carry flaws in them. Moreover, the digital records they create do not carry the full benefits of digitization as they are mostly scanned versions of paper records with limited searchability (searching using specific fields) and integration (ability to integrate multiple data sources using common fields) features.

Several other policy initiatives such as recording changes in land use as well as encumbrances or liens on land and property are either poorly designed or implemented across states.[8] Legislative remedies such as the recently passed Rajasthan Urban Land (Certification of Titles) Act,

---

Growth%20imperative%20for%20India/MGI_The_growth_imperative_for_India.ashx.

[7] Kavya Murthi, *Land and the Courts* (Daksh, 2018), http://dakshindia.org/land-and-the-courts/.

[8] Deepak Sanan, D.B. Gupta, and Prerna Prabhakar, *A Pilot Impact Assessment of the Digital-India Land Records Modernisation Programme* (NCAER, 2017), http://www.ncaer.org/publication_details.php?pID=284.

2016 to introduce state-guaranteed titles often raise more questions than answers. For example, the Rajasthan Act neither defines what a title is nor makes it clear whether the title to be provided is presumptive or conclusive.[9] Such vagueness could only lead to disputes that will continue to clog the courts, something that the legislation was meant to overcome. More recent solutions such as the use of blockchains stem from a misconceived notion that technology can solve all land-related issues without addressing root causes such as a highly compromised or constrained governance structure.[10]

The fact that land market distortions continue to persist suggest that these interventions have had only limited success. As a result, we continue to see reduced lending against land, underinvestment in property, increased search and due diligence costs for new investors, and unchecked rent-seeking behaviour from vested interests that stifles the ease of doing business.

We describe the Indian land markets along with its distortions in greater detail below. In addition, we present a framework to categorize and evaluate these distortions. Subsequent sections discuss possible solutions (including legislative remedies) that have been implemented with varying degrees of success. We close with recommendations that we believe will work well in a multilayered governance setup like in India.

LAND MARKETS IN INDIA

We examine Indian land markets using a simple 4 Ps framework—the *parcel*, the *purpose*, the *person*, and finally the *price*—to better understand the extent to which distortions afflict them.[11]

---

[9] Amlanjyoti Goswami and Deepika Jha, 'Your Title Is Not Ready Yet: Rajasthan's Land Titling Legislation', *Economic & Political Weekly* LI, no. 34 (2016): 26–9.

[10] K.V Kurmanath, 'In AP Capital, Blockchain Technology Secures Land Records', *The Hindu Business Line*, 8 January 2018, https://www.thehindu-businessline.com/info-tech/in-ap-capital-blockchain-technology-secures-land-records/article10020465.ece.

[11] These 4 Ps represent the most important factors behind a real estate appraisal according to the International Valuation Standards Council. See https://www.ivsc.org/files/file/view/id/677.

We take the perspectives of a buyer and a lender, two key stakeholders in these markets, for this assessment. A significant part of annual household savings in India are still allocated to land and real estate. As much as 58 per cent of annual Indian household savings are still invested in physical assets including land and real estate.[12] Similarly, credit against land and real estate is also high.[13] About 40–50 per cent of all corporate debt is secured against land and buildings,[14] while nearly 50–60 per cent of all retail loans are indexed to real estate as collateral in one form or the other in the formal market.[15]

But before we get into the 4Ps, it is important to recognize some key features of our land markets. The land market in India, is not a single homogenous market that envelops the entire country. It is, in fact, a series of micro-markets, each within the state's purview but grouped under different, disparate administrative entities. This is because land is predominantly a state subject under India's constitution.[16] States have,

---

[12] Reserve Bank of India (Mumbai), *Handbook of Statistics on Indian Economy* (2017).

[13] Krishnan, Panchapagesan, and Venkataraman, 'Distortions in Land Markets and their Implications for Credit Generation in India'.

[14] L.M. Bhole and Jitendra Mahakud, 'Trends and Determinants of Corporate Capital Structure in India: A Panel Data Analysis', *Finance India* 18, no. 1 (2004): 37–46; Basudeb Guha-Khasnobis and Saumitra N. Bhaduri, 'Determinants of Capital Structure in India (1990–1998): A Dynamic Panel Data Approach', *Journal of Economic Integration* 17, no. 4 (2002): doi:10.11130/jei.2002.17.4.761.

[15] Reserve Bank of India (Mumbai), *Basic Statistical Returns of Scheduled Commercial Banks in India* (2017).

[16] Land figures in entry 18 of list II (list of items to be regulated by the states) which deals with 'land, that is to say, rights in and over land, land tenures including the relation of landlord and tenant, and the collection of rents; transfer and alienation of agricultural land; land improvement in agricultural loans; colonization'. Entry 45 of the same list discusses aspects of 'land revenue, including assessment and collection of revenue, the maintenance of land records, survey for revenue purposes and record of rights, and alienation of revenues,' and entry 49 of the same list further goes on to mention 'taxes on lands and buildings'. Certain items like the acquisition and requisition of property fall under the Concurrent List that provides powers to both the Union and state governments to make laws.

therefore, the right to legislate on land, decide its best possible use, as well as determine the magnitude of revenues that it can generate.

The sheer variations in how rules are formed and enforced, as well as in the quantity and quality of information provided across states, make distortions a natural outcome. For example, each state has evolved its own land registration system independently, supporting its own language, and taking into consideration the customary laws/practices prevalent in that state. Individuals who wish to transact on landholdings across different states do not have a mechanism whereby all this information can be obtained at a single point of access. Each state has specific restrictions and costs involved in accessing their land registration records. Moreover, records on registrations and disputes can be accessed only through the state machinery, requiring a local presence. The units of measurement for each state are different, and transactions still use local units and measures, for instance, bigha in Assam and cent in Telangana/Tamil Nadu.

While such differences were less consequential in the past as interest in land was mostly local, they now represent major bottlenecks for industrial growth and labour mobility across the country. Most key stakeholders today are not local, be it lenders, investors, or companies that need land for operations. In many cases, they may even be from outside the country. There is very little choice that states have, therefore, other than to address these distortions head on. Some of the larger investor-friendly states like Maharashtra and Gujarat have already started this process along with others like Rajasthan and Andhra Pradesh, which are aggressively seeking non-local help in their development.

Now we examine each of the four dimensions separately.

Parcel

Most of the distortions that occur in the real estate space centre around the lack of a single comprehensive view of parcel-level information, including the physical contours of the land along with information on built structures that rest on them. Typically, each parcel is identified by a unique survey number (recorded by the survey department of the state government) that delineates the boundaries of the parcel clearly. Some of the questions that a buyer or a lender engages with are:

1. What are the contours of the parcel? Is the parcel clearly and unambiguously identified?
2. Is the area on the record the same as the area on the ground (ground truthing)?
3. Has the sequence of amalgamation and separation of the parcel been documented clearly, and geo-spatially identified?
4. Is the parcel located in a flood plain or subject to any other natural hazard?
5. How many distinct properties are built on each individual/jointly owned parcel of land, especially for multistorey apartments?

Unfortunately, several legal, regulatory, or information-based lacunae in our land records make it difficult to answer these questions in many states today.[17]

Firstly, most state governments do not do regular surveys as mandated, and survey maps that contain parcel information are often outdated as a result. In rural areas, where survey numbers constitute large parcels, there is still some clarity in being able to overlay maps of different eras to identify land parcels. However, in urban areas, surveys have simply been unable to keep pace with the change in development and contours of parcels.

Parcels are split or rejoined all the time, and the finer and finer cuts of parcels, especially to accommodate multistorey housing, are often times not reflected in the official survey maps. For instance, the city of Bengaluru, a fast-growing cosmopolitan city with over 10 million people, was last surveyed in the 1930s, much before all the growth had taken place. Recently, Bengaluru's urban local body, the Bruhat Bengaluru Mahanagara Palike (BBMP), faced criticism for basing its demolition drive of properties that encroached storm-water drains (rajakaluves) on village maps drawn in 1904.[18] Moreover, land records

[17] A recent initiative by the Department of Land Resources in the Ministry of Rural Development conducted pilot studies in three states to determine the quality of their rural land records. The synthesis report highlights not only systemic issues, but also significant ground-level variation across these three states. See Sanan, Gupta, and Prabhakar, *A Pilot Impact Assessment of the Digital-India Land Records Modernisation Programme.*

[18] K. Jaiprakash, 'Maps to Nowhere: Village Surveys of Little Help in Marking Encroachments', *The Times of India*, 11 August 2016.

in most states continue to use landmarks and neighbouring parcel information to pinpoint the geographical location of the land despite tremendous advances in geo-spatial mapping technology.

Secondly, there are a multitude of agencies that handle each parcel of land—the survey is conducted by the survey department of the state government; the parcel's possession/ownership is recorded in the village-level revenue records by a functionary of the state government department of revenue; changes in this are registered with the land records registration office of the state; tax collection statistics are maintained at the property tax offices of the municipality/village panchayat, and so on. The siloed nature of these departments means that it is well-nigh impossible to get a single view of the transactions and rights pertaining to a parcel. The process of updating land records is often cumbersome, and involves several manual processes conducive for corruption. Lastly, several key pieces of information related to the parcel often go unrecorded. For example, encumbrances other than mortgages, easement rights, and mutations are not usually included in land records, especially in the rural areas.

Many states recently have started computerizing (scanning physical copies into digital files) their cadastral data without making them truly digital with searchability and filtering features. Also use of local language and units of measurement make searching these records an impossible task, especially in the absence of software that can transliterate multiple languages. Some states like Karnataka have undertaken pilots to create Aadhaar-like property IDs with embedded geo-spatial and encumbrance information. Such efforts are commendable but they remain limited to pilots because of the exorbitant cost, and an underlying lack of political will to comprehensively resurvey, especially in dense urban areas.

All these issues suggest that lenders seeking to lend against land and property must perform extensive due diligence on their own, that could even include a physical survey on the ground. This drives up the transaction/process cost of lending as well as the underlying risk from impairment of collateral.

Purpose

There is often a significant variation between how a parcel of land can be used and how it is actually being used in India. The former comes from master plans of urban local bodies (ULBs) and town planning departments that lay out a planned approach to development. These plans provide a clear indication of dos and don'ts in land use, and are used by government agencies as a benchmark for issuing development permits and other kinds of usage licenses.

The specific questions that would interest a buyer or a lender would be:

1. Have all the required approvals been obtained before development?
2. Is the development within zoning norms? Is the construction within the building code?
3. For secondary market transactions, what is the deviation/violation that is present in the property currently?
4. What is the cost and risk in regularizing such deviations?
5. What is the structure worth if such deviations were to be removed (is it possible to value the asset independent of the deviation after demolishing it)?[19]

In reality, large tracts of land development violate approval norms and plans since enforcement is poor. It is estimated that at least 80 per cent of the structures across East Delhi suffer from either zoning violations or Development Control Regulations (DCR) violations.[20] Moreover, retrospective changes to acceptable land uses make it difficult to establish whether violations happened before or after such changes.[21] Governments swing from ad-hoc clearing drives to regularizations through penalties for dealing with violations, but implementation usually is selective, costly, and riddled with corruption.[22]

---

[19] There is the anecdotal evidence of a hotel in Bengaluru that had built a mezzanine floor without approval. The building's value without the mezzanine floor was nil since it was part of the load-bearing structure.

[20] Alok K.N. Mishra, 'It's a Disaster in the Making: 80% of Buildings in East Delhi "Illegal"', *The Economic Times*, 4 July 2017.

[21] The 2016 National Green Tribunal order widening the no-development zone near Bengaluru lake bodies from 30 metres to 75 metres caused much confusion since many development projects were already underway based on the old threshold.

[22] The Government of Karnataka has introduced schemes (called Akrama–Sakrama) to regularize unauthorized constructions at least three times over

While violations are rampant, some question whether our planning process is adequate to meet our rapid growth. In fact, it is often cited that poor planning such as inadequate FSI (floor space index) norms have constrained land supply significantly, making land-use violations inevitable. By the government's own estimate, all urban growth can be easily accommodated in just 2.25 per cent of the country's land mass if properly planned.[23]

Poor planning and weak enforcement of land-use norms have facilitated the growth of informal land markets where the underlying land is impaired in some form or the other. For example, in Bengaluru, vast tracts of peri-urban land outside municipality jurisdiction are transacted upon, with active connivance of various stakeholders including government employees. These areas do not have proper civic amenities, and are usually built in violation of existing master plans.[24]

Violations impact both collateral value, as well as the long-term sustainability of the underlying land and its surrounding infrastructure. Property-level violations dampen potential property tax revenue collections since violating owners rarely declare non-allowable areas as part of self-assessment. Low revenues force local governments to underfund infrastructural development, triggering a fresh cycle of sub-optimal outcomes (poor planning → new violations → low future revenues → future poor planning). The 2016–17 Economic Survey of India estimated that the city of Bengaluru is possibly collecting just 5 per cent of its property tax revenues based on the gap between

---

the last decade, with the latest being in 2015. While the earlier schemes were implemented, the latest one has been stayed by a high court order.

[23] Ministry of Rural Development, Department of Land Records, *National Land Utilization Policy: Framework for Land Use Planning & Management:* Policy Draft (Government of India, 2013), https://smartnet. niua.org/sites/default/files/resources/draft_national_land_utilisation_policy_july_2013.pdf, 14.

[24] Properties that are within ULB governance and have approved development permits were issued clean records for the purpose of assessment of tax (A-khata), while those that do not have approval were issued acknowledgements with no development privileges (B-khata). In reality, there is an active market for B-khata lands, with several gullible buyers building upon them after purchase.

potential properties from geo-spatial density maps and properties pay-ing actual tax.[25]

Person/Possession

'Person' here refers to the individual/entity with rights over the prop-erty and parcel. Property rights are an important class of institutional arrangement, whereby an individual or community entity is able to enjoy, as per Alchian and Demsetz, 'a bundle' of rights:[26] exclusivity, inheritability, transferability, and enforcement mechanisms. Thus prop-erty rights define legitimately exclusive uses, and identify the indi-vidual/entity who has these exclusive rights.

As societies mature and individuals external to the community start transacting in land assets, states develop sophisticated arrangements for recording and enforcing land rights through a centralized public record of land tracts. This record—the land registry—is necessary but not sufficient for a well operating land market. As Feder and Feeny note: 'A central record is of course only one of the many institutions designed to reduce uncertainty. A functioning legal system and effective enforcement mechanisms are necessary as well.'[27] They go on to cau-tion that in the absence of such public services as the police, judiciary, and so on, individuals will over-invest in securing their rights through fencing, armed guards, and so on, and underinvest in developing the property since it could be seized from them anytime.

Where land is collateralized, its usefulness as collateral is contingent on the borrower and lender having homogenous valuations on the land. Since land is valued as a bundle of rights, particularly transfer rights and occupancy rights, the lender needs to be secure that in case of default, the land can be appropriated, and the borrower indeed has the right to dispose the property by sale or by transfer to the lender.

---

[25] Government of India, *Economic Survey 2016–17* (2017).

[26] Armen A. Alchian and Harold Demsetz, 'The Property Right Paradigm', *The Journal of Economic History* 33, no. 1 (1973): doi:10.1017/s0022050700076403.

[27] Gershon Feder and David Feeny, 'Land Tenure and Property Rights: Theory and Implications for Development Policy', *The World Bank Economic Review* 5, no. 1 (1991): doi:10.1093/wber/5.1.135.

The documentation of land rights in a central registry is the first step towards being able to identify the claims that the borrower has on the land, and in transferring such rights to the lender in a systematic way at the time of initiation of the collateralization process.[28]

Each state has evolved its own processes for land record management, some more robust than others. However, there are generic shortcomings in state records, foremost among them being the intent of the registration process itself.

The registration process in India is meant to be a process of record keeping to identify the property tax payer rather than the owner of the property: it was never meant to convey possessory or ownership rights. Since the process evolved from a tax-administration standpoint, the central land registry is more focused on registering high-value transactions that would generate revenue rather than registering all transactions that identify transfer of usage rights in land. This has resulted in certain lacunae: for instance, lease agreements and mortgage agreements below a certain threshold do not require registration by law. The onus is on the property owner to establish indefeasible title, and this is currently done more in a manner of proving there are no challengers to the title rather than establishing conclusive title.

As registration records are incomplete, chances of impaired title are high. For instance, if a certain party has been in possession of a parcel of land for a long period of time (say more than 30 years), they can challenge ownership on grounds of reversionary interest and investments in the land. There are many anecdotal cases where members of a Hindu Undivided Family claim recompense against sale of land to a third party many years after the said sale claiming lack of prior knowledge of the transaction. When land is divided amongst members of a family, mutation does not automatically get triggered in most states, causing inconsistency between Tax/Revenue records and Planning Survey databases. The role of the documentary evidence going back many years becomes very important in ruling out such encumbrances to land transactions.

Even where solid land registry details are available in a structured format, there could be issues. Due to format changes, lack of a property ID,

---

[28] Gershon Feder, Tongroj Onchan, and Tejaswi Raparla, 'Collateral, Guaranties and Rural Credit in Developing Countries: Evidence from Asia', *Agricultural Economics* 2, no. 3 (1988): doi:10.1016/0169-5150(88)90005-9.

and technology issues, matching prior transactions to current transactions may not be possible. Agricultural or peri-urban land that is absorbed into cities is especially affected by these changes in jurisdiction.

All of these have led to a multitude of tenure and usage combinations in India. At the top in terms of title and usage rights lie approved and well-planned land developments with clear titles. These lands form the best collateral in the market place, and lenders in formal credit markets compete to provide mortgages at the lowest cost of capital possible. A second combination is that of formal tenure but impaired usage, in unplanned urban layouts, also called 'revenue layouts' on non-converted agricultural land. Here, ownership and possession is established, but usage rights are often in violation of the zoning rules. This segment is typically serviced by Non-banking Finance Companies (NBFCs) and private moneylenders that are more expensive and less efficient than formal credit markets.

The third combination is where land usage rights as well as land tenure are unsupported, which typically happens in slums. Here too, there are a variety of shades to the usage and tenure rights. Some slum dwellers have formal tenure documents that confer ownership, while in other cases, state governments confer proof of possession without ownership. Some slum dwellers pay property tax and rents on utilities, though formal tenure documents or possession documents are not available to them. In some cases, no tenure rights exist, as in the case of squatter settlements. In these cases, there is no formal market for collateralization of land rights, but transactions in land rights (or occupancy rights to be more precise) do take place, though with elements of coercion and enforcement by non-state actors.

It is in the interests of lenders to be able to verify the authenticity of the land tenure and usage rights of the borrower. Moreover, improper recording of rights, like an unregistered long-term contractual rental agreement, could expose lenders to unwanted risks like the inability to negotiate or remove the tenant even after foreclosure.

Lenders, to protect themselves against these inefficiencies, typically reduce the LTV of loans based on the usage and title rights that they can establish. In addition, lenders may seek personal guarantees, above and beyond the value of the property. Though such personal guarantees are difficult to enforce at times of default, they are quite prevalent in India unlike in other countries.

Price[29]

The valuation of land is a nuanced exercise which feeds into the collateralization process of land, and impacts its appropriability. Like any other asset, the value of land is determined by its production potential, by the present or future services it incorporates, as well as the bundle of rights attached to it in the specific usage/planning zone. Valuation is established by the parcel, the property usage, and the rights of the person who is transacting in it, and the value of the loan provided is determined by the value of the collateral that is estimated.

There are several estimates of value associated with a land parcel that a lender has to contend with. The simplest, and the only one that is used in other parts of the world, is the *transaction price*. This refers to the price at which a parcel has recently changed hands. In India, most land transactions have to be registered at the transaction price, and a stamp duty with a registration charge (usually calculated on the transaction price and changing by jurisdiction) is to be paid to the state revenue department.

Unfortunately, under-reporting of transaction prices is rampant across India. One obvious reason is the high stamp duty (anywhere from 3–12 per cent), which represents a significant source of revenue for states.[30] Though several government schemes such as the Jawaharlal Nehru National Urban Renewal Mission (JNNURM) have tried to incentivize states to reduce their stamp duties, high stamp duties continue to foster under-reporting.

To overcome loss of revenues due to under-reporting, state governments use their own estimates of market values for the purpose

---

[29] We do not make a distinction between price and value for this study. Value refers inherently to the fundamental value of an asset, while price refers to what buyers are willing to pay for it under the current circumstances. For a variety of factors including liquidity, price can differ from value, and stay different for long periods of time.

[30] Land-related stamp duty and registration charges contributed, on average, about 7 per cent of a state government's revenues in 2015–16. (Authors' own calculations from data provided by the RBI on State Finances: A Study of Budgets, https://rbi.org.in/Scripts/AnnualPublications.aspx?head=State%20 Finances%20:%20A%20Study%20of%20Budget).

of computing stamp duty. These *'guidance values'* (or circle rates or ready-reckoner rates as they are sometimes called) are computed at the block- or street-level with adjustments for variations in amenities and property structures. They are based on a combination of broker inputs and past registration values. While these values represent an improvement over self-reported registered values, they are still inefficient for various reasons.[31]

Firstly, governments do not update these values on time, especially where market rates have dropped.[32] Secondly, estimates are derived at block level, leading to horizontal and vertical inequity in taxation, that is, some locations achieve favourable taxation while some others have unfavourable taxation due to clustering of market values at block level. The process and timing of updating these guidance values is arbitrary owing to non-economic or political considerations.

The third source of price is from the lenders themselves, who undertake their own valuation exercise before they provide a loan against property. This is done using empaneled valuers who estimate market value using a variety of factors including comparable recent transactions and current listings. The Reserve Bank of India mandates that banks must take the lower of this valuation and the self-reported registered value to determine the LTV ratio. Given that registered values are almost always lower than lenders' valuations, LTVs remain naturally depressed.

Aside from providing the best possible estimate of market values, the *bank valuation* exercise (in its current form) also provides for geo-tagging of land parcels along with ground-truthing, making it the most comprehensive data on land records currently available in India. Unfortunately, this data is not available to the market at large. Every lender needs to undertake the expensive exercise of creating this data. It is astonishing to see multiple lenders valuing properties in the same apartment complex around the same time with no coordination.

---

[31] For lack of alternatives, a variety of market participants have come to use the government's guidance value as the de-facto market value for land. For example, courts use them routinely to determine fair value or compensation while income tax authorities use them to detect capital gains avoidance. Even some municipalities use them for assessing property tax liability.

[32] The Government of Haryana recently lowered circle rates in Gurugram, in the face of falling prices, which remain more of an exception than a rule.

Price opacity and lack of easy access to transaction records within the government systems ensure that lenders (and investors) remain conservative when it comes to lending against land and property.

DISTORTIONS INDUCED BY LAWS AND REGULATIONS

There are many laws and regulations that impact Indian land markets. Many of them are legacies of our colonial past when land was an important instrument to raise revenue for the administration. Some of these laws have created unintended distortions, both in their objectives as well as in their enforcement. We discuss some of them below.

The Registration Act of 1908[33]

The Registration Act, 1908 is the legal foundation for the governance of sale or transfer of any immovable property in India. This Act was introduced by the British, and its focus was more on collecting the right amount of revenue, and less on authenticating information provided on the underlying land parcels. This meant that the government was required to act only as a recorder of information that may or may not be accurate. Only the identity of the buyer and seller is verified as they need to report in person during the registration process. There is no requirement to ensure that the seller is indeed the true owner of the underlying land or property before registering the transaction. The dimensions of the property are also not physically verified, nor is the land use for the property.

Moreover, the Act does not make it mandatory to register all transactions that pertain to land—for instance, rentals below a certain threshold, mortgages below a certain value against the land, and so on, do not need mandatory registration. Also, in case of lands held by a Hindu Undivided Family, partitions do not need registration, and the

---

[33] The Registration Act, 1908, Ministry of Law and Justice, https://india-code.nic.in/acts/7.%20Registration%20Act,%201908.pdf.

land can be subdivided through multiple generations without a single record entering the land registry. Lack of effective enforcement means that many transactions can go unregistered, or are registered at lower values, to avoid paying the high registration charges.

The Act is sought to be modified by the Registration (Amendment) Bill, 2013[34] to address some of these concerns.

The Stamp Act of 1899[35]

The Stamp Act, 1899 (with its last amendment in 2006) is another colonial-era legislation that afflicts Indian land markets even today. Transactions on property and related mortgage deeds are taxed through ad-valorem stamp duties which are a significant source of revenue in state budgets. High stamp duties encourage evasion through under-reporting of transaction values, which can be as high as 50 per cent.[36] Under-reporting in property transactions not only facilitates the creation and storage of black money, but also makes markets inefficient as prices no longer represent the underlying values accurately. Several government committees, starting with the Wanchoo Committee in 1971, have tried to suggest ways to discourage under-reporting that sadly remain on paper, except for the idea to use the government's own estimate of market value for computing stamp duties. Every state now uses 'guidance' values instead of self-reported registered values, but unfortunately, the method adopted and the frequency at which they get updated widely vary from state to state.

---

[34] The Registration (Amendment) Bill, 2013, http://www.prsindia.org/billtrack/the-registration-amendment-bill-2013-2851/.

[35] The Stamp Act of 1899, Ministry of Law and Justice, http://www.legislative.gov.in/sites/default/files/The%20Indian%20Stamp%20Act%2C1899%282%20of%201899%29.pdf.

[36] A. Das-Gupta and S. Gopalakrishnan, *Stamp Duties and Registration Fees in West Bengal* (Report Prepared for the Government of West Bengal, National Institute of Public Finance and Policy, 1986), http://www.nipfp.org.in/media/medialibrary/2014/10/STAMP_DUTIES_AND_REGISTRATION_FEES_IN_WEST_BENGAL__DRAFT_REPORT_.pdf.

The Right to Fair Compensation and Transparency in Land Acquisition, Rehabilitation and Resettlement Act of 2013[37]

This Act, commonly referred to as LARR, regulates land acquisitions by the state under eminent domain, and sets down the mechanism for granting compensation, rehabilitation, and resettlement to the landowners. For the first time, LARR formalizes what has been well known on the ground—that there is extensive under-reporting in property transactions, and that guidance values are often only poor substitutes for actual market values. While the formalization comes in the form of providing compensation that can be as much as *four* times the guidance values in peri-urban areas, the process by which that factor was established was quite arbitrary, and does not distinguish between cities that are land constrained (such as Mumbai) and cities that are not. The opportunity to fix the process of valuing land was yet again missed with one ad-hoc method replaced by another.[38]

The Securitisation and Reconstruction of Financial Assets and Enforcement of Security Interest Act of 2002[39]

The Securitisation and Reconstruction of Financial Assets and Enforcement of Security Interest (SARFAESI) Act, 2002 was originally conceived to permit banks and other financial institutions to seize and auction residential or commercial properties that have been

---

[37] The Right to Fair Compensation and Transparency in Land Acquisition, Rehabilitation and Resettlement Act, 2013, Ministry of Law and Justice, http://legislative.gov.in/actsofparliamentfromtheyear/right-fair-compensation-and-transparency-land-acquisition-rehabilitation.

[38] We have heard anecdotal evidence of politically connected agents forcing guidance-value revision in areas prior to announcements of land acquisitions in them.

[39] The Securitisation and Reconstruction of Financial Assets and Enforcement of Security Interest Act, 2002, Ministry of Law and Justice, GovernmentofIndia,http://legislative.gov.in/hi/actsofparliamentfromtheyear/securitisation-and-reconstruction-financial-assets-and-enforcement.

pledged against loans under default.[40] Until then, delinquent borrowers often used legal forum shopping (choosing a more favourable legal option) to delay resolution and prolong their control over the asset.

But despite much promise, the SARFAESI Act has not helped substantially in mitigating the bad debt problem of banks. The average recovery under the SARFAESI Act has come down from upwards of 50 per cent in 2007–8 to less than 10 per cent in 2016–17.[41] This is because the SARFAESI Act requires adherence to provisions like getting the district magistrate's approval and local police help before taking possession, or providing sufficient time for tenants to vacate before auctioning, which can be unfavourable to banks in practice. In addition, borrowers can stay proceedings under the SARFAESI Act by filing writ petitions in high courts, though the Supreme Court has directed the high courts to be selective in entertaining such petitions.[42]

The Real Estate (Regulation and Development) Act of 2016[43]

The Real Estate (Regulation and Development) Act, 2016 (popularly referred to as the RERA) is the newest legislation that directly impacts development and selling of real estate (both commercial and residential) across the country. The Act presents a model legislation empowering consumers against developers that is supposed to be adapted by each state to suit their needs. It provides for threshold-level compliance that makes it difficult for states to dilute their versions.

---

[40] The Securitisation and Reconstruction of Financial Assets and Enforcement of Security Interest Act, 2002. The SARFAESI Act does not cover agricultural land.

[41] Reserve Bank of India (Mumbai), *Trend and Progress of Banking in India* (2017).

[42] *United Bank of India v. Satyawati Tondon & Ors*, 26 July 2010.

[43] The Real Estate (Regulation and Development) Act, 2016, Ministry of Law and Justice, http://www.legislative.gov.in/actsofparliamentfromtheyear/real-estate-regulation-and-development-act-2016.

The biggest contribution of this Act is the high degree of transparency and accountability that is imposed upon builders. Not only do they need to provide plan and approval documents, they also need to provide a timeline for the completion of construction. Furthermore, they need to disclose details on sales that have been notoriously difficult to obtain in the past. Funds received from customers are protected from being used for purposes other than for development. To ensure compliance, stiff penalties, including revoking of registrations, are imposed for violations.

From a collateralization perspective, reducing risk for buyers effectively reduces risk for lenders as well, thereby setting the stage for large amounts of capital to flow into land development. More accurate information on demand and supply will also enhance price discovery, and reduce the cost of gathering information for lenders.

The Prohibition of Benami Property Transactions Act of 1988[44]

The Prohibition of Benami Property Transactions Act, 1988 (recently amended via the Benami Transactions (Prohibition) Amendment Act, 2016[45]) is another legislation that has been tweaked recently to discourage using property markets to store black money. If properly enforced, this Act can eliminate several distortions related to identification of ownership. In addition, the Standing Committee on Finance (2015) has suggested enabling online registration of immovable property with personal identification (Aadhaar and PAN), and sharing of databases between land registration and taxation departments.[46] Lenders are likely to benefit indirectly rather than directly from the effects of these initiatives.

---

[44] The Prohibition of Benami Property Transactions Act, 1988, Ministry of Law and Justice, http://www.legislative.gov.in/sites/default/files/A1988-45A.pdf.

[45] The Benami Transactions (Prohibition) Amendment Act, 2016, Ministry of Law and Justice, http://www.prsindia.org/uploads/media/Benami/Benami%20Transactions%20Act,%202016.pdf.

[46] See http://164.100.47.193/lsscommittee/Finance/16_Finance_28.pdf.

The Rajasthan Urban Land (Certification of Titles) Act of 2016[47]

The Rajasthan Urban Land (Certification of Titles) Act, 2016 is a pioneering attempt by a state to provide clear land titles. This follows the Model Land Titling Bill of 2011 by the Government of India that provided a template for introducing a Torrens-based 'conclusive' titling system to replace the 'presumptive' titling system that is common in India. However, the Rajasthan legislation does not state that its title is conclusive and cannot be contested in a court of law.[48] One can only presume that it is probably a 'clear presumptive' title that it is ensuring.

***

The above represents a snapshot of key pieces of legislation that either create or eliminate distortions in land markets. Apart from these, academics and policy-makers have also proposed solutions for reforming land markets, some of which have been tested through pilots. We discuss some of these solutions in the next section.

MITIGATING LAND MARKET DISTORTIONS

Though not a legislation, the *Digital India Land Records Modernization Programme* (DILRMP) is a large government initiative aimed at modernizing land records management, with an intent to reduce disputes, enhance transparency, and to eventually set the ground for conclusive titling.[49] More specifically, it was designed to impact *four* major areas:

- Computerization of all land records including mutations, along with standardization of information within each record.
- Digitization of maps and integration of textual and spatial data.
- Survey/resurvey and updating of all survey and settlement records, including creation of original cadastral records wherever necessary.

[47] The Rajasthan Urban Land (Certification of Titles) Act, 2016, http://rajassembly.nic.in/BillsPdf/Bill9-2016.pdf.

[48] Goswami and Jha, 'Your Title Is Not Ready Yet'.

[49] The DILRMP was earlier called the National Land Records Modernisation Programme, or NLRMP, when it was first conceived in 2008.

- Computerization of registration, and its integration with the land records maintenance system.

In addition, the programme was meant to develop core geographic information system (GIS) capabilities along with capacity building to address resource needs at the state level for land record management.

Table 9.1 provides the range of tasks covered by the DILRMP, and their completion record as of September 2017:

TABLE 9.1   Status of Land Data Digitization, 2018

Computerisation of land records	86%
Mutation computerized	47%
Issuance of digitally signed Record of Rights (ROR)	28%
Cadastral maps digitized	46%
Spatial data verified	39%
Cadastral maps linked to ROR	26%
Real time updating of ROR and maps	15%
Number of villages where survey/resurvey work completed	9%
Area surveyed	35%

Source: Department of Land Resources, Ministry of Rural Development; PRS, https://www.prsindia.org/policy/discussion-papers/land-records-and-titles-india.

Recently, the Department of Land Resources undertook an impact assessment of the DILRMP programme in three states—Rajasthan, Maharashtra, and Himachal Pradesh.[50] The findings—that the impact was muted—highlight the difficulty of bringing large-scale reforms in Indian land markets. Several factors, ranging from misalignment of incentives among key stakeholders to poor capacity and institutional governance, impede such reforms from fulfilling their potential. It is, therefore, not surprising that the DILRMP was able to spend only 64 per cent of its allocated funds despite the crying need to modernize Indian land records.[51]

[50] Sanan, Gupta, and Prabhakar, *A Pilot Impact Assessment of the Digital-India Land Records Modernisation Programme.*

[51] Department of Land Resources, Ministry of Rural Development, Digital India LR Modernisation Program, http://dilrmp.nic.in/.

A more successful project on digitization of land records was the *Bhoomi* project in the state of Karnataka. The project involved computerizing 20 million land records, including Record of Rights (ROR) and Record of Tenancy and Crops (RTC) of 6.7 million farmers, and making them available easily through kiosks throughout the state. It curtailed discretionary powers of local officials in recording mutations and transfers, and enabled farmers to get copies of their land records for a nominal fee.

Another impactful development in land markets relates to the creation and sharing of mortgage data among lenders. The *Central Registry of Securitisation Asset Reconstruction and Security Interest* (CERSAI) became operational from 2011 with data on mortgage, and borrower- and lender-level information provided by banks and housing finance companies. The introduction of CERSAI has drastically reduced the ability of borrowers to obtain multiple loans against the same property. Data on CERSAI are accessible online by any lender for a fee.

Other structural reforms that have either been proposed or implemented include:

a. *Tying Central Government aid with reforms*: The JNNURM initiative sought to incentivize states to introduce several land-related reforms, including reducing stamp duty to 5 per cent, initiating rent control reforms, and streamlining property taxes. While the incentive was binding on the states initially, it is less so once aid has been disbursed. Not surprisingly, some states are considering raising these duties after a few years.[52]

b. *Creating Aadhaar-like unique property IDs with or without verified property title cards*: Certain states like Karnataka have experimented with introducing unique property IDs for properties in pilot areas.[53] These IDs include all information related to the property, including geo-spatial information, encumbrance, and property characteristics (usage, size, and ownership). As part of the issuing process, extensive resurveying was done ensuring that land records matched

[52] Maharashtra increased its stamp duty on property purchase in Mumbai in 2015.

[53] Government of Karnataka, Urban Property Ownership Records Project Overview, http://www.upor.karnataka.gov.in/.

with ground realities in area and usage. Unfortunately, for reasons best known only to the government, this initiative has not been expanded to cover larger urban centres.

c. *Streamlining the property registration system to make it easier to register and to access transaction-level data*: Most states have digitized their registration data, and have made them available online. Karnataka introduced 'anywhere' registrations in 2011 whereby property transactions can be registered with any sub-registrar's office within the state. The initiative was designed to discourage rent-seeking behaviour during registrations.

d. *Formalizing tenancy through contractual lease agreements:* The government tabled a model Land Leasing Act that requires all tenant lease agreements to be formal, and provides for tenant farmers to access credit without compromising the ownership claim of the landlord. Formal agreements allow lenders to size up total credit exposure, of both tenant and the owner, against a particular piece of land (the collateral).

While these reforms are steps in the right direction, there are some pragmatic reforms that can be adopted as well.

Central Repository for Land and Property Valuations Undertaken by Banks and Housing Finance Companies

Coordination among lenders to share independent property valuations of properties that are currently in the market could help lower costs and reduce variability in valuations of similar properties across lenders. Lenders can leverage this information to simulate mark-to-market benchmarks for their collateral so they can be better prepared for real estate market downturns. Currently, valuations are done at the time of loan origination and after default has happened, but not in between. The success of CERSAI shows that pooling and sharing of data among lenders could benefit all of them.

Use of Blockchains for Land Records with the Banking System

Blockchain technology has been suggested as a transparent and low-cost way to track property-level details, including ownership and encumbrance details. While the current system of land record management requires centralized capture of and access to information, recording based on blockchains would distribute the responsibilities across multiple stakeholders without compromising integrity or security. New information such as a transaction could only be added by selected agents to the chain, making it instantly visible to the entire market.

While the technology is available, it is not clear that it could overcome all the distortions that permeate our land records today. For example, much of the underlying data needed to define a land record could be missing or incomplete for many land parcels today. Creating blockchains to store poor quality information would only carry the current problems onto a newer platform.

Despite these limitations, blockchains represent an opportunity. Banks and other formal lenders today undertake extensive due diligence to ascertain the validity of the information for lands that they are lending against. For example, they use legal professionals to validate ownership and encumbrance history by piecing together data across multiple departments and across time. Land areas are geo-coded, and violations of zoning and other usage norms are ascertained through ground-truthing. In short, records for lands pledged within the formal financial system would be the most complete, and less contentious to transition out to a blockchain.

By incentivizing formal lenders to encourage blockchain creation for lands within their system, the government can clean up land records for little more than half of the land in the market quickly. Borrowers could be incentivized through interest rate subsidies to adopt this system, leading to an end-user driven adoption as opposed to a top–down approach to implementation. Public enterprises with large landholdings (including the Railways, Defence, and Ports) could also take the initiative to use blockchains with relative ease. Recently, the government of Andhra Pradesh has engaged private players to help secure as many as 100,000 land records in its newly created city Amaravati with blockchains, paving the way for other states to consider using this novel solution as well.[54]

[54] Kurmanath, 'In AP Capital, Blockchain Technology Secures Land Records'.

Rather than top–down approaches like state-guaranteed titling, this approach of 'nudging' participants through incentive alignment may actually work in countries with a federal setup like India. Moreover, it can be done in stages, ensuring that reforms don't get stuck for the entire land market because of ownership or other issues that plague a small percentage of the market.[55]

Promoting Paralegal Titles

Yet another way to clean up land records using an organic bottom–up approach is the concept of 'paralegal titling,' where the community (or local governing body) certifies ownership of a particular land parcel. While this may not have the legal standing of a state-guaranteed title, it could be a good start, especially in rural areas where community governance is strong and effective. This method is quite like what courts use in case of title disputes. By obtaining a voluntary affidavit, the owner can claim documentary proof that can later be converted to a clear title or can be used to collateralize their landholdings. Non-governmental organizations (NGOs) and other grassroots players like microfinance companies can be used to facilitate this process to ensure greater coverage.

★★★

Land markets across India are severely distorted, constraining land from being effectively used as collateral. These distortions impact every aspect of land—its ownership, possession, usage, size, value, and prior encumbrances—that matters to lenders. Poor record keeping coupled with disaggregated storage of such data makes verification of information time consuming and expensive. Given that land issues remain largely a state subject, variability across states is also significant. Lenders rationally respond to these enhanced risks by lowering the extent of credit they offer, and by increasing the cost of borrowing against land.

[55] The recent NCAER-coordinated pilot assessments of land records in three states suggest that differences between ownership information in land records and what can be ascertained from the ground are quite small. Sanan, Gupta, and Prabhakar, *A Pilot Impact Assessment of the Digital-India Land Records Modernisation Programme.*

We have examined these distortions in detail in this chapter using a simple framework, and discussed reforms and solutions that have been either proposed or implemented to overcome them. However, the impact of these solutions has been erratic at best. Most of the suggested reforms have taken the top–down approach, and often ignore issues at the local level where much of the data are gathered and used. We propose some simple suggestions that break away from this approach, and use 'nudging' and incentive alignment for owners and lenders instead to seek changes on their own. We believe that our organic approach would be better suited for a large and diffusely governed country like India.

10 The Effect of Urban Land–Use Regulations on Density

The Case of Selected Indian Cities

Kala Seetharam Sridhar[1]

While India is only 31 per cent urban as of 2011, the country's urban areas contribute nearly two-thirds of the country's gross domestic product (GDP), emphasizing their role as engines of economic growth. Urban land is key to economic productivity and growth, given that a lot

[1] An earlier version of this chapter was written for, and presented at the Tenth International Conference of the Institute of South Asian Studies (ISAS), National University of Singapore. I thank Professor Subrata Mitra for the motivation to write the first version of this chapter, given that I already had new data and analysis. The data for the Bengaluru part of this chapter was gathered when the author was with the Public Affairs Centre (PAC). Thanks are due to the PAC, and Sheeba for her assistance with calling the various ward officials and recording the width of the largest roads in each of the 198 wards in Bengaluru, which enabled me to compute the floor area ratio (FAR) for all the wards, subject to these parameters. I am grateful to the numerous ward-level officials in the Bruhat Bengaluru Mahanagara Palike (BBMP) for their patience with our questions, and their responses. I thank Matthew Holian at San Jose State University for his spreadsheet implementation of the spherical law of cosines, which enabled me to calculate distances from each of the wards to the city centre. I am grateful for comments received at the ISAS Tenth

of land-intensive economic activity takes place in cities.[2] A McKinsey[3] report on India's urbanization estimates that India's requirements for built area are about 700–900 million square metres of residential and commercial space every year to accommodate various urban activities. Land-use regulations are needed in the interests of inclusive growth to protect the urban poor, and should also be guided by social and environmental considerations in the Indian context. But they create distortions in the land market, and usually become counterproductive.

Indian cities are characterized by strong urban land-use controls, a legacy of the country's socialistic and planned economy. One instance of the strongly controlled planned economy was the Urban Land Ceiling and Regulation Act (ULCRA) of 1976, which was intended to prevent land hoarding, and to facilitate equitable distribution of land for executing social and welfare schemes. Under this law, no individual or enterprise could hold beyond a certain amount of land (this 'ceiling' varied across metropolitan areas); if they did, they had to 'declare' the amount of land held by them, and sell the extra land to the government at a price considered to be low by market standards.[4]

However, this law restricted greatly the supply of land, and became a charter for corruption. The 'taking' of all surplus urban land by the

---

International Conference, and to Sanjoy Chakravorty at Temple University for motivating me to submit to this volume. Ms. Shanthi M helped to format the chapter as per the requirements, I am thankful to her. Any errors remain mine.

[2] Bertaud gives the example of furniture-making, which is a land-intensive activity, which therefore, has no reason to locate in a large city, where land would be expensive. These types of firms would tend to locate their manufacturing activities in smaller cities, where land is relatively cheaper. Alain Bertaud, 'Cities as Labor Markets', Working Paper #2 (New York: Marron Institute of Urban Management, New York University, 2014). http://marroninstitute.nyu.edu/uploads/content/Cities_as_Labor_Markets.pdf.

[3] McKinsey Global Initiative, India's Urban Awakening: Building Inclusive Cities, Sustaining Economic Growth (Washington, DC: McKinsey & Co, April 2010).

[4] The maximum compensation under the law was INR 10 per square metre (approximately USD 0.35), and the total compensation could not exceed INR 2 lakhs (approximately USD 7010, being based on the exchange rate of 1 USD=INR 28.53, approximately in 1977) per owner.

government under this law, and the absence of a system to incentivize the entry of the vacant urban land into the land market through
appropriate fiscal or other measures, resulted in limiting the supply
of urban land. Further, there was no empirical evidence regarding
the land thus usurped by the government, and the number or scope
of 'public purposes' to which they were apparently put. As Bertaud[5]
highlighted, the most significant impact of the ULCRA was to lock
up large areas of valuable urban land in legal disputes, which were thus
not available for development or redevelopment. Further, the ULCRA
prevented private developers from assembling land for the next stage
of development. Hence the ULCRA effectively decreased the supply
of urban land, and bid up its prices in large cities of India, most notably
Mumbai.

The government realized the pitfalls of the ULCRA and made its
repeal mandatory in all states in 1999, as a result of which by 2007,
most states (except Andhra Pradesh, Assam, Bihar, and West Bengal)
repealed it, since the repeal of the Act was also linked to funding states
could receive under the Government of India's prior urban renewal
programme, the Jawaharlal Nehru National Urban Renewal Mission
(JNNURM).

While the now-repealed ULCRA (save in a few states) is an example
of one aspect of the strong land-use regulations present in urban India
until recently, draconian land-use regulations that continue to exist
in India's cities are rent control and highly restrictive floor area ratios
(FARs), when compared with those in cities internationally.[6] However,
data on these FARs are not routinely gathered at the city level, making it difficult to assess their magnitude, let alone their impact. In this
context, this chapter makes use of extremely rare and valuable data on
FARs at the intra-city (census ward) level for a prominent Indian city

---

[5] Alan Bertaud, 'The Economic Impact of Land and Urban Planning
Regulations in India', 11 April 2002, http://alain-bertaud.com.

[6] Throughout this chapter, the terms FAR (floor area ratio) and FSI (floor
space index) are used interchangeably; in states such as Maharashtra, FSI is used.
Floor area ratio refers to the extent of built area permissible when compared to
the plot area. For instance, if the extent of permissible built area is 500 square
feet on a plot of 100 square feet, the FAR is 5; if the permitted built area is 350
square feet on a plot area of 100 square feet, the FAR is 3.5; and so forth.

to enable an understanding of its impact on density in the context of the standard urban model.

In this chapter, I focus on land-use regulations as they relate to FARs in Indian cities primarily, for several reasons:

1. Floor area ratios are highly restrictive and floor area consumption really low in Indian cities, compared with international standards.
2. Restrictive FARs impact the suburbanization of India's cities. Sridhar[7] found that population suburbanized in response to a relaxation of FAR norms in the suburbs, but that restrictive FARs had no impact on suburbanization of jobs in India's cities.
3. Further, FARs impact the spatial area of Indian cities, and make them unnecessarily large.[8]

I focus on rent control in Indian cities only to a limited extent, in this chapter, given the lack of adequate data to examine its impacts.

OVERVIEW

This chapter is organized as follows. The next section summarizes the objectives, and the rationale for choice of the selected cities, followed by a section that describes the land-use regulations in Indian cities—FAR and rent control—which have been studied here. After this, I present the literature on the subject briefly followed by a description of the relevant theoretical framework (for each of the two regulations considered), model, and data sources. Then the findings from each of the two cities—first Bengaluru and then Mumbai—are presented after which a section discusses the findings from both cities, and relates them to the policy implications of the research. Finally, the chapter summarizes the caveats of the research and concludes.

---

[7] Kala Seetharam Sridhar, 'Impact of Land Use Regulations: Evidence from India's Cities', *Urban Studies* 47, no. 7 (2010): 1541–69.

[8] Jan K. Brueckner and Kala Seetharam Sridhar, 'Measuring Welfare Gains from Relaxation of Land-use Restrictions: The Case of India's Building-height Limits', *Regional Science and Urban Economics* 42, no. 6 (2012): 1061–7, doi: 10.1016/j.regsciurbeco.2012.08.003.

OBJECTIVES

Given the importance of FARs, in this chapter, I answer the question: What is the impact of FARs on population and household density, in the context of the standard urban framework? The standard urban framework refers to the monocentric urban model defined by the population density function for various locations within a given city, dependent on its distance from the city centre, given the tradeoffs between land and commuting costs. The incorporation of land-use regulations in this standard urban framework is necessary, since high FARs are a measure of capital-land ratio, are meant to lead to higher densities, and encourage higher floor area consumption. I examine the impact FARs have on population and household density, in the context of the standard urban framework, taking the case of Bengaluru, where ward-level data have been recently put together on FARs, and Mumbai, two large cities in the country.

It is relevant to study these cities, given their growth and characteristics. Bengaluru grew at an average of 55 per cent during 1981–2011, with the 2001–11 increase being 97 per cent, and is characterized by a density of 11,470 persons per square kilometre, as per the Census of India 2011, while Mumbai has been the subject of extensive academic research and policy debates, given its peculiar topography and land-use policies. Further, Mumbai is denser at a 2011 density of 15,517 persons per square kilometre,[9] and real estate in Mumbai is prohibitively expensive, comparable with that in London, Paris, or New York. In Mumbai, the FSI had been declining over time, until recently. In the case of Mumbai, I am unable to estimate the impact of FSI on density, given the small number of (24) wards.[10] For this reason, the case of Mumbai has been discussed anecdotally, using qualitative evidence.

Hence for Bengaluru the chapter uses quantitative data, while for Mumbai this chapter relies on anecdotal evidence. In this way, the chapter makes a strong contribution to the academic debate on urban land-use regulations in India, relevant for planners and policy experts

---

[9] Census of India Primary Census Abstract, 2011 (New Delhi: Registrar General of India).

[10] Bengaluru was divided into 198 wards, the level at which the FAR and density data were available, at the time of finishing this chapter, ahead of proposals for the civic body's restructuring.

to consider. I find in Bengaluru that FARs impact both population and household density negatively, consistent with what other studies have found. In the context of Mumbai, I use anecdotal evidence to examine FSI, where the effects are compounded by the existence of other distortions such as rent control and topography.

FLOOR AREA RATIO AND RENT CONTROL IN INDIA'S CITIES

The FAR in Indian cities is dependent on several factors—including land use (residential, commercial, or industrial), plot area, road width, and setbacks, among others. In India's cities, the FAR determines the total built-up space on a plot, subject to the following, as per the Town and Country Planning Organisation (TCPO):

a. Land availability and estimated requirements;
b. Housing densities and dwelling sizes; and
c. Availability of parking.

Most planners across Indian cities cite the lack of existing infrastructure in them for absorbing higher densities, typically implied by a higher FAR, which appears to be the basis of the TCPO's guidelines stated above. However, it should be noted that with an increase in the maximum permissible FAR/FSI, the population or household density tends to actually decrease, as Sridhar[11] points out. While this might seem counterintuitive, this occurs since an increase in FAR/FSI usually leads to an increase in floor space per person or per household, with more floor space built on the same unit of land. So people and households consume more of it and population and household density actually decline. As Sridhar points out, what happens to density following an increase in FAR/FSI, depends on the FAR-elasticity of demand for built area.[12] If, in response to an increase in the FAR/FSI, there is a more than proportionate increase in built area, then density increases. There is no need to say that the infrastructure will have to be spruced up in areas where a large FAR increase is expected. If the

---

[11] Sridhar, 'Impact of Land Use Regulations'.
[12] Sridhar, 'Impact of Land Use Regulations'.

actual increase in floor area built is less than that permitted in the FAR regulation, density decreases, as Sridhar points out.[13]

Any land-use regulation that specifies a maximum limit on built area can be held to be restrictive from a free market perspective. However, this requires a specific definition of what is and what is not reasonable, hence criteria for discerning such a difference. Many market-focused scholars could consider any restrictions on FAR/FSI as an impediment to the operation of a 'free' market. However, being more objective, judging by World Bank standards,[14] when we examine central-city FAR values for several cities around the world, the mean and median cluster around 9. So it may be argued that any city which has a maximum permissible FAR of substantially less than 9, should be considered as having a restrictive regulation, despite the political discussion centred around the issue. Having said this, urban land-use regulations are not only restrictive in the context of developing countries such as India, but also in developed countries such as the United States (US) where land-use controls are characterized by zoning, and minimum lot-size restrictions.[15]

The floor area consumption in various cities across the world, including Mumbai in India, is summarized in Table 10.1. Indian cities including Mumbai are characterized by their extremely low floor area consumption, partly due to the low FSI permitted, not only in comparison to 'northern' cities, but also in comparison to cities in China including Shanghai.

---

[13] Sridhar, 'Impact of Land Use Regulations'. It is to be noted, nonetheless, that in older parts of Mumbai, roads and plot sizes are so small that any increase in FAR may not lead to increased density as the capacity for expansion is physically constrained, given Mumbai's topography. However, such reasoning applies to other Indian cities, except those characterized by topography similar to that of Mumbai.

[14] World Bank, *India: Urbanization beyond Municipalities* (Washington, DC: World Bank, 2012).

[15] However, we note here the underlying assumption that land-use regulations are solely negative in their impact, and that unregulated markets would be an ideal solution to 'efficient' land use. This assumption may be questionable when we take into account cultural, social, and environmental considerations, as in the initial discussion.

TABLE 10.1   Floor Area Consumption, Selected Cities across the World

City	Floor Area per Person (in sq. m)
Copenhagen	43.9
Stockholm	41.0
Berlin	37.9
Helsinki	34.2
Warsaw	24.5
Shanghai	34.0
Mumbai	5.0*

Source: Brueckner and Sridhar, 'Measuring Welfare Gains from Relaxation of Land-use Restrictions' (2012); Bertaud, 'Mumbai FAR/FSI Conundrum' (2011); and Patel, 'Life between Buildings' (2013): 68–74.

Note: *Given that both Mumbai and Bengaluru are studied in this chapter, it would have been instructive to have Bengaluru's floor area consumption. However, this is extremely rare data, not easily available for cities, let alone for those in India. Further, a major caveat is that the data in this table do not compare income levels, and demand for and supply of land in each case, which would be different. The available data on floor area consumption, relevant for the purposes of this chapter, have been summarized, where available, for cities through the world from various sources.

The Indian constitution makes housing a 'state subject'. Further, Indian cities also have little capacity or autonomy to set their own rent control legislation, with the result that these laws are typically formulated by the state governments (see Dey and Dev[16] for a summary of rent control legislation in all Indian states). The relevant laws for Bengaluru and Mumbai are formulated by the states of Karnataka and Maharashtra, respectively.

The state of Karnataka (of which Bengaluru is the capital) does have a rent control act, amended most recently in 2001. While in theory, all properties come under the purview of this Act, any building whose rent exceeds INR 3,500 (roughly USD 51.35, based on the exchange rate

---

[16] Paramita Datta Dey and Satvik Dev, 'Rent Control Laws in India: A Critical Analysis', Working Paper WP06-04 (New Delhi: National Institute of Urban Affairs, December 2006), www.niua.org.

between INR and USD on the Reserve Bank of India website on 27 January 2017) per month is exempt. Further, any building, for a period of 15 years from the date of completion of construction or 'substantial renovation' is exempt from the Act. This clause of the Karnataka Rent Control Act essentially renders the Act ineffective in Bengaluru, given the rental prices in the city, and hence does not warrant further discussion. However, the Maharashtra (of which Mumbai is the capital) Rent Control Act, 1999, does not exempt any property, except those which are built and owned by the central or state housing authority. Hence rent control is for all practical purposes, more important in Mumbai than in Bengaluru.

EXISTING LITERATURE

While the monocentric model of urban spatial structure was originally developed by Alonso,[17] Mills,[18] and Muth,[19] there is a stream of literature which investigates the impact of urban land-use regulations on urban form in the US. These include Brueckner and Fansler,[20] McGrath,[21] Spivey,[22] Deng et al.,[23] and Paulsen,[24] who assume that

---

[17] William Alonso, *Location and Land Use: Toward a General Theory of Land Rent* (Cambridge, MA: Harvard University Press, 1964).

[18] Edwin S. Mills, 'An Aggregative Model of Resource Allocation in a Metropolitan Area', *The American Economic Review* 57, no. 2 (1967): 197–210.

[19] Richard F. Muth, *Cities and Housing: The Spatial Pattern of Urban Residential Use* (Chicago: University of Chicago Press, 1969).

[20] Jan K. Brueckner and David A. Fansler, 'The Economics of Urban Sprawl: Theory and Evidence on the Spatial Sizes of Cities', *The Review of Economics and Statistics* 65, no. 3 (1983): 479–82.

[21] Daniel T. McGrath, 'More Evidence on the Spatial Scale of Cities', *Journal of Urban Economics* 58, no. 1 (2005): 1–10.

[22] Christy Spivey, 'The Mills–Muth Model of Urban Spatial Structure: Surviving the Test of Time?', *Urban Studies* 45, no. 2 (2008): 295–312.

[23] Xiangzheng Deng, Jikun Huang, Scott Rozelle, and Emi Uchida, 'Growth, Population and Industrialization, and Urban Land Expansion of China', *Journal of Urban Economics* 63, no. 1 (2008): 96–115.

[24] Kurt Paulsen, 'Yet Even More Evidence on the Spatial Size of Cities: Urban Spatial Expansion in the US, 1980–2000', *Regional Science and Urban Economics* 42, no. 4 (2012): 561–8.

spatial areas of cities are dependent on variables identified in the relevant theory: income, commuting cost, and population. Further, Wassmer[25] and Geshkov and DeSalvo[26] estimated the effects of land-use regulations on urban footprints. Along with the FAR, Geshkov and DeSalvo included other land-use regulations such as urban growth boundaries and minimum lot-size restrictions in their regression of the spatial area of cities, while Wassmer used more general indicators to point to the presence of urban growth policies.

Sridhar[27] investigated the impact of FAR limits on population- and employment-density gradients (rather than spatial areas) of India's cities, while Brueckner and Sridhar[28] examined the impact of restrictive land-use regulations on the spatial area of Indian cities. Bertaud, Buckley, and Owens[29] examined the incidence and scale of FAR effects by contrasting the situation in Mumbai and Bengaluru. There is also a stream of literature which understands the effect of urban land-use regulations on housing prices. This literature includes Pollakowski and Wachter,[30] who focused on zoning restrictions and development ceilings, measured by the number of approved housing units, and found a price elasticity of 28 per cent with respect to zoning restrictions in Montgomery county, Maryland. Quigley and Raphael[31] measured the impact of controls on housing prices

---

[25] Robert W. Wassmer, 'The Influence of Local Urban Containment Policies and State Wide Growth Management on the Size of United States Urban Areas', *Journal of Regional Science* 46, no. 1 (2006): 25–65.

[26] Marin V. Geshkov and Joseph S. DeSalvo, 'The Effect of Land-use Controls on the Spatial Size of US Urbanized Areas', *Journal of Regional Science* 52, no. 4 (2012): 648–75.

[27] Sridhar, 'Impact of Land Use Regulations'.

[28] Brueckner and Sridhar, 'Measuring Welfare Gains from Relaxation of Land-use Restrictions'.

[29] Alain Bertaud, Robert Buckley, and Kathryn Owens, 'Is Indian Urban Policy Impoverishing?', Paper presented at the World Bank: Urban Research Symposium (December 2003).

[30] Henry O. Pollakowski and Susan M. Wachter, 'The Effects of Land-use Constraints on Housing Prices', *Land Economics* 66, no. 3 (1990): 315–24.

[31] John M. Quigley and Steven Raphael, 'Regulation and the High Cost of Housing in California', *The American Economic Review* 95, no. 2 (2005): 323–8.

in California, and reported a 3-4.5 per cent increase in the price of owner-occupied housing, and 1-2.5 per cent increase in the price of rental housing, in response to each additional regulatory measure. Ihlanfeldt[32] used the number of land-use management restrictions adopted by the jurisdiction (referring to permit, compliance, and review costs), and found that a unit increase in the restrictiveness increased the price of housing by 5 per cent, taking the case of Florida cities. Glaeser and Ward[33] examined lot-size restrictions and other land-use controls in Boston' such as those pertaining to wetlands, septic systems, and subdivision requirements (which are all restrictive in some way or other), and found that each additional restriction reduced new construction by 10 per cent.

Thus most of the studies in the context of the US generally concur that restrictive land-use regulations increase housing prices. Even in the context of developing countries such as India, Brueckner and Sridhar[34] found that relaxing the FAR by one unit led to the spatial reduction of a city's area to the extent of 20 per cent, which led them to compute welfare gains to the extent of INR 106 million per city.

Since FARs measure capital-land ratio, they are an important part of the standard monocentric model. McMillen[35] rightly pointed out the prediction of the model that low commuting costs for locations close to the city centre lead to high land values, which result in high FARs. He reported the findings from a regression where the natural log of the FAR was dependent on distance from the central business district (CBD), taking the case of Chicago. He found that FARs declined by 5.5 per cent, with every extra mile from the Chicago CBD, as the monocentric model predicts. He experimented with many functional

[32] Keith R. Ihlanfeldt, 'The Effect of Land Use Regulation on Housing and Land Prices', *Journal of Urban Economics* 61, no. 3 (2007): 420–35.

[33] Edward L. Glaeser and Bryce A. Ward, 'The Causes and Consequences of Land Use Regulation: Evidence from Greater Boston', *Journal of Urban Economics* 65, no. 3 (2009): 265–78.

[34] Brueckner and Sridhar, 'Measuring Welfare Gains from Relaxation of Land-use Restrictions'.

[35] Daniel P. McMillen, 'Testing for Monocentricity', in *A Companion to Urban Economics*, eds Richard J. Arnott and Daniel P. McMillen (Oxford: Blackwell, 2006), 128–40.

forms, including the cubic spline,[36] finding all to be consistent with the predictions of the monocentric city model.

A paper by White and Allmendinger[37] comparing the US and United Kingdom (UK) housing markets, found differences between planning approaches in the two countries; however, in both, it was found that planning constraints increased prices, reduced the supply of housing, and, in the UK, reduced choice for consumers.

While a majority of the literature from the West focuses on the effects of land-use controls on housing prices (Glaeser and Ward;[38] Quigley and Rosenthal[39]), Bertaud and Brueckner[40] focus on Bengaluru, and estimate the welfare loss per household between INR 700-2100, representing anywhere in the range of 1.5-4.5 per cent of income, due to the FAR restriction.[41]

As Brueckner and Lall[42] also point out, by enabling people's location closer to the centre, rising density actually saves commuting costs.

---

[36] For improving the fit of urban spatial relationships such as the land value and distance from the city centre, functional forms such as the cubic spline are employed. In this approach, as McMillen points out, the distance variable is split into equal intervals and a separate cubic function is applied to each region, giving rise to the name.

[37] Michael White and Philip Allmendinger, 'Land-use Planning and the Housing Market: A Comparative Review of the UK and the USA', *Urban Studies* 40, nos 5–6 (2003): 953–72.

[38] Glaeser and Ward, 'The Causes and Consequences of Land Use Regulation'.

[39] John M. Quigley and Larry A. Rosenthal, 'The Effects of Land Use Regulation on the Price of Housing': What Do We Know? What Can We Learn?', *Cityscape: A Journal of Policy Development and Research* 8, no. 1 (2005): 69–137.

[40] Alain Bertaud and Jan K. Brueckner, 'Analyzing Building-height Restrictions: Predicted Impacts and Welfare Costs', *Regional Science and Urban Economics* 35, no. 2 (2005): 109–25.

[41] Bertaud and Brueckner take the view that floor area restrictions lead to an increase in the spatial area of the city, by limiting densities near the centre, hence result in higher commuting costs. Hence the welfare loss is computed as the increase in commuting cost resulting from the restriction.

[42] Jan K. Brueckner and Somik Lall, 'Cities in Developing Countries: Fueled by Rural–Urban Migration, Lacking in Tenure Security, and Short of Affordable Housing', in *Handbook of Regional and Urban Economics*, eds Gilles

The role of the FAR should ideally be to increase density and encourage densification. However, in determining the FAR, the objective of planners in Indian cities has been to inadvertently decrease population and household densities.[43] It should be mentioned that the debate on the FAR/FSI is quite polarized in Indian cities. Indian urban planners strongly believe that increased density results in reduced environmental quality, increased congestion, and problems with water supply, electricity, and parking. In addition, the practical view of typical Indian planners is that higher densities place tremendous demands on urban infrastructure, which the cities are unable to provide as per existing guidelines, given that they are characterized by inadequate revenues and technical capacities.

Unfortunately, there are not many scholarly papers on this issue in the Indian context, except the paper by Bertaud and Brueckner,[44] which develops and simulates an analytical model for Bengaluru, without actual data. Brueckner and Sridhar[45] use actual data to estimate these welfare gains resulting from relaxing building-height restrictions in Indian cities. Patel[46] criticizes Brueckner and Sridhar,[47] and refutes the recommendation that increasing FSI across the board in Indian cities would result in an overall welfare gain, which the latter counter[48]

Duranton, J. Vernon Henderson, and William C. Strange (Amsterdam: Elsevier, 2015), 1399–455.

[43] However, we note a high FAR alone does not necessarily reduce unit costs of land or housing, as Manhattan testifies. There are possibly other factors at work which have led to escalation of housing prices in Manhattan—the local economy tends to become more buoyant, creating more opportunities, and amenities improve over time, capitalizing in increasing housing prices. But for the high FAR permitted, I would argue that Manhattan prices would have been even higher.

[44] Bertaud and Brueckner, 'Analyzing Building-height Restrictions'.

[45] Brueckner and Sridhar, 'Measuring Welfare Gains from Relaxation of Land-use Restrictions'.

[46] Patel, 'Life between Buildings'.

[47] Brueckner, and Sridhar, 'Measuring Welfare Gains from Relaxation of Land-use Restrictions'.

[48] Jan Brueckner and Kala S. Sridhar, 'Response to Patel: In Defence of Relaxed FSI Limits', *Economic & Political Weekly*, XLVIII, no. 39 (2013): 82.

saying that Indian cities should be open to change, given the long traf-
fic gridlocks, to reduce commute times, make housing more affordable,
and improve the financial viability and convenience of public transport.
Nonetheless, Patel[49] proposes a more useful metric for Indian cities
enabling comparisons, called crowding, defined as the residents or jobs
per acre/hectare of home or jobs built-up area, respectively. However,
this is not practical data to get in the context of Indian cities, where
even basic data such as area are subject to varying estimates, as the work
with the data for this chapter demonstrated.

THEORY, MODEL, AND DATA SOURCES

In the urban monocentric model, employment is assumed to be
located in the CBD, hence the locational choice of households which
are assumed to be identical, is modelled entirely on the basis of access
to employment. Other locational considerations are ignored. In the
monocentric model, centrally located housing is expensive; hence
households save on land and live in smaller houses, if they live near
the centre. Households that incur higher commuting costs experience
decreased housing prices far from the CBD, and hence consume larger
houses. As Brueckner[50] found, given certain preferences and technology, population density has an exponential form, as in the following
equation, which we use here as the theoretical basis for the estimations:

$$D(r) = D_o e^{-br} \qquad [1]$$

In equation [1], r is the distance of a given location (in miles or kilometres) from the CBD, D_o refers to population density at the edge of
the metropolitan area, and b is the density gradient, which represents
the change in population (or employment) density per unit of change
in distance from the CBD. It should be clear that the density gradient
b and D_0 are constants to be estimated from the data, if available at a
highly disaggregated level (usually census-tract or ward within cities).

[49] Patel, 'Life between Buildings'.

[50] Jan K. Brueckner, 'A Note on Sufficient Conditions for Negative
Exponential Population Densities', *Journal of Regional Science* 22, no. 3 (1982):
353–9.

Equation [1] is typically estimated in log linear form, as in equation [2]:[51]

$$Ln\ D(r) = Ln\ D_o - br \qquad\qquad [2]$$

Given the polarized debate about FAR/FSI in Indian cities and their impacts on density, I econometrically study the impact of FARs on both population and household density, in the context of equation [2], along with distance. I examine the effect of land-use regulations (FAR) on household density, since the urban model relates more to the locational choice of the household.

For obtaining data on FARs at the ward level in Bengaluru, first, the zoning regulations of the city were used to arrive at the maximum permissible FAR value, dependent on plot size, land use, and road width. For getting information on road width, each of the 198 wards of the city was contacted for the broadest road in the ward and its width, such that the FAR value could be attributed accordingly. Then the transfer of development rights (TDR) permitted was added to the FAR value, to arrive at the maximum permissible value of the FAR for every ward.

The imposition of a legal maximum (ceiling) on rent is called rent control. If the ceiling determined by rent control is above the market rent (recognizing that different rental housing markets possibly have different market clearing rents), then the ceiling has no effect. If the rent control ceiling were to be set at a level below the market rent, then it leads to conditions of excess demand or shortage, which has characterized most Indian cities. If the legal maximum rent is set below the equilibrium rent, then the landlords would not have the incentives to renovate/rehabilitate their property, with the result that such properties would move out of the rental market, artificially restricting the supply of rental housing.

The econometric estimations are the focus of the next section, taking the case of Bengaluru, using ward-level data from the Census of India 2011.

[51] In a double log equation, as is the case with equation [2], the estimated coefficients are interpreted as elasticities.

THE CASE OF BENGALURU: THE IMPACT
OF LAND–USE REGULATIONS ON DENSITY

For Bengaluru, as described, there was a unique dataset put together at the ward level, for 198 wards, containing information on population density from the 2011 Census, their distances from the city centre, and FARs. The maximum value of the permissible FAR in the city's wards has been included to reflect the additional FAR permissible for TDRs. Transfers of development rights reflect the reality when the government gives additional built-up area in lieu of the area surrendered by the landowner. In this situation, the landowner can either use the additional built-up area obtained himself or *transfer* it to a different landowner, who may need the additional built-up area, for an agreed sum of money. In Bengaluru, the TDR is 1.6 times the FAR.

Table 10.2 summarizes the descriptive statistics for the variables used in the regressions. Tables 10.3 and 10.4 report the results of regressions of FARs and distance on population and household density, respectively, assuming various city centres.

I computed three measures of a city centre for Bengaluru—one is the conventional centre where the state's secretariat (called the Vidhana Soudha) sits; the second centre that is considered is the city's railway station (located in Majestic, traditionally known to be the city centre); yet another centre that is taken into account is the ward that has the maximum population density. I calculated distance from each of the wards to the chosen centres 'as the crow flies'. Table 10.4 presents the

TABLE 10.2   Summary Statistics for Variables

	Average	Maximum	Minimum	Std. Deviation
Pop Density	26,549	1,24,478	2,096	20,823
HH density	6,376	24,836	499	4,621
FAR+TDR	3.99	5.20	2.80	0.89
Dist-Vidhana Soudha (ward 110)	5	18	0	4
Dist-Majestic (ward 95)	5	21	0	4
Dist-max density (ward 135)	5	23	0	5

Source: BBMP and author's computations.

TABLE 10.3 Impact of Distance and Floor Area Ratios on Population Density in Bengaluru

	Parameter Estimates[a, b]					
	Distance from City Centre (majestic (ward 95))	Distance from City Centre (ward with maximum density (ward 135))	Distance from City Centre (ward containing Vidhana Soudha (ward 110))	FAR	R^2	Model F Value
Model 1	-0.10 (-7.61)★★★	NA	NA	-0.17 (-2.73)★★	0.24	31.41
Model 2	NA	-0.09 (7.60)★★★	NA	-0.16 (-2.53)★★	0.24	31.31
Model 3	NA	NA	-0.09 (-5.16)★★★	-0.16 (-2.44)★★	0.14	15.42

Source: BBMP and author's computations and analyses; Number of observations=198.

Notes: a. The dependent variable is the (natural) log of population density for all regressions, as in equation [2].

b. Intercepts not reported for any regression.

TABLE 10.4 Impact of Distance and Floor Area Ratios on Household Density in Bengaluru

	Parameter Estimates[a, b]					
	Distance from City Centre (majestic (ward 95))	Distance from City Centre (ward with maximum density (ward 135))	Distance from City Centre (ward containing Vidhana Soudha (ward 110))	FAR	R^2	Model F Value
Model 1	-0.10 (-7.27)★★★	NA	NA	-0.15 (-2.56)★★	0.23	28.51
Model 2	NA	-0.09 (7.52)★★★	NA	-0.14 (-2.40)★★	0.24	30.37
Model 3	NA	NA	-0.08 (-4.61)★★★	-0.15 (-2.26)★★	0.11	12.45

Source: BBMP and author's computations and analyses; Number of observations=198.

Notes: a. The dependent variable is the (natural) log of household density for all regressions, as in equation [2].

b. Intercepts not reported for any regression.

effect of distance and land-use regulations (as measured by the FAR) on household density, given that the standard urban model is more about household location decisions. Here also, I examine the impact of distance assuming various centres as with population density, along with the FAR.

The several regressions of the population or household density as dependent on distance from the city centre (all measures) (Tables 10.3 and 10.4) show negative effects on population and household density, of the distance from the city centre as we expect, consistent with the standard urban model, strongly suggesting that density declines as one moves farther from the city centre, irrespective of which location is considered as the centre.

The regressions in Tables 10.3 and 10.4 show a negative and statistically significant impact of the FAR on both population and household density, with all measures of the city centre in each of the specifications. There are several possible reasons why we find this negative impact (while we expected a positive coefficient) of the FAR on density:

First, FARs in Indian cities are low everywhere, and are not at a threshold where we can expect them to unleash their positive impacts on (population or household) density. For instance, the FAR varies only from a low of 2.8 to a maximum of 5.2 within Bengaluru, with a standard deviation of 0.89 (Table 10.2), which shows not much variability. Had there been a greater variability in the FARs across the wards, then we may have seen the expected high density impacts of a higher FAR.

Second, the negative impact could be due to the fact that FARs are determined to be lower where population or household density is higher, to 'reduce congestion', so there could be a two-way relationship.

Third, in the light of the earlier discussion, if the actual FAR (built space)–elasticity of demand for built area is less than 1, the actual increase in floor area consumption would be less than that specified by the FAR regulation, then population or household density declines.

Finally, it is possible that if actual building heights rather than the permissible FARs were used, the impact of FARs on population or household density may have been positive, as expected.[52]

---

[52] It is possible to get the actual building heights, based on a 'street view'. However, at the time the research for this chapter was completed, the Government of India was contemplating introducing a Geospatial Information

Nonetheless, these findings are consistent with those in Sridhar,[53] who found that the FAR had a negative effect on the population density gradient, indicating that Indian cities suburbanized in response to a relaxation of building heights, which usually happens in the suburbs, since the central cities are already 'congested'. Further, these findings support the studies in the international context that the literature review has described.

In order to understand the impact distance from the city centre has on land-use policies in the context of Indian cities such as Bengaluru, taking advantage of the data I had both on FARs and distance from the city centre at the ward level, I estimated a McMillen-type regression of FAR on distance from the city centre, assuming again the three different city centres—Majestic, Vidhana Soudha, and the area with the maximum population density.[54] However, in each of these cases, the coefficient on the distance variable was negative, being statistically and economically insignificant. This is good news for one reason, since it shows that there is no collinearity between the distance from the city centre and the FAR. The insignificant effect of the distance from the city centre on the FAR in the Indian context also implies that actual market forces, commuting, and land costs have little impact on the way in which land-use regulations are actually formulated. This makes sense, given that we know that India was strongly planned for a long time, and its socialist policies with constraints largely conditioned its other policies including those pertaining to land use.

IMPACTS OF RENT CONTROL IN BENGALURU

There is not much research on the effects of rent control in Bengaluru. A World Bank study by Malpezzi and Tewari[55] estimated that in the

---

Regulation Bill, which implied that any addition or creation of anything that has to do with any geospatial information—or location—within the territory of India will need the permission of the government.

[53] Sridhar, 'Impact of Land Use Regulations'.

[54] McMillen, 'Testing for Monocentricity'.

[55] Stephen Malpezzi and Vinod K. Tewari, *Costs and Benefits of Residential Rent Control in Bangalore, India* (Washington, DC: World Bank, Policy, Planning and Research Staff, Infrastructure and Urban Development Department,

absence of controls and other regulations, while the typical[56] household would consume 133 units (in 1974 rupees) of housing, households were actually consuming only 65 units of housing. The study found that while the tenants benefitted from the lower rent, they also lost since they were consuming less housing than they would otherwise, in the absence of such restrictions. As per their estimates, the loss to households was greater than the benefit derived from lower rent; hence they concluded that the tenant in the rent-controlled housing unit was worse off than if s/he were in equilibrium at market prices. This study is of course dated, but there are no recent studies of the impact of rent control in Bengaluru. In the context of this chapter, there was no secondary data available on rental prices, by ward, to examine the impacts of FAR. Moreover, the state's rent control act exempts all properties with a monthly rent of greater than INR 3,500; hence effectively, rent control has no impact on the city's density, as discussed earlier.

THE CASE OF MUMBAI: FLOOR SPACE INDEX AND RENT CONTROL

Mumbai is the one Indian 'maximum city' which is dotted by skyscrapers. However, there is a strange story to the unduly low FSI permitted in Mumbai, where contrary to international evidence, the FSI declined continuously since 1964 when it was fixed at 4.5 at Nariman Point, the central point of the city. Mumbai's draft development plan for 2034 (Chapter 17 on FSI) gives reasons as to why this was the case.[57] The high land values, inflated property prices, and high cost of construction, justified the higher FSI in the 1960s. An FSI of 2.45 was retained for developed areas like Colaba and Marine Drive, which, according to Mumbai's draft development plan, was an outcome of the earlier

---

Report INU 82, 1991), http://documents.worldbank.org/curated/en/817011468772802607/pdf/multi-page.pdf.

[56] They used the term 'ordinary controlled' household, defined as those 'controlled housing units' whose rents were frozen, and whose rents were not 'fair rents' set by rent control.

[57] Municipal Corporation of Greater Mumbai, *Draft Development Plan for 2034* (Mumbai: Municipal Corporation of Greater Mumbai, 2014).

set of Development Control Rules. Surprisingly, however, for more densely built-up areas such as Mandvi, and Kalbadevi, an FSI of 1.66 was specified, against the actual consumed FSI of over 3. By specifying lower than the existing FSI, planners expected redevelopment of these areas at lower densities. For areas around Sion, Dadar, and Worli, an FSI of 1.33 was set with a view to allowing one additional floor where buildings were constructed as per earlier rules (which implied an FSI of only 1).

In this 'maximum city,' it is interesting to note that many buildings were built prior to the imposition of the recent FSI regulation, therefore had an FSI higher than 1.33. The intriguing outcome is that no renovation of old buildings would be possible without entailing a loss of floor space. Hence any renovation or redevelopment, given the high price of floor space in Mumbai, is uneconomical. Bertaud[58] notes that at the time dilapidated buildings in the city had to be rebuilt, the urban local body (the Brihanmumbai Municipal Corporation) permitted the FAR to increase from 1.33 to roughly 3.2 (Phatak[59]), sensing that it was not practical to relocate the tenants in situ without increasing the FSI. This is one reason which explains how and why many dilapidated buildings are not renovated in the central city of the metropolitan area, due to the loss of FSI, if such structures were to be demolished.

However, in the metropolitan area, the trading of FARs is allowed, which is referred to as TDRs, which the city's urban local body (ULB) permitted, in lieu of land or public facilities which it could not afford. However, this was discretionary, and failed to eliminate the negative impacts of a uniformly low FSI everywhere. As Bertaud[60] points out, this was not a way of improving land-use efficiency, but only a way of generating additional funds for the cash-strapped local body.

Mumbai is also a strange case where rent control worsened the effects of an already low FSI. Dey and Dev[61] point out that the initial

---

[58] Bertaud, 'Mumbai FAR/FSI Conundrum'.

[59] V.K. Phatak, 'Land Based Fiscal Tools and Practices for Generating Additional Financial Resources', *Capacity Building for Urban Development project*, Ministry of Urban Development, Government of India and World Bank, New Delhi, India, 2013.

[60] Bertaud, 'Mumbai FAR/FSI Conundrum'.

[61] Dey and Dev, 'Rent Control Laws in India'.

rent control legislation in India was put in place for the first time in the then Bombay[62] in 1918, immediately following the First World War. As Mumbai's draft development plan (for 2034) notes, many rent-controlled tenanted buildings in the island city[63] were in acute need of repair as the landowners had deliberately neglected these properties which did not yield them any returns. So in 1969, the state government (of Maharashtra) decided to interfere, and constituted the Bombay Building Repairs and Reconstruction Board, which found it difficult to reconstruct these buildings within the existing FSI, while accommodating the existing tenants; hence the Board allowed 2.4 times the permissible FSI.

As reported by Mumbai's draft development plan, a study in the context of Mumbai of the relationship between FSI and density found a weak correlation between the two (with an R^2 of 0.08). Nonetheless, the draft development plan of Mumbai recognizes that it is imperative to seek a 'new paradigm' for the FSI. It reflects the understanding that FSI was construed as a tool for containing density, but that it did not have the desired effect. As the draft development plan itself recognizes, the uniformly low FSI throughout the city led to the underutilization of the development potential of existing land, which led to a distorted land market and artificial increase in property prices.

For instance, in Colaba, at the southern tip of the peninsular city, a two BHK (Bedroom Hall Kitchen) flat sells for INR 35,714 per square foot (GBP 350 or USD 540), or a sale value of INR 2.5 crores (about GBP 248,000 or USD 378,000), as per www.magicbricks.com. Further, this is the only property that pops up when a hypothetical search is done for property in this area. In Worli, north of the CBD, a two BHK flat costs INR 3.0 crores (about GBP 297,000 or USD 454,545) (making for INR 20,704 per square foot (GBP 205 or USD 315)).[64] Even the draft development plan of Mumbai notes that in both city and suburbs, while the construction cost increased at the rate of about 10 per cent per annum over a 14-year period of 2000–14, the residential prices increased by nearly 25 per cent per annum. According

[62] In 1995, Bombay was renamed Mumbai.

[63] The inner part of the city, south Mumbai, is called the island city.

[64] These prices were retrieved from the website of magicbricks.com on 29 August 2015.

to a study by Jones Lang Lasalle (JLL) India, more than 66 per cent of the unsold housing inventory in Mumbai is priced above INR 1 crore, which is well beyond the affordability of most of the city's homebuyers. That study found that only 3.2 per cent of the apartments in the city were in the INR 31–65 lakh range. Further, out of a total of 44,032 units, about 33,500 (76 per cent) residential apartments were priced above INR 1 crore. By June 2015, nearly 83 per cent of the housing units were in the category of INR 1 crore or above, even while this proportion declined from 90 per cent in April 2015, due to new project launches in the city's suburban locations.[65] Such high prices are clearly unaffordable for a country which has about USD 1,500 average per capita income,[66] if we were to go by the definition of affordable housing, which states that housing should constitute no more than 30–40 per cent of the monthly income of the buyer.[67]

Clearly, the draft development plan recognizes that with the flat low FSI, development rights became scarce, which in turn created space for rent seeking. Hence Mumbai's draft development plan proposes that the present FSI should be approximately equal to 70 per cent of the new FSI with a maximum FSI of 8 (summarized in Table 17.2 in the draft development plan).

DISCUSSION, POLICY IMPLICATIONS, AND CAVEATS

Summarizing, the evidence from Bengaluru is that FARs have a negative impact on population and household density, which is consistent with the evidence from other studies. Given the exemptions allowed in the Karnataka Rent Control Act, it is unlikely that rent control has significant impacts in Bengaluru, as discussed. In Mumbai, it has been found that the relationship between FAR and density is weak, but the impacts of rent control cannot be underestimated. However, this

[65] 'In City of Dreams, Home Ownership's a Nightmare for Many', *The Economic Times*, 21 September 2015.

[66] The median income is much lower, on which data were not available for any country, until recently.

[67] Jones Lang Lasalle and PHD Chamber of Commerce and Industry, *Affordable Housing: The Indian Perspective & Future Outlook: Building Change & Sustainable Communities* (New Delhi: March 2018).

should not deter Indian policy-makers and urban planners from being open to the theory and international experience regarding opening up of the FAR/FSI regime, as Mumbai's current draft development plan itself testifies. With respect to rent control, sometime in 2016, the Ministry of Housing and Urban Affairs, Government of India, was considering finalizing a model tenancy act, which among other things, would permit the owners of prime properties in Delhi and Mumbai to charge market rates of rent to their tenants, which of course, would have to be enacted by their respective state governments, to be implemented. While a steep rise in the rent could result in large-scale evictions or voluntary relocations as people are unable to afford dramatically increased rents in prime locations, gradual increases in rents are typically absorbed. For instance, in most areas of Bengaluru, Chennai, and other major Indian cities, which are not in the jurisdiction of rent control legislation, there is an in-built annual increase of a certain percentage in the rent, as per the lease agreement, which is agreed to at the time of moving in. However, there is no question that dramatic increases in the rent, in the post-rent-control regime, would have major political and social implications.

While higher inner-city density reduces the need for urban fringe development and acquisition of 'new' land for urbanization, there was a proposal to amend in 2015 India's old (1894) Land Acquisition Act to remove the provision of 'consent' of 70 per cent of urban landowners for public–private-partnership (PPP) projects. However, this amendment was not approved by the houses of parliament, though some states have amended their relevant legislation along similar lines. While such land acquisition could be viewed as being at the expense of local farmers and controversial, Chakravorty[68] asks why there was no fuss about land acquisition in the India of the 1950s when it was highly inequitable, but why there is a big hue and cry about land acquisition in India currently, when the compensation is lucrative, and farmers are being made stakeholders in the infrastructure projects for which their land is acquired.[69]

[68] Sanjoy Chakravorty, 'Land Acquisition in India: The Political-economy of Changing the Law', *Area Development and Policy* 1, no. 1 (2016): 48–62, doi: 10.1080/23792949.2016.1160325.

[69] This research points to the fact that in the mid-1980s, compensation was only INR 12,000 per acre in well-located Saidapet in Chennai, on which the

In India, policies adopted to tackle housing are also typically in the nature of incentives to developers to initiate low-income housing projects (on the supply side), and provide easier access to finance (on the demand side), although these categories are too neat to describe the actual interventions. A Real Estate Regulation and Development Act was passed in 2016, which protects the interests of homebuyers (a supply side regulation). A major benefit in the Act for consumers is that builders will have to quote house prices based on carpet area (which refers to usable spaces like kitchens and toilets), and not super built-up area (which presumably includes stairways and other common areas). Further, this Act helps to establish state-level regulatory entities to oversee residential and commercial real estate transactions to guarantee their timely completion, and timely handover to home or apartment buyers.

However, this chapter has looked at a neglected aspect of land-use regulation in India's cities. As is clear from this chapter, increasing the FAR/FSI reduces the demand for land, by encouraging a high capital-land ratio and vertical growth. Further, the government could also offer higher FSI to the landowners, in addition to handing back a certain proportion of developed land to the owners who benefit from the capitalization. There is already precedence of such practices in the example of Navi Mumbai's City and Industrial Development Corporation Ltd (CIDCO).[70]

Madras Export Processing Zone was established (where the land cost skyrocketed to more than INR 150 million/acre in 2016). This research also reports that in the decade of the 2000s, the Indian courts increased compensation by 15-20 times or even higher in many cases; and refers the reader to an analysis of land acquisition litigation and compensation by the Haryana, Punjab, and Delhi high courts by Ram Singh. Ram Singh, 'Inefficiency and Abuse of Compulsory Land Acquisition: An Enquiry into the Way Forward', *Economic & Political Weekly* XLVII, no. 19 (2012): 46–53.

[70] As per a newspaper report, CIDCO offered 22.5 per cent developed plots as compensation to landowners whose land had been acquired. Sanjay Jog, 'Cidco Claims It Has Started Giving Developed Plots to Affected People', *Business Standard*, 12 July 2016, http://www.business-standard.com/article/economy-policy/cidco-claims-it-has-started-giving-developed-plots-to-affected-people-116071100473_1.html.

Such a practice could encourage more efficient urban land use in India's cities, by stimulating vertical growth, making the process of land acquisition and compensation more equitable, and urbanization more inclusive, and environmentally sustainable. It is, however, necessary to acknowledge social, economic, and environmental considerations in the Indian context. Social considerations mean that heritage conservation, especially those structures belonging to the ancient monarchy and history of the country need to be preserved, which imply that height restrictions cannot be relaxed drastically. Further, environmental considerations mean that in cities which are in ecologically vulnerable areas, those characterized by loose soil, FARs cannot be very high. Finally, state agencies and private developers in countries such as India do not release land to the extent desirable, the reason being that they hold on to the land for the gain in land-value capitalization they are likely to reap, when the area is well developed with infrastructure. Further, while one may argue that the traditional econometric models of monocentric urban form are rarely applicable in practice, Brueckner and Sridhar,[71] within the framework of the standard monocentric city, demonstrate the policy relevance of relaxing building-height restrictions in India's cities. They report that for every one unit relaxation in the city's FAR/FSI, the city's spatial area is reduced by 20 per cent, which translates into saving in commuting (both time and fuel) costs for the edge resident, and compute a welfare gain of INR 106 million per city based on the spatial reduction in area of the city, which can be partially used for financing the infrastructure needed to support a higher FAR.

★★★

This chapter extends our knowledge of the impact of excessively restrictive land-use regulations on density, and thus housing, in the context of Indian cities.

Such policies as those described in the real estate regulation legislation treat the symptoms, not the underlying causes of the malady. The research in this chapter shows that attempts by India's policy-makers

---

[71] Brueckner, and Sridhar, 'Measuring Welfare Gains from Relaxation of Land-use Restrictions'.

to fix problems with housing affordability may be futile, unless the underlying causes of the housing scarcity (excessively restrictive land-use regulations) are addressed. There are other policy/regulatory issues such as the license raj as applicable to housing, which this chapter has not examined. A simple example of the license raj with respect to housing is the fact that at every stage of the building process, a developer has to obtain several permits (including those from the National Green Tribunal, infrastructure-related permits), and other clearances, the transaction costs of which contribute to increasing the price of the 'affordable' house by several times, and make it actually unaffordable for the buyer.

Hence despite the social and contextual reservations, I conclude that the FARs in Indian cities, as applied currently, have not helped them to develop in the most effective manner, and need to be relaxed.

Future research should work on the caveats and limitations of data reported in this chapter. The impacts of strong land-use policies should be examined for other large Indian cities for which similar data is gathered/computed. It is possible that using the actual height of buildings, rather than the maximum permissible value of the FAR/FSI, may yield the desired impacts on densification. While technology permits us to do this, government regulation should enable more precise quantification of such data, in addition to relaxing the controls.

11 Towards a Market for Land in India

Post-LARR Development Makes It Necessary

Subhomoy Bhattacharjee

LIFE AFTER LARR

By December 2016, the Supreme Court registry showed there were 280 cases which had been filed under the Right to Fair Compensation and Transparency in Land Acquisition, Rehabilitation and Resettlement Act, 2013 (LARR), since it was notified on 1 January 2014. The cases challenge the acquisitions made under LARR.[1] The numbers are big, when one compares them with the total land acquisition disputes under the older Land Acquisition Act of 1894 (LAA) in the same apex court. Between 1950 and 2016, there were 1,269 of them. Though the numbers are dominated by cases filed against one agency, the Delhi Development Authority (200 out of 280[2]), yet when they are read with the relaxations in LARR made by at least six state governments,

---

[1] N. Wahi, A. Bhatia, D. Gandhi, S. Jain, P. Shukla, and U. Chauhan, *Land Acquisition in India: A Review of Supreme Court Cases from 1950 to 2016* (New Delhi: Centre for Policy Research, 2017), 12.

[2] Wahi et al., 'Land Acquisition in India'.

the potential of the new Act to provide a lasting solution to the basic problem of land transfer in India, is quite doubtful.

The Government of India framed LARR to solve one of the most iniquitous problems of the Indian economy. The problem is how to transfer land held by farmers or others for building manufacturing units and associated infrastructural projects ranging from cities to even standalone substations for electric transmission lines. A bit of background to the dispute is in order here. In the late-nineteenth century, as the demand for land to lay railway lines, a postal network, and new industrial units began to surface, the colonial government of India found it expedient to pass an omnibus LAA that was just marginally removed from the concept of eminent domain, to acquire land. The LAA established a procedure for the state acting through the district magistrates to take over land after giving the affected parties the right to object, and made provisions for paying of compensation to the land-losers.

The distress element in the LAA pirouetted on the asymmetry of information between the acquiring authority and the selling party. In addition, the acquirer or the state was specifically authorized to ignore the commercial value of the land in question. This created a producer surplus for the state in most transactions, and through it that of the private entity which got the land. The lack of information and the unfair producer surplus vitiated the transactions that led to a build-up of resentment among the sellers. Over the successive decades of independent India, as the Government of India moved to acquire more land, the resentment reached several flash points creating sizeable political storms. Those storms forced the Government of India to come up with a new act by 2013 for land acquisition. This was LARR.

The 2013 LARR has moved to the other extreme in the business of acquisition of land. Enumeration of the details of the Act is beyond the scope of this chapter[3] but each of its provisions including that of social impact assessment that brings in a much larger body of people than the owners of the land into the process of decision-making, the rules for declaration and award of compensation, followed by clear rules relating

---

[3] The Right to Fair Compensation and Transparency in Land Acquisition, Rehabilitation and Resettlement Bill, 2013 (PRS Legislative Research), http://bit.ly/2zp1uuN.

to rehabilitation and resettlement are meant to ensure that an acquisition should only be the last resort, especially in tribal areas.[4]

Economists have pointed to a key area of concern from LARR. 'By trying to bring in transparency [LARR] introduces new rigidities. With its provision for overlapping layers of diligence by committee [sic], it will markedly slow down the pace of land acquisition and lead to further choking of supply and escalation in the price of land.'[5] The concern about escalation of price of land is made vividly by Sanjoy Chakravorty.[6] He shows through careful measurement of land prices since the 1990s, especially around the key metro markets, that India has entered a permanent regime of high land prices. He goes on to establish that the high prices now and in future make it difficult for the state or a private party to acquire land.

Chakravorty and Rajaraman's thesis is disputed by Wahi et al.[7], who argue:

a. data on reported land prices is no indicator that such prices are actually paid by the government for land acquisition.
b. due to evasion of registration fees, most lands are undervalued before the government, and therefore, more often than not, the government would pay less than the market value of the land.

In such circumstances, a land acquisition process mediated by the state with safeguards as laid out in LARR is desirable, they argue. However, they have offered no evidence that evasion of registration fees is so widespread nationally that sellers would lose out in any deal without the detailed intermediation as prescribed by LARR. Taking the argument to the next stage, they note that any deviation from LARR made by some of the states would be suboptimal for the sellers, and consequently for the larger interests of equity for the nation.

[4] 'Acquisition of Tribal Land', Press Information Bureau, Government of India, 11 March 2015, http://pib.nic.in/newsite/PrintRelease. aspx?relid=116797.

[5] Indira Rajaraman, *Economically Speaking* (New Delhi: Academic Foundation, 2016), 203.

[6] Sanjoy Chakravorty, *The Price of Land: Acquisition, Conflict, Consequence* (New Delhi: Oxford University Press, 2013).

[7] Wahi et al., 'Land Acquisition in India'.

This position has been espoused by civil society groups too. With reference to the Telangana Land Acquisition Amendment Act, 2016, an umbrella group of such organizations notes: 'States have absolutely no power to execute a "state" Act vis-à-vis "land acquisition," under Section 107 of [LARR]…The field is already occupied by the central…Act, and the state necessarily has to comply with all the procedural requirements.'[8] The petitioners are clear that not only should there be no dilution of LARR, they also take the position, as the above quote shows, that in their opinion there is no space available for states to alter LARR as per the Constitution of India. Yet Telangana joins the rank of states that have decided they have the authority to do so. We shall not examine the question of constitutional rights in this chapter. Instead we shall examine if LARR has led to an improvement in the handling of land-related questions in India.

DEVIATIONS FROM LARR

Right from the date LARR was notified on 1 January 2014, states have expressed their displeasure with the law. This was on two counts. First, more than one state expressed their displeasure over the Centre passing a law that was clearly a subject for the state legislature.[9] To assuage them even before the bill became a law, the Government of India noted that LARR was a model law for states to apply as they deem fit as Jairam Ramesh said in an *Economic Times* report on 21 May 2012.[10] Second, more states—nine when this chapter was completed—have amended LARR, typically dropping the sections on social impact assessment and that of mandatorily obtaining consent from the landholders and project affected people (PAP).

As per the changes, Andhra Pradesh, Haryana, and Maharashtra have introduced the concept of land pooling. Landowners retain their

---

[8] Counterview.org, 'States have no Power to Have their Land Acquisition Law under Section 107 of Centre's 2013 Act', http://bit.ly/2xGjUoE.

[9] Constitution of India, Seventh Schedule, List II, Entry 18.

[10] https://economictimes.indiatimes.com/opinion/et-commentary/support-flixibility-to-state-governments-on-land-acquisition-jairam-ramesh/articleshow/13350713.cms.

right over the land, but pool contiguous pieces for handing over to the government and earn development rights on those. Uttar Pradesh has allowed direct negotiations between the buyers and sellers which was put to use to build its 303-kilometre long expressway between Lucknow and Agra. The state claims the policy allowed the expressway company to buy 3,400 hectares from 30,700 farmers in just six months. According to a Business Standard report of 17 July 2015,[11] the policy has been extended to all government departments, local bodies, autonomous institutions, municipal boards, and respective development authorities for their projects.

Both Telangana and Tamil Nadu have crafted exemptions to LARR, especially on social impact assessments, and on the consent clause. In Tamil Nadu, three acts, the Tamil Nadu Highways Act, 2001, the Tamil Nadu Acquisition of Land for Industrial Purposes Act, 1997, and the Tamil Nadu Acquisition of Land for Harijan Welfare Schemes Act, 1978 have been exempted from the purview of the consent and social impact assessment clauses. Tamil Nadu was the first mover among states to amend LARR.

Similarly, the states of Gujarat, Rajasthan, Maharashtra, Jharkhand, and Telangana have also brought in new laws to override LARR. These changes have been approved by the NITI Aayog (National Institution for Transforming India), in principle. The projects for which the exemptions were made are those on national security, defence, rural infrastructure, affordable housing, industrial corridors, and other infrastructural projects, including projects under public–private-partnerships (PPPs). For instance, in Maharashtra, the Mumbai–Nagpur Super Communication Expressway needs consent from 354 villages for land pooling to acquire 20,820 hectares of land.[12] To build the capital of Andhra Pradesh, Amaravati, the same model has been used. On the other hand, the Rajasthan Urban Land (Certification of Titles) Act, 2016 gives the state government the power to enter into any property or premises for the purpose of survey after giving its owner prior notice. It is part of two bills the state legislature cleared in 2016 to

---

[11] https://www.business-standard.com/article/pti-stories/niti-aayog-praises-land-pooling-method-for-ap-capital-116093001137_1.html.

[12] Subhomoy Bhattacharjee, Presentation at ISAS, National University of Singapore (October 2016).

create special investment regions (SIR). With the power under this Act, the state can map out a set of plots to build such regions. The pooling of the plots once the titling is done will be made possible by a second act, the Rajasthan Land Pooling Scheme Act. The veracity of the title deeds will be underwritten by the state government.[13]

There have been changes made in the rules for return of land to the sellers too. Odisha and Jharkhand do not allow the land to revert to the sellers if a project does not materialize. It only goes back to the land bank of the state.[14] The legal position is quite similar to that under the Coal Bearing Areas Act, 1957. The latter was one of 13 pieces of legislation promulgated by the Government of India since 1885 to provide separate rules for taking of land by the state for different purposes ranging from railways to defence. While LARR did not cancel out the operation of these acts (the amendment to LARR brought by the National Democratic Alliance (NDA) government in 2015 tried to amalgamate them[15]), through a subsequent notification, the Government of India's Department of Land Resources has clarified that LARR provisions will apply to these Acts, too.[16] While civil society has taken umbrage at what they reckon is a dilution of the intention of LARR, the Bombay High Court has stood behind the position of these states. In a case in Mumbai, where the Brihanmumbai Municipal Corporation (BMC) had delayed taking over possession for more than five years even after paying compensation to the owners, the Court held there was no reason for the state to begin the process of acquisition all over again.[17]

[13] Sahil Makkar, 'Rajasthan Govt Does It Again, Ushers in Crucial Land Reforms', SmartInvestor.in, 10 April 2016, http://bit.ly/2hHGgA8.

[14] Manju Menon, Kanchi Kohli, and Debayan Gupta, 'In State-level Changes to Land Laws, a Return to Land Grabbing in Development's Name', *The Wire*, 28 September 2017, http://bit.ly/2gGolKz.

[15] The Right to Fair Compensation and Transparency in Land Acquisition, Rehabilitation and Resettlement (Amendment) Ordinance, 2015, Press Information Bureau, Government of India, 30 May 2015, http://pib.nic.in/newsite/PrintRelease.aspx?relid=122149.

[16] Order, Ministry of Rural Development, Government of India, 28 August 2015, http://bit.ly/2kPTVtA.

[17] 'Owner Can't Reclaim Land Even if Government Fails to Acquire it in 5 Years', *The Times of India*, 14 October 2017, http://bit.ly/2zav06g.

The states hastened their amendments once the Government of India-sponsored change to LARR was aborted. The changes brought in by them make it clear that for the foreseeable future they will remain deeply involved in the process of land acquisition. While the pace of acquisition has come down, post-LARR, this trend has not changed. The reasons for the slower pace are two. The first is the slowdown in the economy. It has definitely contributed to the slower pace. The second is no state has found it easy to undertake acquisition within the full rubric of LARR. States like West Bengal and Bihar which have adopted LARR in toto have not been able to pick up a single parcel of land beyond what they already hold. Even in others, the pace has not picked up. Most of the acquisitions as a note on the proposed Dholera city shows, predate LARR.[18]

This is despite the changes made by nine states to ease the restrictions imposed by LARR. The one major exception is the construction of the new state capital by the Andhra Pradesh government. The data from Land Conflict Watch and another study, Land Disputes and Stalled Investments in India, that uses data from the Centre for Monitoring Indian Economy's (CMIE) database for the years 2000–16, show big acquisitions date back primarily to the period before LARR.[19] In Gujarat for instance, a big challenge looms. Plans for a bullet train from the state capital Ahmedabad to Mumbai envisage land acquisition of at least 825 hectares along the length, and already there are reports of obstacles being raised by land-holders along the course of the 500-kilometre line.[20] The railway ministry envisages it will be able to complete the project by 2022. One of the reasons for its optimism is that the full blown impact of LARR will not be in operation, thanks to the exception carved out for infrastructure projects in the amendments made by the Gujarat government. In a subsequent section, we discuss more of the strategies the Government of India has adopted to work within the constraints of LARR.

---

[18] Rishit Neogi, 'Gujarat's One-sided Land Policy', *Economic & Political Weekly* LII, no. 38 (2017): http://www.epw.in/engage/article/gujarats-one-sided-land-policy.

[19] https://www.downtoearth.org.in/news/governance/land-conflicts-affect-over-3-2-million-people-in-india-56318.

[20] Rina Chandran, 'India's Bullet Train Project Reignites Debate on Land for "Public Purpose"', Reuters, 25 September 2017.

LARR VERSUS MARKET FOR LAND

There has been no estimate of the costs the Indian economy has suffered because of the lack of a well-run market for land in India. The Government of India itself acknowledges that 'Studies show that tribal people who account for 8.6% of the population (Census 2011) experience much higher displacement burden'.[21] However, there have been estimates of the benefits such a market would bring for the economy. It has often been posited that due to the scarcity of land relative to the size of the population of India, a market for land would exacerbate the inequalities in the distribution of this resource. On the contrary, we argue that a market for land will actually reduce the cost of transaction for those whose principal economic asset is a piece of land.

A data set created by Land Conflict Watch demonstrates that most land conflicts are about rights on common land. Examining 289 land-related conflicts in India that span 1.2 million hectares till the end of 2016, it notes that of them, '32 per cent of land conflicts involved only common lands and another 42 per cent involved both common and private lands'.[22] So three-fourths of the land conflicts in India are about common lands—areas which are either government held or else have no single property holder who claims them as their own.

Note that the LARR provisions contemplate compensation mainly for land held as private property. While section 3 (c) (iii) and (iv) extend the Act to the acquisition of forest and common land, there are no clear principles within the Act to value those tracts. The work is left to the expert body to be drafted with regard to the social impact assessment. 'There are no guidelines to determine the methodology for such assessment and the Bill does not provide for such guidelines to be delegated to the Rules. This could lead to lack of consistency in the assessment of projects by different expert groups.'[23] It is not that

---

[21] See 'Acquisition of Tribal Land'.

[22] Ankur Paliwal, *Land Conflicts in India: An Interim Analysis* (Rights and Resources Initiative, Washington, DC, United States & Tata Institute of Social Sciences, Mumbai, 2016), 7, http://bit.ly/2zo4yHx.

[23] Pallavi Bedi and Sana Gangwani, 'The Right to Fair Compensation and Transparency in Land Acquisition, Rehabilitation and Resettlement Bill, 2013', PRS Legislative Research, http://bit.ly/2zp1uuN.

there are no global benchmarks for evaluating forests or commons.[24] But loading all of that on to an act creates an intolerable strain on delivery. In the absence of a market for even privately held land, Wahi et al. argue that the circle rates used as proxy are a poor substitute.[25] How does one value common land without even larger divergences? Yet the entire burden of relief and rehabilitation as a percentage of the cost of acquisition will depend on the price arrived at. We argue that it is this weakness in pricing that has encouraged six states (at the last count) to amend LARR. Effectively then, LARR's formula to offer compensation thus has little salience here. The land that is held by the government is not being alienated, and it will be extremely difficult to figure out who are the ones to be compensated for common land. These are, for instance, the areas of tribal landholdings in the country.

Here, one must put on record a key issue about livelihoods in India. As the data set put together by Land Conflict Watch shows, the critical question among those affected is about security of livelihood. Questions on management of land ought not to be confused with that of security of livelihood. There is no doubt that the Government of India must be concerned about the economic security of people when it decides to change the land-use pattern in any area. These have to be addressed in a robust way by enveloping, those whose livelihoods get altered, in a blanket of social security measures. This is a fundamental responsibility of the state. But to load land transactions with these objectives does the reverse. It absolves the responsibility of the state, and instead raises the cost of the transfer for both the buyer and the seller by prolonging the time period of the award. There is no way a tribal assembly in a gram sabha can say yes to a land alienation project unless they have already been provided alternatives. Those alternatives, however, cannot run on the back of a land acquisition act, no matter how well intentioned. Instead, making the pricing of land responsive to supply and demand offers a valuable piece of information to those affected on what they should demand from the

[24] Joshua T. Bishop, 'Valuing Forests: A Review of Methods and Applications in Developing Countries' (Environmental Economics Programme, International Institute for Environment and Development (IIED), July 1999), http://bit.ly/2yqpMpQ.

[25] Wahi et al., 'Land Acquisition in India'.

government for security of their livelihood. It is also not clear to what extent Parliament has the right to decide that a private land acquisition project should be compelled to offer a relief and rehabilitation scheme. Instead of going to court to challenge the same, since the passage of LARR, developers have opted to lobby with the state governments to dilute the same. As a result, despite the passage of four years since the enactment of LARR, there has hardly been any social impact assessment report for any major land project in India.

Let us now look at the data on court cases relating to private land that has been acquired by the state. This is the data that the study by Wahi et al.[26] throws up. Court cases are a proxy indicator of the perceived divergence felt by those who transact in the market for land from what they feel is the true value of their holdings; in other words, the producer surplus which they forego.

The statistical breakdown of the land-related cases brought before the Supreme Court shows that most of the cases involved acquisitions that were initiated during the decades 1960–89. Of these, '63.4% of the total cases in [the] dataset numbering 805 cases, that is roughly two thirds of all cases involved claims by land losers seeking enhanced compensation under the Land Acquisition Act'. The litigants did not question the locus standi of either the Government of India or the states to acquire land. They are interested in the price at which it should be bought. The same trend can be spotted in the cases decided by the Supreme Court under LARR. 'Almost 83% of the challenges before the Supreme Court involved instances where no compensation had been paid to the land losers.'[27] Also remember that land-related cases have a long gestation period of at least 15–20 years in the courts. This implies that much of the litigation involving acquisitions post-1991 has not yet been decided by the Supreme Court. Those cases too, when they are decided upon, are likely to reinforce this trend further. In this context, one notices the same trend with respect to private landholdings in tribal areas too. In a first of its kind study done in Mandla district of Madhya Pradesh on the basis of sale deeds of land in a 30-year period, it was found that price

---

[26] Wahi et al., 'Land Acquisition in India'.
[27] Wahi et al., 'Land Acquisition in India', 34.

discovery was as robust as evident in districts near metro cities.[28] Those who have brought the cases are clear why they have knocked the doors of the court. It is about deciding the price which should be paid. Given the need to ensure fair pricing of land, a market-based mechanism would obviously provide a more satisfactory solution to these plaintiffs.

Transactions on land have everything to do with the price paid for it. The concern raised by LARR for bringing a larger body of people affected by the acquisition of land to the fore by mandating safeguards for them, only serves to prolong the process of acquisition but does not settle the key issue of pricing of land satisfactorily. Rather it can be said that compared with capital and labour, the pricing of land has suffered because there is no move even now to create a market for it. Yet, as of now, no state has made market pricing one of the key ingredients for transfer of land.

The key action area then is to disengage the state from the role it sets itself as provider of land for industry. This position incidentally is quite at variance with the rules in force for other factors of production. No company in India would ask the state to provide capital at a reasonable cost to finance a project. Even if it did, the state would have no options to offer. Similarly, the state does not provide subsidized workers to work at a factory. In the same vein, it is not necessary for the state to provide land to an entity. The situation has come about because the Government of India has not worked to set up a market for land in India. The lack of movement has also suited segments of the industry as they have been shielded from the necessity to pay the real price for the land that they acquire.

So we arrive at four conclusions from the above analysis:

a. The subtext of the land conflicts in India is about the issue of livelihood security. LARR does not provide the answer to these issues.
b. Instead, as the overwhelming majority of court cases demonstrate, sellers see the process before and after the passage of LARR as asymmetric.

---

[28] S. Bhattacharjee, R. Sinha, and K. Dutta, 'Fair Pricing of Land and Its Compensation in an Emerging Economy: Case for India', http://bit.ly/2zb2Ic8.

c. Just like the earlier Act of 1894, LARR encourages private developers to depend on the Government of India or state governments to
   acquire land for them.
d. The process can only be radically changed by developing a national
   market for land under preferably, a common regulator, to ensure
   uniformity of rules.

As the Make in India, Smart Cities, and Affordable Housing for All programmes, and the bullet train project begin to translate into renewed
demands for land, this is something that needs to be taken forward
with gusto. Significantly, some of the fresh incidents of protests have
begun to affect state-run companies, too. In West Bengal, PowerGrid
Corporation has seen one of its land acquisitions for a substation
come under dispute that has led to two deaths; in Tamil Nadu and
Puducherry, renewed exploration plans for gas by the Oil and Natural
Gas Corporation Ltd (ONGC) led to protests by farmers. It shows that
the definition of 'public purpose' which offered a wider shoulder for
state-run companies to acquire land has begun to lose acceptability
among the land-losers.

OPTIONS FOR MARKET PRICING OF LAND

So far we have examined the options the Government of India and the
states have deployed to apportion land between competing claimants
in the country. But, we discovered that solutions which bypass the
market mechanism yield suboptimal results. While LARR has certainly
ensured a drastic improvement in equity, it still falls short in being a
long-term solution for acquisition of land. In this section, we study the
alternatives the Government of India along with the state governments
could deploy as forward-looking strategies, which also in pari passu
reduce corruption in the business of land. These options would deliver
a healthy welfare outcome to the Indian people.

In this connection, one has to refer to a seminal report produced
by the NITI Aayog on leasing of land. The report examines how
agricultural land can be made more productive by offering farmers
firm leasing rights. The expert committee recommends bringing in
a uniform set of laws to legalize land leasing so that there is both,

'a complete security of land ownership right for land owners and security of tenure for tenants for the agreed lease period'. It also suggests removal of the clause of adverse possession of land from the land laws of various states as it interferes with the free functioning of the land-lease market.[29]

The report pivots on the right to hold and sell agricultural land without any encumbrances by farmers. And this is where the advances made by most Indian states in the recognition of landholdings through digital technology come in. According to the Department of Land Resources in the Ministry of Rural Development, at least 20 states have already computerized their land records. Of them, more than half now issue a sale letter for land only through their digital land record system. This is a huge revolution in India's centuries-old convoluted landholdings system.

For example, in the case of Rajasthan, as mentioned above, the state has had to pass a special law to assure buyers of land that their sale deeds will be recognized by the state government. This has been the experience of all state governments, and one of the key reasons why the Department of Land Records is usually held as one of the portfolios of the chief minister. This is also the reason why industries prefer to involve the state administration in their acquisition of land, besides of course the attraction of securing a lower price for the land. Digital land records largely do away with the need for such state support. Land can be bought and sold easily.

There are, however, several shortcomings in the switch over of land records to a digital world. Land is a state subject. As the website of the Department of Land Resources of the Government of India admits, it can only assist the states to make the switch.[30] It cannot direct them even though it can provide generous financial support. Yet, given the massive advantage of such a switch, it is necessary to encourage the states to ask for help. As of now, 26 states have discontinued

---

[29] T. Haque, *Report of the Expert Committee on Land Leasing* (NITI Aayog, Government of India, 31 March 2016), http://niti.gov.in/writereaddata/files/document_publication/Final_Report_Expert_Group_on_Land_Leasing.pdf.

[30] Frequently Asked Questions on the National Land Records Modernisation Programme, http://dolr.nic.in/dolr/FAQ.asp.

handwritten records, but only four of them have linked the records with the respective courts.[31]

The pace of change can become noticeably faster if the NITI Aayog's proposed changes in land-leasing laws are adopted by the states en masse. It is a rare lessee who will venture to rent farmland without clear land records. But once the law is changed, there would be demand and supply of such land. It would push up the demand for availability of unencumbered records that in turn can be provided only digitally. Those records will supply the lessee with all the information needed before taking the land on rent. The success of the reforms in leasing laws is therefore a precondition for the digitalization of land records. Once these two take place, India will be on its way to develop a market for land.

The final element in the emergence of a land market in India is the need for titling of lands. Even after making the records digital, there is no conclusive evidence that a piece of land rightfully belongs to the person who declares it is so (Rajasthan government guarantee, for instance). It is only through a mixture of technological change in cadastral maps allied with ground mapping that a full-fledged titling of all land can happen in India. This requires an intensively collaborative programme between the states and the Government of India. The economic implications that would follow from such a titling exercise are immense. Of course there are risks to titling in a land-scarce country like India since the premium for such titles can create an adverse market.[32] While safeguards can be built for the same, the current situation of nil records cannot be maintained.

For instance, for most retail loans, Indian banks demand and obtain land as a key collateral. Yet when, like in the current situation, banks are forced to sell the land parcels in auctions to recover the loans, they have begun to discover that the records are illusory. Many of them are

---

[31] Digital India Land Records Modernization Programme, Government of India, http://nlrmp.nic.in/faces/rptPhysicalHome/rptStateGenericDetail.xhtml?id=./../master/physical.xhtml.

[32] P. Annez, B. Bhatt, and B. Patel, 'What Getting Land Title Really Means' (New York: Marron Institute of Urban Management, New York University, May 2014), http://bit.ly/2gbSr7P.

subject to disputes, yet none of those disputes had come to light when the loans were negotiated.[33]

The lack of scientific land records therefore cripples the ability of small landholders to either lease out their land or sell in an informed market to the highest bidder. Instead they are forced to depend on the state to obtain the best possible price for their land in an 'acquisition' rather than a sale in a free market.

★★★

Till now we have examined why LARR despite its promise has not met the needs of the land economy in India. We have looked at the reasons why the state governments have deviated from this piece of legislation. We have also examined why rather than these laws the welfare outcome for each segment will be better served by establishing a national market for land.

There is meanwhile a via media that the Government of India can exploit in the interregnum. The subsequent analysis draws heavily from a report led by Shubhashis Gangopadhyay, research director of the India Development Foundation (IDF). This report shows that a lot of constraint in making land available can be sorted out if the Government of India taps into its own landholdings.[34] It is not referring to the land banks for industries the various state governments own but those held unused, by their agencies. These are massive tracts, mostly held within municipal limits, and so should be eminently attractive for industries. Releasing them can avoid demands for fresh land acquisition.

A pilot inventory of public lands in the Ahmedabad Municipal Corporation indicates that 32 per cent of all developed and developable land—that is, excluding the road network, water bodies, and railway

---

[33] For an excellent exposition on the same please, refer to the speech by K.P. Krishnan, Additional Secretary, Department of Land Resources, Government of India, https://www.youtube.com/watch?v=mv97JjGdUbA.

[34] P. Annez and S. Gangopadhyay, eds, *India's Public Lands: Responsive, Transparent, and Fiscally Responsible Asset Management* (Gurgaon: IDF), idfresearch.org/download.php?pid=240&page=race.

lines—is public land with the Corporation. The Union Government departments and organizations are the largest landowners in the country. There is no definitive publicly available inventory of central landholdings, but a study of published sources indicates that these holdings are very large and potentially underutilized. The 13 major Port Trusts hold around 100,000 hectares of land in all. The Airports Authority of India controls 20,400 hectares of high-value land surrounding major airports. The Indian Railways has identified 43,000 hectares of its massive landholdings as unnecessary for railway service, and has estimated the value of this excess land at some USD 40 billion. The Ministry of Defence is India's largest landowner. Its holdings amount to over 283,280 hectares, of which about 0.28 lakh hectares are out of cantonments—many of them in prime urban areas. 'A pilot public land inventory for Ahmedabad estimates that the relatively small but very well located Ahmedabad cantonment occupies about 7 per cent of the total developed and developable land in the city'.[35]

What the exercise revealed was gargantuan. It excluded all cemeteries, parks and gardens, heritage buildings, slums, land used for utilities, infrastructure lands, and industrial estates. Again, the authors discarded unused lands already earmarked for public purposes from the valuation exercise. Yet after cutting all of them, 'the value of potentially marketable excess land is still substantial—ranging from a low of Rs 20,000 crores at jantri[36] rates to Rs 55,000 crores at market rates'. This amount is 'between 84 per cent and 225 per cent of the about Rs 43,000 per capita needed for all urban infrastructure investments over the next twenty years in Ahmedabad'.[37]

The data is the same for all cities, by and large, Annez and Gangopadhyay say. There are two advantages to quantifying and managing these tracts. It will free up fiscal resources for investments in other areas, and it will make the governments able to provide land to companies without making fresh acquisitions. According to former finance secretary Sumit Bose, this is a practical suggestion. If the municipal bodies, states, and Centre sit on such vast tracts and do not

---

[35] Annez and Gangopadhyay, *India's Public Lands.*

[36] The term refers to a legal document in Gujarat specifying the value of land and buildings at any point of time.

[37] Annez and Gangopadhyay, *India's Public Lands,* 3.

make those data public, there is a huge scope for corruption, in parcelling out tracts to favoured parties without public scrutiny. 'It is a regulatory risk,' he said.[38]

At the same time, unlocking government land is not easy. Annez and Gangopadhyay say a policy announced by the Prime Minister's Office in August 2012 aims to unlock centrally controlled land for infrastructure projects. The policy authorizes central institutions to transfer land to other departments of the government, to sub-national governmental units, and (even) to public–private-partnerships (PPPs), where the land will be used for infrastructure projects. In practice, the Cabinet freeze on public land disposition remains. They describe it as a choke point. 'Cabinet has become the centralised choke point holding back public land-use decisions and critical infrastructure projects. This highly centralised approach is causing very substantial delays.'[39]

The best way, the IDF study suggests, is to identify 'surplus' land that is not needed for provision of public services. They assure there is plenty of it as the Ahmedabad exercise shows. 'Once a list of "surplus" land has been identified, market forces and perhaps other agents of government can focus on the most attractive or useful surplus parcels, and express demand for them. There is [sic] plenty of similar efforts made abroad in Germany, Canada, and Australia to show this is a practical way out.'[40]

Wahi et al.[41] quoted earlier in the chapter show land acquisition cases take on an average 20 years to navigate the courts. Worse, for the state authorities, the courts have become harsher on lands acquired—nearly 95 per cent of acquisition cases brought after LARR was enacted were shot down by the Supreme Court. Once shot down, it is back to the drawing board for all those cases, a long drawn out affair. Instead, land parcels held by government bodies in urban and peri-urban areas can be offered to industry at market rates, even as a national market for land is put in place.

---

[38] Seminar on 'Public Lands for Public Needs: How We Can Optimise Returns from a Dormant Asset for National Needs', India Development Foundation, New Delhi, 28 February 2017.

[39] Annez and Gangopadhyay, *India's Public Lands*, 8.

[40] Annez and Gangopadhyay, *India's Public Lands*.

[41] Wahi et al., 'Land Acquisition in India'.

12 Land in India

Meddling in Muddled Markets

Amitendu Palit[*]

Very few pieces of public policy legislation in India have been as debated and discussed as the Land Acquisition Act of 1894 (LAA), and its successor, the Right to Fair Compensation and Transparency in Land Acquisition, Rehabilitation and Resettlement Act of 2013 (LARR). The latter replaced the former after extensive consultations among various stakeholders, and more than five years of rigorous background work within the government. But even five years after the enactment of LARR, nagging doubts remain over the benefits it has delivered.[1] These doubts assume significant proportions in the context of the greater objective of the growth of land markets in India, and the role of the state in this regard.

[*] The author acknowledges the support of the National Research Foundation of Korea Grant funded by the Korean Government (NRF - 2017S1A6A3A02079749) in this work.)
[1] 'Five Years On, Has Land Acquisition Act Fulfilled Its Aim?', *The Economic Times*, 1 September 2018, https://economictimes.indiatimes.com/news/economy/policy/five-years-on-has-land-acquisition-act-fulfilled-its-aim/articleshow/65639336.cms.

LARR: POLITICAL OPTICS AND ABORTIVE AMENDMENTS

The 2013 LARR had a straightforward objective: to prevent acquisition of land by Central and state governments for 'public purpose', and concomitant utilization of the acquired land for industrial purposes, particularly by private developers. By drastically increasing the cost of acquisition for public purpose—not just through the higher compensation to be paid to the original owners, but also the mandatory need for obtaining prior consent from the community,[2] and carrying out social impact assessments—land acquisition was intended to become the last resort for obtaining land by the state. The purported goal behind making the cost of land acquisition significantly higher so as to disincentivize the process was consistent with the view held by some experts that original landowners are deprived of the benefits of appreciation in the value of acquired land once it is designated for industrial use.[3]

The enactment of LARR did not encounter any major hurdles in either house of the Indian Parliament. This wasn't surprising. No party—most so the ruling Congress and the main opposition party, the Bharatiya Janata Party (BJP)—wanted to be coloured 'anti-farmer' at a time when the next elections to the lower house were to be held in less than a year. But once these were held, and the BJP came to power with a comprehensive majority, it changed tack on the Act. It tried to do away with some of the provisions of the Act that made land acquisition heavily restrictive. Within a year of coming to power, the BJP-led National Democratic Alliance (NDA) attempted to introduce amendments to LARR for exempting land acquired for some categories of industrial projects, notably defence, rural infrastructure, affordable housing, industrial corridors, and social infrastructure, from the

---

[2] Consent is required for public–private partnership (PPP) and privately developed projects, not government ones.

[3] The predecessor of LARR, the LAA prevented original landowners from approaching courts for benefitting from future appreciation in land value emanating from its new use. Many experts found the limitation distinctly 'anti-farmer'. See Amitendu Palit, 'Land and Food Acts: Trading Economic Pragmatism for Political Gain', in *India's Fiscal Policy: Prescriptions, Pragmatics and Practice*, ed. Supriyo De (Cambridge: Cambridge University Press, 2017), 138-55.

requirements of social impact assessment and obtaining prior consent. The costs of acquisition, however, were left unchanged.

The political logic of the BJP would ostensibly have been to adjust provisions in a manner that would allow the government to acquire large-scale land for building infrastructure by attracting private investment. This was necessary as the new government was widely perceived to have a wholesome commitment to the agenda of rapid industrial development—a view strengthened by the announcement of the flagship 'Make in India' initiative—aiming to make India a manufacturing powerhouse. But the government was unsuccessful in proceeding with the amendments, in spite of attempting to do so through multiple fixed-term ordinances. The numerical imbalance between both houses of Parliament as reflected in the heavy majority of the NDA in the lower house as opposed to it being in the minority in the upper house was a key legislative hurdle. But even greater difficulties were perceived from the political damage of attempting to amend an Act that was widely seen as 'pro-farmer'.

With more and more state elections coming up in the country's ceaseless electoral cycle and the opposition gunning the government for its pro-industry, anti-farmer posturing, a hasty retreat on amending LARR was considered the best political ploy. Farmer distress in the country was being emphasized by the opposition as an area to which the government was turning a blind eye, reflected perhaps most categorically in the leader of the opposition Rahul Gandhi's famous 'suit–boot ki sarkar' jibe on the floor of the Parliament,[4] where Prime Minister Modi was described as 'pro-corporate' and 'anti-poor' for, among others, his efforts to dilute LARR. Amendments to the latter obviously have no direct connection to agrarian distress in the country, which is largely driven by miniscule plot sizes, lack of access of growers to open market sales, a distorted procurement pricing system, weather fluctuations, and mounting indebtedness. However, such factors, which have prevailed for years and have hardly been addressed satisfactorily either by the BJP or its predecessor the Congress, did not deter the latter from characterizing the BJP as 'anti-farmer' because of its efforts to amend LARR.

---

[4] 'Rahul Gandhi Tears into Modi's "Suit–Boot ki Sarkar"', *The Times of India*, 21 April 2015, https://timesofindia.indiatimes.com/india/Rahul-Gandhi-tears-into-Modis-suit-boot-ki-sarkar/articleshow/46993611.cms.

On the other hand, the BJP withdrew from proceeding on the amendment because it did not wish to surrender any political capital. In the months and years that have followed since the amendments were submitted to a Joint Parliamentary Committee (JPC) for its recommendations in 2015,[5] the Modi government's interest in the amendments has also dwindled, evident from the infrequent meetings the JPC has had. At the same time, agrarian distress in the country has not shown signs of abating; while such distress has not translated into major electoral losses for the BJP across the country, even in elections in 'committed' BJP states like Gujarat, it has affected their electoral performance.[6]

With elections to the Parliament for 2019 drawing closer, the BJP has been careful in not magnifying the impression that it is unable to safeguard the country's farmers. After all, some of the Modi government's ability to deliver during its term will be judged on the basis of whether it gets close to the claim of doubling farmer incomes by the year 2022.[7] Farmer support schemes and a farmer-friendly image are therefore the order of the day. As a result, the government has stayed away from all efforts that might contradict such an image, most notably amending LARR.

Whether LARR would change in any way after the next general elections is difficult to say. But given that both major national parties of the country consider it a pro-farmer legislation, or at least a legislation that is 'rights-based' and justiciable as far as farmers are concerned, major changes—like on obtaining prior consent, carrying out

[5] 'Joint Parliamentary Committee Meeting on Land Acquisition Bill Not Held Due to Less Member Turnout', *The Times of India*, 27 February 2018, https://timesofindia.indiatimes.com/india/joint-parliamentary-committee-meeting-on-land-acquisition-bill-not-held-due-to-less-member-turnout/articleshow/63101188.cms.

[6] 'Why BJP Lost Rural Gujarat', *Rediff.com*, 21 December 2017, http://www.rediff.com/news/interview/must-read-why-bjp-lost-rural-gujarat/20171221.htm.

[7] 'PM Modi Promises Farmers Low Input Costs and Good Price for Harvest', *The Economic Times*, 21 June 2018, https://economictimes.indiatimes.com/news/politics-and-nation/our-government-to-double-farmers-income-by-2022-narendra-modi/articleshow/64658335.cms.

social impact assessments, and altering the costs of compensation—are unlikely. The Act continues to remain in force in its present form.

What have been the implications of LARR? Irrespective of what political parties champion as pro-farmer, which the Act could well be from the perspective of 'land-losers,' who, historically, have often been forced to give up their land due to the state employing eminent domain for 'public purpose', and have been short-changed on compensation, there are serious difficulties that have emerged on the supply-side. Most notably, the prospect of obtaining land for new uses has become much more onerous than before. The difficulties are not only procedural, but also financial, given the higher compensation involved. Indeed, various estimates, including those by government agencies like the NITI Aayog (National Institution for Transforming India), point to land acquisition under LARR taking more than four years, thereby creating major delays and project overruns.[8] As a result, there are two obvious implications. The first of these is an attempt on the part of several state governments in India to dilute the provisions of LARR. The second—an effect with greater long-term implications on the character of the Indian land market—is the difficulties imposed on the evolution of a land market encouraging transaction of land according to market forces.

STATES BECOME CENTRAL

The responsibilities of the Centre and states on land regulation follow a complex allotment under the Indian constitution. 'Land' and 'land reforms' are 'state' subjects, allowing the state to legislate on these issues, while 'land acquisition' figures among concurrent subjects, thereby allowing both the Centre and states to legislate. While Central laws on concurrent subjects are superior to individual state laws, states can seek Presidential assent for amending the overriding Central laws. The provisions actually endow the states with a significant amount of authority to introduce land acquisition legislation different from Central acts such as LARR.

[8] 'Land Acquisition: Rationale and the Way Forward', NITI Aayog, 18 October 2016, http://niti.gov.in/content/land-acquisition-rationale-and-way-forward; 'Doing Business in India', *the PRS Blog*, 1 November 2017, http://www.prsindia.org/theprsblog/?tag=land-acquisition.

In the past, the LAA was employed by several states for acquiring land for 'public purpose', which was used by private developers for industrial and commercial development. Such instances, on several occasions, created major uproars and public outcry, and were also disapproved of by the courts—for example, in the case of the Uttar Pradesh government's acquisition of land in Noida and Greater Noida.[9] The LAA was a much easier legislation to acquire land, as opposed to LARR. So while the former saw active use by states, the latter has created difficulties. States, therefore, have been taking steps to dilute the provisions of LARR.

Over the last three years, several Indian states have sought to deviate from LARR. The most notable deviations are those with respect to avoidance of mandatory social impact assessment. Gujarat, Maharashtra, Tamil Nadu and Telengana have endeavoured for the exclusion of social impact assessment for several categories of projects, while some others like Andhra Pradesh, Jharkhand, Sikkim, and Uttar Pradesh have attempted to 'tweak' social impact assessment requirements. States like Chhattisgarh, Haryana, and Tripura have also lowered the compensation requirement for land acquired in rural areas.[10] The active role of states in framing their own land acquisition rules by avoiding some of the most stringent provisions of LARR, is also consistent with the Central Government encouraging them to do so, including the public expression of such views by important figures like the Finance Minister and the Deputy Chairman of the NITI Aayog.[11]

---

[9] 'Supreme Court Quashes Land Acquisition for Jail in UP', *The Hindu*, 4 August 2011, https://www.thehindu.com/news/national/supreme-court-quashes-land-acquisition-for-jail-in-up/article2319906.ece.

[10] Kanchi Kohli and Debayan Gupta, 'Mapping Dilutions in a Central Law: A Comparative Analysis of Rules Made under the Right to Fair Compensation and Transparency in Land Acquisition, Rehabilitation and Resettlement (LARR) Act, 2013', Occasional Paper, Centre for Policy Research, India (2017), http://cprindia.org/system/tdf/working_papers/Mapping%20Dilutions%20in%20a%20Central%20Law%20(final).pdf?file=1&type=node&id=6455.

[11] 'Some States Keen to Bring Their Own Land Acquisition Laws', *The Times of India*, 15 July 2015, https://timesofindia.indiatimes.com/india/Some-states-keen-to-bring-own-land-acquisition-laws-Arun-Jaitley/articleshow/48084200.cms; 'Land Act Bit Draconian, Frame Own Laws: Arvind Panagariya to States', *The Economic Times*, 10 September 2015, https://

The further interesting point to note is that while the Centre fought shy of pushing the amendments to LARR after a point of time, it did not come in the way of the states doing so at their own level. Indeed, BJP-ruled states like Gujarat, Maharashtra, and Haryana have not refrained from diluting the provisions of LARR, and have not been dissuaded by the Centre from doing so. The opposition Congress too has not been particularly 'agitated' over the states amending LARR.

These developments certainly make one wonder whether the entire fuss created by the Congress over LARR being a pro-farmer legislation was essentially political optics; and whether the BJP too appreciated the importance of sustaining such optics, while allowing states to pursue their own agendas. Whatever it be, it is becoming evident that several states in India are increasingly beginning to assume primary authority in acquiring land according to their own requirements and circumstances. This might well be the way things shape out in the years to come.

BUT HOW TO GET LAND?

Notwithstanding the states assuming greater roles in acquiring land through individual legislation, the development of a land 'market' in India remains a questionable proposition. The price explosion in land markets has already been discussed in the introductory chapter. But the implications of LARR are also very significant in this regard.

One of the key features of LARR was to implant a formula for determining the cost of acquiring land. In the first instance, the Act expanded the cost of acquisition to include direct compensation, payment for damage to land and crops in the process of acquisition, cost of acquiring land and building for accommodating affected families, costs for developing infrastructure for resettlement, and cost of rehabilitation.[12] The overall cost, according to the Act, turns out to be a formula

---

economictimes.indiatimes.com/news/economy/policy/land-act-bit-draco-nian-frame-own-laws-arvind-panagariya-to-states/articleshow/48901548.cms.

[12] The Right to Fair Compensation and Transparency in Land Acquisition, Rehabilitation and Resettlement Act, 2013, section 3, http://www.legislative.gov.in/sites/default/files/A2013-30.pdf.

that for rural areas includes the market value of land multiplied by 1.0 to 2.0 (based on the distance of the land from the urban area), plus the value of assets attached to land or building, plus a solatium (two times the market value); and for urban areas, market value of land multiplied by 1.0 plus value of assets attached to land or building plus solatium (equal to the market value).[13] These formulae, both for rural and urban areas, have become the floor for determining the price of land. The minimum price for rural land, according to the formula specified, is likely to be almost as much as four times the market value, while that of urban land is twice the market value.

The clear implication of the above, from the perspective of states as well as project developers, is to face the prospect of land prices having become significantly higher. This is evident from the way costs of obtaining land for road construction and highways have shot up in India. Developer estimates of acquisition costs that were just under 10 per cent in 2009, are found to have increased to as much as 40 per cent, or even more.[14] The impact of such rise would be felt hard on returns on investments in industrial projects at a time when many of these are suffering from lack of funds. This becomes a 'chicken and egg' situation as banks are unwilling to lend further to these projects that are stuck, or not able to service their debt obligations, for fear of aggravating non-performing loans.

Is outright purchase of land a better option for Indian states and infrastructure agencies? Ideally, land, irrespective of its end-use, should be available for transaction with sufficient information and flexibilities on part of both buyers and sellers, if the markets are functioning well. Such markets would have largely eliminated the need for acquisition. More importantly, the role of the state—and in the present instance,

[13] 'Compensation for Land Owners', The Right to Fair Compensation and Transparency in Land Acquisition, Rehabilitation and Resettlement Act, 2013, The First Schedule. 'Solatium' is provided for in Chapter 4, Section 30 of the Act. It is to be a part of the final award of compensation to be determined by the Collector, and will be 100 per cent of the compensation amount, in addition to the compensation determined.

[14] 'Steep Climb: Land Cost of Road Projects Rises to Whopping 55 pct from 9 pct in 2009', *The Financial Express*, 28 December 2017, https://www.financialexpress.com/industry/steep-climb-land-cost-of-road-projects-rises-to-whopping-55-pct-from-9-pct-in-2009/992540/.

the role of the state governments in India—as facilitators, or 'honest brokers', could have been avoided. Unfortunately, that is hardly the case. Acquisition legislation in India has perpetuated situations in which the role of the state governments and state agencies remains fundamental in the land market.

Earlier, at the time of the LAA, the role of the state in acting as a virtuous intermediary was important given that it was necessary to ensure that information asymmetries between buyers and sellers did not end up in creating adverse outcomes; but, of course, they did, and the state was anything but a virtuous intermediary. But even now, the role of the state remains essential, even if it is viewed from the perspective of outright purchases. With private investors now practically squeezed out of the land market due to the high costs of acquisition and other requirements (for example, prior consent, social impact assessment), states have little option other than garnering land on their own. Many states are considering outright purchase of land in this regard. But the floor on land prices brought in by LARR is affecting such purchases. In order to avoid the 'issues' involved in acquisition, particularly overcoming the long delays involved in social impact assessments and other formalities, states are settling for outright purchases by paying owners more than what the cost of compensation would have entitled them to. Roadway projects in Maharashtra, for example, have had state agencies buying rural land by paying five times the market value—more than what the compensation would have been if there was acquisition.[15]

As would have been expected, the imposition of an imputed floor through the perceived computation of compensation from the perspective of landowners has introduced another layer of complication in land transactions. Owners are now not only emboldened to ask for higher prices for their land, but are also encouraged to do so by property agents, who hope to benefit from the process by capitalizing on the long-standing problem of information asymmetry. Agents are prepared to pay premiums to landowners over and above what could have been the acquisition price, and sell the same to government

---

[15] As reported by a senior official of the Maharashtra State Road Development Corporation (MSRDC) with respect to the purchase of land for the Mumbai–Nagpur Super Communication Expressway. See 'Steep Climb'.

agencies given the urgency in expediting infrastructure projects. This is evident in a state like Uttar Pradesh where a major infrastructure project like the development of an international airport at Greater Noida is a keenly awaited mission given the beneficial impact it can have on the state in terms of generating more livelihoods and incomes. The issues being encountered by the state agencies in their decision to purchase land, as opposed to its acquisition, reflect the mentioned intentions of landowners and property agents.[16] It is indeed remarkable how LARR—arguably a pro-farmer and rights-based legislation—is also being subjected to comprehensive rent-seeking through the collusion of various actors.

IMPERFECT MARKET, SCARCE RESOURCES

As a supply-side issue, the problem of states obtaining land through outright purchase is beginning to assume serious proportions drawing attention to the deep imperfections plaguing land markets in India, most ostensibly in pricing. The role of state governments in purchasing land for making it available for building infrastructure and other public goods remains imperative. Indeed, non-state actors, particularly the Indian private sector, are hardly in a position to bypass state governments and purchase land directly from the owners. The 'deep pockets' needed for that are conspicuously scarce in today's India, given the high land prices—driven northwards, among others, by the conditions under LARR—as well as the reluctance of banks to extend liberal credit to industrial developers. With the creditworthiness of private investors dropping fast from a lender's perspective, not only are private projects finding it difficult to take off, but even public-private-partnerships (PPPs) are limping. Both categories of industrial projects must satisfy the requirements of prior consent, social impact assessment, compensation, and resettlement and rehabilitation under LARR. Furthermore, with private funds running low, the states need to take on the initial investment responsibilities in PPPs, making state

[16] 'Jewar Farmers Demand Rs 5k per sq km for Selling Land for Greater Noida Airport', *Hindustan Times*, 25 April 2018, https://www.hindustantimes.com/india-news/jewar-farmers-demand-rs-5k-per-sqm-for-selling-land-for-greater-noida-airport/story-zYIoRkFpwf4fTkF2GcndiO.html.

governments mandatory 'first movers' in major infrastructure projects in the country. Many states, while accepting their lead role, would be keen on bypassing the mandatory requirements of LARR in the larger interest of avoiding costs incurred in the procedure, and proceed to direct purchase, even by paying higher premiums. The tendency leads to a couple of outcomes that are again typical of the imperfections characterizing India's land markets.

At a time when land prices are at unprecedentedly high levels—as discussed in detail in the introductory chapter—and state government exchequers are under stress, Indian states are eager to hold on to land, even if such land cannot be put to immediate use. Thus unused acquired land is being stuffed into state land banks, ignoring the stipulation that such land should be returned to the original landowners after a minimum period of time.[17] Several states—Jharkhand, Karnataka, Odisha, Tamil Nadu, Telengana, and Tripura—have made rules circumventing the requirement of returning land to the original owners, and instead retaining it with the state.[18] Higher 'hoarding' of land by states—both in rural and urban areas—creates a situation where other land buyers are being typically 'crowded out' of the land market. The scarcity created by government retention of land would have the obvious impact of further raising prices of available land. It also consolidates the state's primacy in landownership given that the government continues to be the largest landowner.[19] Paradoxically, rather than reducing the government's ownership of land and making land markets in India wider and deeper in terms of availability of land, thereby enabling market-driven land pricing, LARR has succeeded in consolidating and

---

[17] Section 101 of LARR directs land acquired thereunder to be returned to the 'original owner, or owners, or their legal heirs' if such land is lying unutilized after five years from the date of acquisition. Section 101 also provides for such land to be returned to the 'Land Bank' of the appropriate government in the prescribed manner. *The Right to Fair Compensation and Transparency in Land Acquisition, Rehabilitation and Resettlement Act, 2013, section 101.* States are framing rules that prefer the second alternative as opposed to the first.

[18] Kohli and Gupta, 'Mapping Dilutions in a Central Law'.

[19] Ram Singh, 'The Problem of Land Hoarding', *The Hindu*, 8 January 2018, https://www.thehindu.com/opinion/op-ed/the-problem-of-land-hoarding/article22391966.ece.

strengthening the command of the government over landownership. This further entrenches market imperfections and corruption through rent-seeking, given that government agencies and other non-state actors, notably developers, can arrive at 'negotiated' prices for using unutilized surplus land from land banks.

Notwithstanding the issues involved, the inevitability of state governments in India continuing to be central actors in the country's land market must be accepted. In this regard, attention must also be focused on the ability of states to keep buying land. In this era of competitive federalism, land has become a major resource on which states seek to compete, given that access to land empowers state governments with a vital scarce resource, essential for generating revenues. The revenue-generating capacity of land is enormous. Stamp duties on land transactions are an important source of revenue for state governments. Although these rates have significantly reduced over the years, they are still at around 4–8 per cent of the cost of property. From the perspective of state public finances, higher cost of property entails higher collections through stamp duties, creating a perverse incentive for states to keep property prices high. States also collect revenue from registration fees on sales, which are of course much less. Again, from a state finance perspective, further reduction in stamp duties might mean loss of state income,[20] unless it is compensated by sufficient increase in other forms of land revenue, notably property and other taxes. On an average, stamp duties contribute around 11 per cent of the aggregate tax revenues of Indian states, while land revenue accounts for only 1 per cent.[21]

The question that assumes critical importance in this regard is, how do the states generate enough revenues so that they have adequate resources for buying land for infrastructure and pursuing other development schemes that require land? The incentive of utilizing land itself for generating revenue for buying more land remains a powerful, if perverse, one. Very few states have been able to mobilize enough revenues from extra-budgetary sources for achieving fiscal sufficiency.

[20] Prachee Mishra and Rupal Suhag, 'Land Records and Titles in India', PRS India (September 2017), http://www.prsindia.org/administrator/uploads/general/1517552636~~Land%20Records%20and%20Titles%20in%20India.pdf.

[21] Mishra and Suhag, 'Land Records and Titles in India'.

Indeed, far-reaching developments like those with respect to the introduction of the goods and services tax (GST) make the situation even more complex as states do not have individual flexibilities now on a number of items for deciding their revenue targets.

The GST has been a remarkable development in India's public finance. It has subsumed a variety of indirect taxes that were earlier levied by the Central and state governments on goods and services into a unified system of taxes, split into a few slab rates. By doing so, the effort has been to move towards a consolidated pool of revenues, from which states would be allotted their shares. In order to allow states flexibility for choosing their own rates on some specific items, like refined petroleum products and alcohol for human consumption—items that fetch states considerable revenue—these have been kept outside the purview of GST. There have been some ambiguities with respect to the impact of GST on land transactions. Since sale and purchase of land are already subject to stamp duties, these don't attract GST. However, GST is attracted by the renting out of immovable property. The point to ponder is whether land and real estate transactions, including buying/selling/renting and leasing, can, in some way come within the scope of GST and fetch larger revenues for state governments. Indeed, in this respect, it is further worth considering if it is possible to introduce innovative nuances in the GST, so that collections from land and real estate, while being transparent and predictable, contribute exclusively to state government coffers. The issue is worth considering in the light of the long-term sustainability of state government public finances, and the imperative for them to keep buying land, if not acquiring it.

NOT LAST WORDS

India's quest for transitioning to market-based economic mechanisms has had mixed results. The successes have been noticeably more in product markets. However, in the critical factor markets of land, labour, and capital, results have been suboptimal in many instances. Land is perhaps the best example of such suboptimality.

The aggressive employment of eminent domain by the state, through the convenient language of 'public purpose', for obtaining land, was always vulnerable to the growth of collusions between state and non-state actors for maximizing rents and profits in a selective fashion. The

LAA did exactly so, particularly after ownership of land in India was downgraded from a fundamental right to a constitutional right. Lack of proper land records and title deeds, as well as inadequate data on sale deeds and the perverse incentive to suppress sale prices for avoiding taxes, led to situations where compensations to displaced owners were largely inadequate. All these, and more, were expected to be sorted out by LARR. However, what the latter has succeeded in doing is driving the wedge further between a rights-based and markets-based approach to economic development in the country. An overwhelming focus on protection of the rights of landowners and the urge to assure them maximum compensation has deprived land markets in India of the possibilities of discovering the right price signals.

The land markets, therefore, are hardly markets from any standard neoclassical approach. Rather, they are arenas of vicious imperfections, where, as the earlier discussions have noted, state governments remain imperative for the procurement of land for industrial use by private investors. The overriding legislation on acquisition in the country is an overarching framework that various states are trying to escape from in a variety of innovative ways. These innovations are essential as they need to keep acquiring, or buying land, at high rates thanks to the floor on land prices set by LARR. Furthermore, the steady decline in revenues from stamp duties and the lack of adequate compensation from other land revenues create a compelling incentive for states to keep land prices high, maybe by resorting to odd practices like hoarding!

The need of the hour, for correcting distortions and moving on to the framework for establishing an efficient land market capable of correct price discovery, is to reach a consensus on avoiding the cumbersome clauses of LARR. Without sacrificing the core objective of the legislation, which is to safeguard the interests of landowners, a way forward needs to be found out for ensuring land is 'available'. Various states have already shown the way in this direction by subtly deviating from some of the more stringent provisions of the Act. The interesting aspect of such deviations is political neutrality. Both BJP and Congress-led states, along with those led by regional parties, have been active in framing their individual pieces of legislation. In doing so, they have not been apprehensive of acquiring 'anti-farmer' identities. They actually cannot, since amending LARR for ensuring quicker supply of land for infrastructure and other developments cannot be an anti-farmer move.

Not at the price levels that exist now. Moreover, more public goods should benefit all, including farmers, as rural communities respond to opportunities for new livelihoods.

As the next elections to the Indian Parliament scheduled for 2019 draw closer, land is expected to assume prominence in the electoral narrative in connection with the discussion on farmers and rural India. Given the proclivities of Indian political parties, particularly the BJP and the Congress, the 'necessary' optics of donning pro-farmer mantles might again mean that work on sorting out the creases in LARR gets shelved for the time being. However, in the foreseeable future, it is necessary to ensure that it is either amended, or its draconian provisions don't affect the development of land markets in India through active encouragement of state-specific legislation. The convergence of across-the-board political urgency in this regard, as seen over the last three years, is a heartening sign.

Bibliography

Albouy, David, Gabriel Ehrlich, and Minchul Shin. 2018. Metropolitan Land Values, *Review of Economics and Statistics*, 100, no. 3: 454–66.

Alchian, Armen A. and Harold Demsetz. 1973. 'The Property Right Paradigm', *The Journal of Economic History* 33, no. 1: 16–27, doi:10.1017/s0022050700076403.

Alonso, William. 1964. *Location and Land Use: Toward a General Theory of Land Rent*. Cambridge, MA: Harvard University Press.

Alston, Lee, Gary Libecap, and Robert Schneider. 1996. 'The Determinants and Impact of Property Rights: Land Titles on the Brazilian Frontier', *The Journal of Law, Economics, and Organization* 12, no. 1: doi:10.3386/w5405.

Angad, Abhishek. 2012. 'Lokayukta Verdict on BMIC "Land Grab" Case on October 4th', *Citizen Matters*, 2 October.

Annez, P. and S. Gangopadhyay. eds. nd. *India's Public Lands: Responsive, Transparent, and Fiscally Responsible Asset Management*. Gurgaon: IDF, idfresearch.org/download.php?pid=240&page=race.

Annez, P., B. Bhatt, and B. Patel. 2014. 'What Getting Land Title Really Means'. New York: Marron Institute of Urban Management, New York University, http://bit.ly/2gbSr7P.

Austin, Granville. 2000. *The Indian Constitution: Cornerstone of a Nation*. New Delhi: Oxford University Press.

———. 2003. *Working a Democratic Constitution: A History of the Indian Experience*. New Delhi: Oxford University Press.

Balakrishnan, Sai. 2019. *Shareholder Cities: Agrarian to Urban Land Transformations along Economic Corridors in Liberalizing India*. Philadelphia, PA: University of Pennsylvania Press (forthcoming).

Bandelj, Nina, Kristen Shorette, and Elizabeth Sowers. 2011. 'Work and Neoliberal Globalization: A Polanyian Synthesis', *Sociology Compass* 5, no. 9: doi:10.1111/j.1751-9020.2011.00408.x.

Banerjee-Guha, Swapna. ed. 2010. *Accumulation by Dispossession: Transformative Cities in the New Global Order*. New Delhi: Sage.

Bedi, Heather Plumridge. 2013. 'Special Economic Zones: National Land Challenges, Localized Protest', *Contemporary South Asia* 21, no.1: doi/abs/1 0.1080/09584935.2012.757582.

Bedi, Heather Plumridge and Louise Tillin. 2015. 'Inter-state Competition, Land Conflicts and Resistance in India', *Oxford Development Studies* 43, no. 2: doi:10.1080/13600818.2015.1035246.

Bedi, Pallavi and Sana Gangwani. 2017. *The Right to Fair Compensation and Transparency in Land Acquisition, Rehabilitation and Resettlement Bill, 2013*, PRS Legislative Research, http://bit.ly/2zp1uuN.

Bertaud, Alain. 2002. 'The Economic Impact of Land and Urban Planning Regulations in India', 11 April, http://alain-bertaud.com.

———. 2011. 'Mumbai FAR/FSI Conundrum', revised 20 July 2011, http://alainbertaud.com.

———. 2014. 'Cities as Labor Markets', Working paper #2. New York: Marron Institute of Urban Management, New York University, http://marroninstitute.nyu.edu/uploads/content/Cities_as_Labor_Markets.pdf.

Bertaud, Alain and Jan K. Brueckner. 2005. 'Analyzing Building-Height Restrictions: Predicted Impacts and Welfare Costs', *Regional Science and Urban Economics* 35, no. 2: 109–25.

Bertaud, Alain, Robert Buckley, and Kathryn Owens. 2003. 'Is Indian Urban Policy Impoverishing?', Paper presented at the World Bank: Urban Research Symposium, December.

Besley, Timothy and Robin Burgess. 2000. 'Land Reform, Poverty Reduction, and Growth: Evidence from India', *Quarterly Journal of Economics* 115, no. 2: 389–430.

Bhattacharjee, S., R. Sinha, and K. Dutta. 2017. 'Fair Pricing of Land and its Compensation in an Emerging Economy: Case for India', http://bit.ly/2zb2Ic8.

Bhole, L.M. and Jitendra Mahakud. 2004. 'Trends and Determinants of Corporate Capital Structure in India: A Panel Data Analysis', *Finance India* 18, no. 1: 37–46.

Bidwai, Praful. 2007. 'From Singur to Nandigram & Beyond: Development as Dispossession', http://www.prafulbidwai.org/index.php.

Bishop, Joshua T. 1999. 'Valuing Forests: A Review of Methods and Applications in Developing Countries'. Environmental Economics Programme, International Institute for Environment and Development, http://bit.ly/2yqpMpQ.

Biswas, Asit and Cecilia Tortajada. 2001. 'Development and Dams: A Global Perspective', *Water Resources Development* 17, no. 1: 9–21.

Block, Fred. 2008. 'Polanyi's Double Movement and the Reconstruction of Critical Theory', *Revue Interventions Économiques* 38: 1–14, http://journals.openedition.org/interventionseconomiques/274.

Block, Fred and Margaret R. Somers. 1984. 'Beyond the Economistic Fallacy: The Holistic Social Science of Karl Polanyi', in Theda Skocpol, ed., *Vision and Method in Historical Sociology*. Cambridge: Cambridge University Press.

———. 2014. *The Power of Market Fundamentalism: Karl Polanyi's Critique*. Cambridge, MA: Harvard University Press.

Borras Jr., Saturnino M., Ruth Hall, Ian Scoones, Ben White, and Wendy Wolford. 2011. 'Towards a Better Understanding of Global Land Grabbing: An Editorial Introduction', *The Journal of Peasant Studies* 38, no. 2: doi: 10.1080/03066150.2011.559005.

Brass, Tom. 1995. *New Farmers' Movements in India*. Ilford, Essex; Portland, Oregon: Frank Cass.

Brueckner, Jan K. 1982. 'A Note on Sufficient Conditions for Negative Exponential Population Densities', *Journal of Regional Science* 22, no. 3: 353–9.

Brueckner, Jan K. and David A. Fansler. 1983. 'The Economics of Urban Sprawl: Theory and Evidence on the Spatial Sizes of Cities', *The Review of Economics and Statistics* 65, no. 3: 479–82.

Brueckner, Jan K. and Kala S. Sridhar. 2013. 'Response to Patel: In Defence of Relaxed FSI Limits', *Economic & Political Weekly*, XLVIII, no. 39: 82.

Brueckner, Jan K. and Kala Seetharam Sridhar. 2012. 'Measuring Welfare Gains from Relaxation of Land-Use Restrictions: The Case of India's Building-Height Limits', *Regional Science and Urban Economics* 42, no. 6: 1061–7, doi 10.1016/j.regsciurbeco.2012.08.003.

Brueckner, Jan K. and Somik Lall. 2015. 'Cities in Developing Countries: Fueled by Rural–Urban Migration, Lacking in Tenure Security, and Short of Affordable Housing', in Gilles Duranton, J. Vernon Henderson, and William C. Strange, eds, *Handbook of Regional and Urban Economics*, pp. 1399–1455. Amsterdam: Elsevier.

Burawoy, Michael. 2010. 'From Polanyi to Pollyanna: The False Optimism of Global Labor Studies', *Global Labour Journal* 1, no. 2: 301–13, doi: 10.15173/glj.v1i2.1079.

Carter, Michael R. and Pedro Olinto. 1998. 'Do the "Poor but Efficient" Survive in the Land Market? Capital Access and Land Accumulation in Paraguay'. Paper presented at the XXIst International Congress of the Latin American Studies Association.

Central Compilation & Translation Press, Central Government of China. 2016. *The 13th Five-Year Plan for Economic and Social Development of the People's Republic of China*, http://ghs.ndrc.gov.cn/ghwb/gjwngh/.

Cernea, Michael M., ed. 1999. *The Economics of Involuntary Resettlement: Questions and Challenges.* Washington, D.C.: World Bank.

Chakravarty, Sukhamoy. 1987. *Development Planning: The Indian Experience.* New Delhi: Oxford University Press.

Chakravorty, Sanjoy. 2003. 'Capital Source and the Location of Industrial Investment: A Tale of Divergence from Post-reform India', *Journal of International Development* 15, no. 3: 365–83.

———. 2013. 'A New Price Regime: Land Markets in Urban and Rural India', *Economic & Political Weekly* XLIII, no. 7: 45–54.

———. 2013. 'On Land, No Lessons Learnt', *The Indian Express*, 30 August, http://indianexpress.com/article/opinion/columns/on-land-no-lessons-learnt/.

———. 2013. *The Price of Land: Acquisition, Conflict, Consequence.* New Delhi: Oxford University Press.

———. 2015. 'Land Acquisition and the Rent-Seeking State', *Seminar* 674 (State of Democracy): 35–9.

———. 2016. 'Land Acquisition in India: The Political-Economy of Changing the Law', *Area Development and Policy* 1, no. 1: 48–62, doi: 10.1080/23792949.2016.1160325.

Chakravorty, Sanjoy, S. Chandrasekhar, and Karthikeya Naraparaju. 2018. 'Income Generation and Inequality in India's Agricultural Sector: The Consequences of Land Fragmentation', http://www.igidr.ac.in/pdf/publication/WP-2016-028.pdf.

Chandran, Rina. 2017. 'India's Bullet Train Project Reignites Debate on Land for "Public Purpose"', *Reuters*, 25 September.

Chitra, K.P. 2013. Politics of Land Acquisition and Conversion: With Reference to Two Development Projects in Kerala. PhD diss. Tata Institute of Social Work.

Dandekar, V.M. and Nilakantha Rath. 1971. 'Poverty in India', *Economic & Political Weekly* VI, nos 1 and 2: 25–7, 29–48, 106–46.

Das, Gurcharan. 2002. *India Unbound: From Independence to the Global Information Age.* New Delhi: Penguin.

Das, Hem Chandra Lal. 1993. *Agricultural Efficiency in India: An Inter-regional Analysis.* New Delhi: Mittal.

Das, S. 2015. 'Sanand: The New Global Auto Hub', *Business Standard*, 23 March, http://www.business-standard.com/article/companies/sanand-the-new-global-auto-hub-115032200818_1.html.

Das-Gupta, A. and S. Gopalakrishnan. 1986. *Stamp Duties and Registration Fees in West Bengal.* Report Prepared for the Government of West Bengal, National Institute of Public Finance and Policy, http://www.nipfp.org.in/media/

medialibrary/2014/10/STAMP_DUTIES_AND_REGISTRATION_
FEES_IN_WEST_BENGAL__DRAFT_REPORT_.pdf.

Dasgupta, Jyotirindra. 1989. 'India: Democratic Becoming and Combined Development', in Larry Diamond, Juan Linz, and Seymour Martin Lipset, eds, *Democracy in Developing Countries*, pp. 53–104. Boulder, CO: Lynne Rienner.

Datta Dey, Paramita and Satvik Dev. 2006. 'Rent Control Laws in India: A Critical Analysis', Working paper WP06-04. New Delhi: National Institute of Urban Affairs, www.niua.org.

Davies, Keith. 1984. *Law of Compulsory Purchase and Compensation*. London: Butterworths.

Deininger, Klaus and Gershon Feder. 2014. 'Land Registration, Economic Development, and Poverty Reduction', in *Property Rights and Land Policies*, pp. 257–91. Cambridge: Lincoln Institute of Land Policy.

Deininger, Klaus, Derek Byerlee, Jonathan Lindsay, Andrew Norton, Harris Selod, and Mercedes Stickler. 2011. *Rising Global Interest in Farmland: Can It Yield Sustainable and Equitable Benefits?* Washington, D.C.: World Bank.

Deng, Xiangzheng, Jikun Huang, Scott Rozelle, and Emi Uchida. 2008. 'Growth, Population and Industrialization, and Urban Land Expansion of China', *Journal of Urban Economics* 63, no. 1: 96–115.

De Soto, Hernando. 2000. *The Mystery of Capital: Why Capitalism Triumphs in the West and Fails Everywhere Else*. New York: Basic Books.

Dhawan, B. 1989. *The Big Dams: Claims and Counter Claims*. New Delhi: Commonwealth.

Djurfeldt G., V. Athreya, N. Jayakumar, S. Lindberg, A. Rajagopal, and R. Vidyasagar. 2008. 'Agrarian Change and Social Mobility in Tamil Nadu', *Economic & Political Weekly* XLIII, no. 45: 50–61.

Dreze, Jean and Amartya Sen. 1990. *Hunger and Public Action*. New Delhi: Oxford University Press.

Duflo, Esther and Rohini Pande. 2007. 'Dams', *Quarterly Journal of Economics* 122, no. 2: 601–46.

Edelman, Marc. 2005. 'Bringing the Moral Economy Back in…to the Study of 21st -Century Transnational Peasant Movements', *American Anthropologist* 107, no. 3: 331–45, doi:10.1525/aa.2005.107.3.331.

Feder, Gershon and David Feeny. 1991. 'Land Tenure and Property Rights: Theory and Implications for Development Policy', *The World Bank Economic Review* 5, no. 1: 135–53, doi:10.1093/wber/5.1.135.

Feder, Gershon, Tongroj Onchan, and Tejaswi Raparla. 1988. 'Collateral, Guaranties and Rural Credit in Developing Countries: Evidence from Asia', *Agricultural Economics* 2, no. 3 : 231–45, doi:10.1016/0169-5150(88)90005-9.

Feng, Yaoyun. 2013. Chongtu de Chixuxing: S Cun Nongmin Yu Zhengfu Zhengdi Jiufen Wenti Yanjiu (冲突的持续性：S村农民与政府征地纠纷问题研究) [The Continuation of Conflict: A Study on Disputes on Land Expropriation between the Peasants and the Government in S Countryside]. PhD diss. Jilin University.

Fernandes, Walter. 1998. 'Development-Induced Displacement in Eastern India', in S.C. Dube, ed., *Antiquity to Modernity in Tribal India*, Vol. 1: *Continuity and Change among the Tribals*, pp. 217–301. New Delhi: Inter-India Publications.

———. 2004. 'Rehabilitation Policy for the Displaced', *Economic & Political Weekly* XXXIX, no. 12: 1191–3.

———. 2007. 'Singur and the Displacement Scenario', *Economic & Political Weekly* XLII, no. 3: 203–6.

———. 2008. 'Displacement and Land Alienation from Common Property Resources', in L. Mehta, ed., *Displaced by Development: Confronting Marginalization and Gender Injustice*, pp. 105–29. New Delhi: Sage.

———. 2008. 'Sixty Years of Development-Induced Displacement in India: Scale, Impacts, and the Search for Alternatives', in H.M. Mathur, ed., *India Social Development Report 2008: Development and Displacement*, pp. 89–102. New Delhi: Oxford University Press.

Fogelsong, Richard. 2014. *Planning the Capitalist City: The Colonial Era to the 1920s*. Princeton, NJ: Princeton University Press.

Foshan New Town. 2016. 'Foshan Xincheng Fazhan Licheng' (佛山新城发展历程) ['The Development Process of Foshan New Town'], http://www.fsnewcity.gov.cn/xwzx/rsdp/lsyg/201605/t20160506_5599133.html.

Frankel, Francine R. 1971. *India's Green Revolution: Economic Gains and Political Costs*. Princeton, NJ: Princeton University Press; Bombay: Oxford University Press.

———. 2005. *India's Political Economy: The Gradual Revolution (1947–2004)*, 2nd edition. New York: Oxford University Press.

Gadgil, Madhav and Ramchandra Guha. 1995. *Ecology and Equity: The Use and Abuse of Nature in Contemporary India*. New York and London: Routledge.

Gemici, Kurtuluş and Manjusha Nair. 2016. 'Globalization and Its Countermovement: Marxian Contention or Polanyian Resistance?', *Sociology Compass* 10, no. 7: doi.org/10.1111/soc4.12389.

Geshkov, Marin V. and Joseph S. DeSalvo. 2012. 'The Effect of Land-Use Controls on the Spatial Size of US Urbanized Areas', *Journal of Regional Science* 52, no. 4: 648–75.

Ghatak, Maitreesh and Parikshit Ghosh. 2011. 'The Land Acquisition Bill: A Critique and a Proposal', *Economic & Political Weekly* XLVI, no. 41: 65–72.

————. 2015. 'Land Acquisition Act: Addressing Both Justice and Prosperity', Ideas for India, http://www.ideasforindia.in/article.aspx?article_id= 1483.

Ghatak, Maitreesh and Sanchari Roy. 2007. 'Land Reform and Agricultural Productivity in India: A Review of the Evidence', *Oxford Review of Economic Policy* 23, no. 2: 251–69.

Ghatak, Maitreesh, Sandip Mitra, Dilip Mookherjee, and Anusha Nath. 2012. 'Land Acquisition and Compensation in Singur: What Really Happened?', http://personal.lse.ac.uk/ghatak/singur.pdf.

Glaeser, Edward L. and Bryce A. Ward. 2009. 'The Causes and Consequences of Land Use Regulation: Evidence from Greater Boston', *Journal of Urban Economics* 65, no. 3: 265–78.

Gopalakrishnan, Shankar. 2012. *Control, Regulation and Expropriation of India's Forest and Common Lands*. Delhi: Rights and Resources Initiative.

Gopalkrishnan, E. 2000. 'ICOLD Comment on Report of World Commission on Dams', www.dams.org/report/reaction/icoldindia.htm.

Gorringe, H. 2005. *Untouchable Citizens: Dalit Movements and Democratisation in Tamil Nadu* (Cultural Subordination and the Dalit Challenge). New Delhi; Thousand Oaks, CA: Sage.

Goswami, Amlanjyoti and Deepika Jha. 2016. 'Your Title Is Not Ready Yet: Rajasthan's Land Titling Legislation', *Economic & Political Weekly* LI, no. 34: 26–9.

Goswami, Bhaskar. 2007. 'Special Economic Zones: Lessons from China', countercurrents.org.

Government of India. 1994. 'Demand for Creating of Tamil Nadu Land Reforms Measure'. Rajya Sabha Secretariat.

————. 2002. *Report on Reforming Investment Approval & Implementation*: Part II: *Downstream Issues: Implementation and Operation*. New Delhi: Planning Commission.

————. 2011. 'Selected Socio-economic Statistics', Ministry of Statistics and Programme Implementation, http://mospi.nic.in/mospi_new/upload/ sel_socio_eco_stats_ind_2001_28oct11.pdf.

————. 2017. 'State-Wise Distribution of Approved SEZs', Ministry of Commerce and Industry, http://www.sezindia.nic.in/writereaddata/pdf/ StatewiseDistribution-SEZ.pdf.

Government of Maharashtra. 1984. *Report of Fact Finding Committee on Regional Imbalance in Maharashtra (under the chairmanship of V.M. Dandekar)*.

————. 2013. *Report of the High Level Committee on Balanced Regional Development Issues in Maharashtra*.

Government of Tamil Nadu. 1971. 'Budget 1971–72 Speech of Thiru M Karunanidhi Chief Minister', Madras.

———. 1975. 'Budget 1975–76 Speech of Thiru M Karunanidhi Chief Minister', Madras.

———. 1980. 'Budget 1980–81 Speech of Thiru V.R. Nedunchezhiyan, Minister of Finance', Ministry of Finance (Madras).

———. 2007. 'The Industrial Policy 2007', Industries Department, http://www.tidco.com/images/industrialpolicy_e_2007.pdf.

Grugel, Jean and Pía Riggirozzi. 2012. 'Post-neoliberalism in Latin America: Rebuilding and Reclaiming the State after Crisis', *Development and Change* 43, no. 1: doi: 10.1111/j.1467-7660.2011.01746.x.

Guangdong Provincial Government. 1993. 'Guangdong Zhengdi Guanli Guiding' (广东征地管理规定) ['Regulations on Land Acquisition in Guangdong'], http://www.gd.gov.cn/govpub/dffg/200606/t20060616_1479.htm.

———. 2005. 'Guangdong Renmin Zhengfu Bangongting Guanyu Zhuanfa Sheng Guotu Ziyuanting Guanyu Shenhua Zhengdi Zhidu Gaige De Yijian De Tongzhi' (广东人民政府办公厅关于转发国土资源厅关于深化征地制度改革的意见的通知) ['Circular on the Opinion on Deepening the Land Expropriation Institutions by the Land and Resource Department'], Issue No. 29.

Guangzhou Government. 2012. 'Yinfa Guangzhou Shi Zhengdi Buchang Baohu Biaozhun Zhidao Yijian (Shixing)de Tongzhi>'(印发《广州市征地补偿保护标准指导意见(试行)的通知》)['Circular on the Tentative Guidelines of the Criterion for Compensation for Land Acquired in Guangzhou'], http://www.gz.gov.cn/gzswjk/2.2.21/201201/42f8ed642461431d8970f1ecc36ed0de.shtml.

———. 2017. 'Guangzhoushi Renmin Zhengfu Bangongting Guanyu Yinfa Guangzhoushi Nongmin Jiti Suoyou Tudi Zhengshou Buchang Shixing Banfa De Tongzhi'(广州市人民政府办公厅关于印发广州市农民集体所有土地征收补偿试行办法的通知) ['Circular on the Interim Measures for Land Expropriation of the Peasants' Collective-owned Land in Guangzhou by the Office of the Municipal Government of Guangzhou', http://www.gz.gov.cn/gzgov/s2812/201708/cb90a3dc1c764b13be-a3688fc9d66687.shtml.

Gudavarthy, Ajay. 2012. 'Can We De-stigmatise Reservations in India?', *Economic & Political Weekly* XLVII, no. 6: 55–62.

Guha-Khasnobis, Basudeb and Saumitra N. Bhaduri. 2002. 'Determinants of Capital Structure in India (1990–1998): A Dynamic Panel Data Approach', *Journal of Economic Integration* 17, no. 4: 761–76. doi:10.11130/jei.2002.17.4.761.

Gujarat Industrial Development Corporation. nd. 'GIDC Land Policy 2010', https://gidc.gujarat.gov.in/pdf/Whats_New/Participative_Policy_Development_New_Estates.pdf.

————. n.d. 'Sanand Industrial Estate', https://gidc.gujarat.gov.in/pdf/gidc-presentation/GIDC_Sanand_Industrial_Estate.pdf.

Gujarat Infrastructural Development Board. 2013. 'Industrial Park Development in the State of Gujarat', last modified 7 October 2013, http://www.igep.in/live/hrdpmp/hrdpmaster/igep/content/e48745/e49028/e56649/e57530/04_GIZintconf710_VR.pdf.

Gupta, Akhil. 1998. *Postcolonial Developments: Agriculture in the Making of Modern India*. Durham, NC: Duke University Press.

Hall, Ruth, Marc Edelman, Saturnino M. Borras Jr, Ian Scoones, Ben White, and Wendy Wolford. 2015. 'Resistance, Acquiescence or Incorporation? An Introduction to Land Grabbing and Political Reactions "From Below"', *The Journal of Peasant Studies* 42, nos 3–4: doi: 10.1080/03066150.2015.1036746.

Haque, T. 2016. *Report of the Expert Committee on Land Leasing*, NITI Aayog, Government of India, 31 March, http://niti.gov.in/writereaddata/files/document_publication/Final_Report_Expert_Group_on_Land_Leasing.pdf.

Harriss, John. 1987. 'Capitalism and Peasant Production: The Green Revolution in India', in Teodor Shanin, ed., *Peasants and Peasant Societies*. London: Penguin.

————. 2009. 'Globalization(s) and Labour in China and India: Introductory Reflections', *Global Labor Journal* 1, no. 1: 3–11, doi: 10.15173/glj.v1i1.1062.

Harvey, David. 1982. *The Limits to Capital*. Oxford: Basil Blackwell.

————. 2003. *The New Imperialism*. Oxford: Oxford University Press.

Heymann, Eric and M. Vaeth. 2007. '450 Billion Reasons to Invest in India's Infrastructure', *Deutsche Bank Research Report, Asia Current Issues*, 28 November.

Hillygus, D. Sunshine and Todd G. Shields. 2009. *The Persuadable Voter: Wedge Issues in Presidential Campaigns*. Princeton, NJ: Princeton University Press.

Hobsbawm, Eric. 1975. *The Age of Capital, 1848–1875*. New York: New American Library.

Ihlanfeldt, Keith R. 2007. 'The Effect of Land Use Regulation on Housing and Land Prices', *Journal of Urban Economics* 61, no. 3: 420–35.

Institute of Applied Manpower Research, Planning Commission, Government of India. 2012. *India Human Development Report 2011: Towards Social Inclusion*. New Delhi: Oxford University Press.

Jaiprakash, K. 2016. 'Maps to Nowhere: Village Surveys of Little Help in Marking Encroachments', *The Times of India*, 11 August.

Jenkins, Rob. 1999. *Democratic Politics and Economic Reform in India*. Cambridge: Cambridge University Press.

————. ed. 2004. *Regional Reflections: Comparing Politics across India's States*. New York: Oxford University Press.

Jing, Jun. 2000. 'Displacement, Resettlement, Rehabilitation, Repatriation and Development: China Report', Contributing Paper to World Commission on Dams.

Jog, Sanjay. 2016. 'Cidco Claims It Has Started Giving Developed Plots to Affected People', *Business Standard*, 12 July, http://www.business-standard.com/article/economy-policy/cidco-claims-it-has-started-giving-developed-plots-to-affected-people-116071100473_1.html.

Johnson, Chalmers. 1983. *MITI and the Japanese Miracle: The Growth of Industrial Policy, 1925–1975*. Stanford, CA: Stanford University Press.

Jones Lang Lasalle and PHD Chamber of Commerce and Industry. 2018. *Affordable Housing: The Indian Perspective & Future Outlook: Building Change & Sustainable Communities*. New Delhi.

Kaushal, Pradeep and Liz Matthew. 2015. 'Land Law: Oppn Staring Down, Govt May Blink', *The Indian Express*, 23 February.

Kennedy, Loraine. 2014. 'Haryana: Beyond the Urban–Rural Divide', in Rob Jenkins, Loraine Kennedy, and Partha Mukhopadhyay, eds, *Power, Policy, and Protest: The Politics of India's Special Economic Zones*. New Delhi: Oxford University Press.

Kohli, Atul. 2012. *Poverty Amid Plenty in the New India*. Cambridge: Cambridge University Press.

Kohli, Kanchi and Debayan Gupta. 2017. 'Mapping Dilutions in a Central Law: A Comparative Analysis of Rules Made under the Right to Fair Compensation and Transparency in Land Acquisition, Rehabilitation and Resettlement (LARR) Act, 2013', Occasional Paper, Centre for Policy Research, India.

Kosalram, S.A. 1973. 'Political Economy of Agriculture in Tamil Nadu', *Social Scientist* 1, no. 12: 3–21.

Krishnan, K.P., Venkatesh Panchapagesan, and Madalasa Venkataraman. 2017. 'Distortions in Land Markets and Their Implications for Credit Generation in India', *Economic & Political Weekly* LII, no. 35: 48–55.

Kumar, Pushpendra and B.K. Sinha. 2000. *Land Reforms in India: An Unfinished Agenda* (Vol. 5). New Delhi: Sage.

Kundu, Amitabh, Girish Kumar Misra, and Rajkishor Meher. 1986. *Location of Public Enterprises and Regional Development*. New Delhi: Concept Publishing Company.

Kurmanath, K.V. 'In AP Capital, Blockchain Technology Secures Land Records', *The Hindu Business Line*, 8 January, https://www.thehindubusinessline.com/info-tech/in-ap-capital-blockchain-technology-secures-land-records/article10020465.ece.

Lakshmikantha, B.K. 2010. 'KIADB Acts Like Real Estate Agent, Says Karnataka High Court', *DNA*, 11 December.

Leaf, Murray J. 1980/1981. 'The Green Revolution in a Punjab Village, 1965–1978', *Pacific Affairs* 53, no. 4 (Winter): 617–25.

Levien, Michael. 2007. 'India's Double-Movement: Polanyi and the National Alliance of People's Movements', *Berkeley Journal of Sociology* 51 (2007): 119–49, http://www.jstor.org/stable/41035623.

———. 2011. 'Special Economic Zones and Accumulation by Dispossession in India', *Journal of Agrarian Change* 11, no. 4: 454–83.

———. 2013. 'The Politics of Dispossession: Theorizing India's "Land Wars"', *Politics and Society* 41, no. 3: 351–94, doi:10.1177/0032329213493751.

Li, Tania M. 2014. *Land's End: Capitalist Relations on an Indigenous Frontier.* Durham, NC: Duke University Press.

Lin, Yibiao. 2011. *Bei Zhengdi Nongmin Chayixing Shouchang Yiyuan Yanjiu*(被征地农民差异性受偿意愿研究) [*Studies on the Willingness of Peasants towards the Compensation in Land Acquisition in the Fujian Provinces*]. Fuzhou: Fujian People Publishing House.

Liu, Shouying. 2014. *Zhimian Zhongguo Tudi Wenti*(直面中国土地问题) [*Land Issue in Transitional China*]. Beijing: China Development Press.

Lobo, Lancy and Shashikant Kumar. 2009. *Land Acquisition, Displacement and Resettlement in Gujarat 1947–2004.* New Delhi: Sage.

López, Ramón. 1997. 'Environmental Externalities in Traditional Agriculture and the Impact of Trade Liberalization: The Case of Ghana', *Journal of Development Economics* 53, no. 1: 17–39, doi:10.1016/s0304-3878(97)00015-1.

Lutringer, Christine. 2010. 'A Movement of "Subsidized Capitalists"? The Multi-level Influence of the Bharatiya Kisan Union in India', *International Review of Sociology* 20, no. 3: doi: 10.1080/03906701.2010.511913.

Madhavan, M.R. 2013. 'Land Acquisition Process Can Take 50 Months', *The PRS Blog*, http://www.prsindia.org/theprsblog/?author=6.

Mahalanobis, P.C. 1961. *Talks on Planning.* Bombay: Asia Publishing House.

Makkar, Sahil. 2016. 'Rajasthan Govt Does It Again, Ushers in Crucial Land Reforms', SmartInvestor.in, 10 April, http://bit.ly/2hHGgA8.

Malik, Arun and Robert M. Schwab. 1991a. 'Optimal Investments to Establish Property Rights in Land', *Journal of Urban Economics* 29, no. 3: 295–309, doi:10.1016/0094-1190(91)90003-p.

———. 1991b. 'The Economics of Tax Amnesties', *Journal of Public Economics* 46, no. 1: 29–49, doi:10.1016/0047-2727(91)90063-8.

Malpezzi, Stephen and Vinod K. Tewari. 1991. *Costs and Benefits of Residential Rent Control in Bangalore, India.* Washington, D.C.: World Bank, Policy, Planning and Research Staff, Infrastructure and Urban Development Department, Report INU 82, http://documents.worldbank.org/curated/en/817011468772802607/pdf/multi-page.pdf.

Mamonova, Natalia. 2015. 'Resistance or Adaptation? Ukrainian Peasants' Responses to Large-Scale Land Acquisitions', *The Journal of Peasant Studies* 42, nos 3–4: doi:10.1080/03066150.2014.993320.

Manikumar, K.A. 1997, 'Caste Clashes in South Tamil Nadu', *Economic & Political Weekly* XXXII, no. 36: 2242–3.

Manoj C.G. 2015. 'Land Bill Sent to Joint Panel, Cong Split on Move', *The Indian Express*, 13 May.

Manthan Adhyayan Kendra. 2009. 'The First Development-Caused Displacements in India: The Forgotten People of Bhakra Nangal', in R. Modi, ed., *Beyond Relocation: The Imperative of Sustainable Resettlement*. New Delhi: Sage.

Mathew, Liz, Pradeep Kaushal, and Maneesh Chhibber. 2015. 'Allies Akali Dal, Sena Join Opp to Push BJP in a Corner over Land Law', *The Indian Express*, 25 February.

Mathur, Shishir. 2013. 'Use of Land Pooling and Reconstitution for Urban Development: Experiences from Gujarat, India', *Habitat International* 38: 199–206.

Mayer, Peter. 2010. 'Are There Political Patterns in Communal Violence in India?', Biennial Conference of the Asian Studies Association, http://test. asaa.asn.au/ASAA2010/reviewed_papers/Mayer-Peter.pdf.

McGrath, Daniel T. 2005. 'More Evidence on the Spatial Scale of Cities', *Journal of Urban Economics* 58, no. 1: 1–10.

McKinsey Global Initiative. 2010. *India's Urban Awakening: Building Inclusive Cities, Sustaining Economic Growth*. Washington, D.C.: McKinsey & Co.

McKinsey Global Institute. 2001. 'India: The Growth Imperative', last modified 2001, www.mckinsey.com/~/media/McKinsey/Global%20Themes/ India/Growth%20imperative%20for%20India/MGI_The_growth_imperative_for_India.ashx.

McMichael, Philip. 2005. 'Global Development and the Corporate Food Regime', in Frederick H. Buttel and Philip McMichael, eds, *New Directions in the Sociology of Global Development* (Research in Rural Sociology and Development, Vol. 11), pp. 265–99. Bingley: Emerald Group Publishing Limited.

———. 2014. 'Rethinking Land Grab Ontology', *Rural Sociology* 79, no. 1: doi: 10.1111/ruso.12021.

McMillen, Daniel P. 2006. 'Testing for Monocentricity', in Richard J. Arnott and Daniel P. McMillen, eds, *A Companion to Urban Economics*, pp. 128–40. Oxford: Blackwell.

Menon, Manju, Kanchi Kohli, and Debayan Gupta. 2017. 'In State-level Changes to Land Laws, a Return to Land Grabbing in Development's Name', *The Wire*, 28 September, http://bit.ly/2gGolKz.

Merrilat, H.C.L. 1970. *Land and the Constitution of India*. Bombay: N.M. Tripathi.

Mills, Edwin S. 1967. 'An Aggregative Model of Resource Allocation in a Metropolitan Area', *The American Economic Review* 57, no. 2: 197–210.

Ministry of Rural Development, Department of Land Records. 2013. *National Land Utilization Policy: Framework for Land Use Planning & Management*, Policy Draft. Government of India, https://smartnet.niua.org/sites/default/files/resources/draft_national_land_utilisation_policy_july_2013.pdf.

Mishra, Alok K.N. 2017. 'It's a Disaster in the Making: 80% of Buildings in East Delhi "Illegal"', *The Economic Times*, 4 July.

Mishra, Prachee and Rupal Suhag. 2017. 'Land Records and Titles in India', PRS India, September, http://www.prsindia.org/administrator/uploads/general/1517552636~~Land%20Records%20and%20Titles%20in%20India.pdf.

Mitra, Subrata. 2011. *Politics in India: Structure, Process and Policy*. London: Routledge.

———. 2017. *Politics in India: Structure, Process and Policy*. London: Routledge.

———. 2018. 'Democracy's Angry Crowds: Civil Society and Legitimacy in India', in Vinod Rai and Amitendu Palit, eds, *Seven Decades of Independent India*, pp. 189–200. Gurgaon: Penguin Viking.

Modi, Renu. ed. 2009. *Beyond Relocation: The Imperative of Sustainable Resettlement*. New Delhi: Sage.

Moore, Barrington. 1966. *Social Origins of Dictatorship and Democracy: Lord and Peasant in the Making of the Modern World*. Boston: Beacon Press.

More, Thomas. 1515 [1988]. *Utopia*, eds George M. Logan and Robert M. Adams, Cambridge Texts in the History of Political Thought. Cambridge: Cambridge University Press.

Moses, Brindavan C. 1995. 'Struggle for Panchama Lands: Dalit Assertion in Tamil Nadu', *Economic & Political Weekly* XXX, no. 5: 47–8.

Mukhopadhyay, Partha and Kanhu Charan Pradhan. 2009. 'Location of SEZs and Policy Benefits: What Does the Data Say?', in Centre for Policy Research, *Special Economic Zones: Promise, Performance and Pending Issues*, pp. 61–84. New Delhi: Centre for Policy Research.

Munck, Ronaldo. 2004. 'Globalization, Labor, and the "Polanyi Problem"', *Labor History* 45, no. 3: doi: 10.1080/0023656042000257765.

Murthi, Kavya. 2018. *Land and the Courts*, Daksh, http://dakshindia.org/land-and-the-courts/.

Muth, Richard F. 1969. *Cities and Housing: The Spatial Pattern of Urban Residential Use*. Chicago: University of Chicago Press.

Myrdal, Gunnar. 1968. *Asian Drama: An Inquiry into the Poverty of Nations.* New York: Pantheon.

Nair, Manjusha. 2016. *Undervalued Dissent: Informal Workers' Politics in India*. Albany, NY: SUNY Press.

————. 2018. 'State-Embedded Villages: Rural Protests and Rights Awareness in India and China', in Prasenjit Duara and Elizabeth Perry, eds, *Beyond Regimes: China and India Compared*. Cambridge: Harvard University Press.

————. 2019. 'Land as a Transactional Asset: Moral Economy and Market Logic in Contested Land Acquisition in India', *Development and Change*, published online 22 February: https://doi.org/10.1111/dech.12494.

Narain, Vishal. 2009. 'Growing City, Shrinking Hinterland: Land Acquisition, Transition and Conflict in Peri-urban Gurgaon', *India, Environment and Urbanization* 21, no. 2: 501–12.

Neogi, Rishit. 2017. 'Gujarat's One-Sided Land Policy', *Economic & Political Weekly* LII, no. 38: http://www.epw.in/engage/article/gujarats-one-sided-land-policy.

Ninan, T.N. 2014. 'The UPA's Worst Legacy', *Business Standard*, 21 March.

Pai, Sudha and Avinash Kumar. 2014. 'Uttar Pradesh: Contrasting Cases from the National Capital Region', in Rob Jenkins, Loraine Kennedy, and Partha Mukhopadhyay, eds, *Power, Policy, and Protest: The Politics of India's Special Economic Zones*. New Delhi: Oxford University Press.

Pal, Mahuya and Mohan J. Dutta. 2013. '"Land Is Our Mother": Alternative Meanings of Development in Subaltern Organizing', *Journal of International and Intercultural Communication* 6, no. 3: 203–20, doi:10.1080/17513057.2013.765954.

Palit, Amitendu. 2017. 'Land and Food Acts: Trading Economic Pragmatism for Political Gain', in Supriyo De, ed., *India's Fiscal Policy: Prescriptions, Pragmatics and Practice*, pp. 138–55. Cambridge: Cambridge University Press.

Palit, Amitendu and Subhomoy Bhattacharjee. 2008. *Special Economic Zones in India: Myths and Realities*. Delhi: Anthem Press.

Paliwal, Ankur. 2016. *Land Conflicts in India: An Interim Analysis*. Rights and Resources Initiative, Washington, DC, and Tata Institute of Social Sciences, Mumbai, http://bit.ly/2zo4yHx.

Parasuraman, S. 1999. *The Development Dilemma: Displacement in India*. Basingstoke: Macmillan.

Patel, Shirish. 2013. 'Life between Buildings: The Use and Abuse of FSI', *Economic & Political Weekly* XLVIII, no. 36: 68–74.

Pathak, M. 2010. 'Gujarat Farmers Turn Film Producers', *Mint*, 11 November.

Paulsen, Kurt. 2012. 'Yet Even More Evidence on the Spatial Size of Cities: Urban Spatial Expansion in the US, 1980–2000', *Regional Science and Urban Economics* 42, no. 4: 561–8.

Phatak, V.K. 2013. 'Land Based Fiscal Tools and Practices for Generating Additional Financial Resources', *Capacity Building for Urban Development project*, Ministry of Urban Development, Government of India and World Bank, New Delhi, India.

Polanyi, Karl. 2001 [1944]. *The Great Transformation: The Political and Economic Origins of Our Time.* Boston: Beacon Press.

Pollakowski, Henry O. and Susan M. Wachter. 1990. 'The Effects of Land-Use Constraints on Housing Prices', *Land Economics* 66, no. 3: 315–24.

Press Information Bureau. 2015. 'Acquisition of Tribal Land', 11 March.

————. 2015. The Right to Fair Compensation and Transparency in Land Acquisition, Rehabilitation and Resettlement (Amendment) Ordinance, 30 May, http://pib.nic.in/newsite/PrintRelease.aspx?relid=122149.

Press Trust of India. 2014. 'Focus on "Skill, Scale and Speed" to Compete with China: PM', *The Hindu*, 8 June.

Pushpendra. 1999. 'Dalit Assertion through Electoral Politics', *Economic & Political Weekly* XXXIV, no. 36: 2609–18.

Quigley, John M. and Larry A. Rosenthal. 2005. 'The Effects of Land Use Regulation on the Price of Housing: What Do We Know? What Can We Learn?', *Cityscape: A Journal of Policy Development and Research* 8, no. 1: 69–137.

Quigley, John M. and Steven Raphael. 2005. 'Regulation and the High Cost of Housing in California', *The American Economic Review* 95, no. 2: 323–8.

Rai, Vinod. 2016. 'The Pradhan Mantri Fasal Bima Yojana: India's New Safety Net for Farmers', ISAS Brief No. 432, June.

Rajaraman, Indira. 2016. *Economically Speaking.* New Delhi: Academic Foundation.

Rajshekhar, M. 2013. 'Great Rural Land Rush: 3 to 100-Fold Rise in Farm Land Prices May Not Bode Well', *The Economic Times*, 12 November.

Ramaswamy, K.V. 2007. 'Regional Dimension of Growth and Employment', *Economic & Political Weekly* XLII, no. 49: 47–56.

Ramesh, Jairam and Muhammad Ali Khan. 2015. *The Making of the 2013 Land Acquisition Law.* New Delhi: Oxford University Press.

Rawal, Vikas. 2008. 'Ownership Holdings of Land in Rural India: Putting the Record Straight', *Economic & Political Weekly* XLIII, no. 10: 43–7.

Ren, Xuefei. 2017. 'Land Acquisition, Rural Protests, and the Local State in China and India', *Environment and Planning* 35, no. 1: 25–41.

Reserve Bank of India. 2014. *Basic Statistical Returns of Scheduled Commercial Banks in India.*

————. 2017a. *Handbook of Statistics on Indian Economy.*

————. 2017b. *Indian Household Finance, Report of the Household Finance Committee.* Mumbai: Reserve Bank of India, https://rbidocs.rbi.org.in/rdocs/PublicationReport/Pdfs/HFCRA28D0415E2144A009112DD314ECF5C07.PDF.

————. 2017c. *Trend and Progress of Banking in India.*

Roll, Richard and John Talbott. 2001. 'Political and Economic Freedoms and Prosperity, previously titled: Why Many Developing Nations Just Aren't', eScholarship, University of California.

Roy, Arundhati. 2011. 'Into the Inferno', *New Statesman*, 20 July.

Roy, Srirupa. 2007. *Beyond Belief: India and the Politics of Postcolonial Nationalism.* Durham and London: Duke University Press.

Rudolph, Lloyd I. and Susanne H. Rudolph. 1987. *In Pursuit of Lakshmi: The Political Economy of the Indian State.* Chicago: The University of Chicago Press.

Rukmini S. 2015. 'India's New Farm Suicides Data: Myths and Facts', *The Hindu*, 24 July, http://www.thehindu.com/data/indias-new-farm-suicides-data-myths-and-facts/article7461095.ece.

Sanan, Deepak, D.B. Gupta, and Prerna Prabhakar. 2017. *A Pilot Impact Assessment of the Digital-India Land Records Modernisation Programme.* NCAER, http://www.ncaer.org/publication_details.php?pID=284.

Sanyal, Bishwapriya. 1991. 'Antagonistic Cooperation: A Case Study of Nongovernmental Organizations, Government and Donors' Relationships in Income Generating Projects in Bangladesh', *World Development* 19, no. 10: 1367–79.

Sarkar, Abhirup. 2012. 'Development, Displacement and Food Security: Land Acquisition in India', in Chetan Ghate ed., *Oxford Handbook of the Indian Economy.* New York: Oxford University Press.

Scott, James C. 1976. *The Moral Economy of the Peasant: Rebellion and Subsistence in Southeast Asia.* New Haven, CT: Yale University Press.

Sen, Amartya. 1982. *Poverty and Famines: An Essay on Entitlement and Deprivation.* Oxford: Clarendon Press.

———. 1985. *Commodities and Capabilities.* Amsterdam: North Holland.

Sharma, H.R. 1994. 'Distribution of Landholdings in Rural India, 1953–54 to 1981–82: Implications for Land Reforms', *Economic & Political Weekly* XXIX, no. 13: A12–A25.

Shiva, Vandana. 1991. *The Violence of the Green Revolution.* London: Zed Books.

Silver, Beverly J. and Giovanni Arrighi. 2003. 'Polanyi's "Double Movement": The Belle Époques of British and U.S. Hegemony Compared', *Politics and Society* 31, no. 2: doi: 10.1177/0032329203252274.

Singh, Ram. 2012. 'Inefficiency and Abuse of Compulsory Land Acquisition: An Enquiry into the Way Forward', *Economic & Political Weekly* XLVII, no. 19: 46–53.

———. 2018. 'The Problem of Land Hoarding', *The Hindu*, 8 January, https://www.thehindu.com/opinion/op-ed/the-problem-of-land-hoarding/article22391966.ece.

Singh, Satyajit. 2002. *Taming the Waters: The Political Economy of Large Dams in India.* New Delhi: Oxford University Press.

Sinha, Aseema. 2005. 'Political Foundations of Market-Enhancing Federalism: Theoretical Lessons from India and China', *Comparative Politics* 37, no. 3: doi:10.2307/20072893.

———. 2005. *The Regional Roots of Developmental Politics in India: A Divided Leviathan*. Bloomington, IN: Indiana University Press.

Sivaramakrishnan, K.C. 1976–7. 'New Towns in India: A Report on a Study of Selected New Towns in the Eastern Region', http://www.cprindia.org/sites/default/files/books/NEW%20TOWNS%20IN%20INDIA_1.pdf.

Spivey, Christy. 2008. 'The Mills–Muth Model of Urban Spatial Structure: Surviving the Test of Time?', *Urban Studies* 45, no. 2: 295–312.

Sridhar, Kala Seetharam. 2010. 'Impact of Land Use Regulations: Evidence from India's Cities', *Urban Studies* 47, no. 7: 1541–69.

Sud, Nikita. 2014. 'Governing India's Land', *World Development* 60, no. 1: url: https://ora.ox.ac.uk/objects/uuid:bbd85621-4b2f-42f5-95b3-3025 6ecad1b4.

Tata Services Limited, Department of Economics and Statistics. 2008. *Statistical Outline of India 2007–08*. Mumbai.

Tewari, Ruhi. 2015. 'Land Bill Clears LS: Consent Clause Stays, Govt Yields on Private Parties', *The Indian Express*, 11 March.

Thakkar, H. 2000. 'Assessment of Irrigation in India', in World Commission on Dams, *Dams and Development: A New Framework for Decision Making*. London: EarthScan Publications, http://www.internationalrivers.org/files/world_commission_on_dams_final_report.pdf

Urban Redevelopment Authority of Foshan New Town, the Dadun Village Committee, Dadun Village Economic Cooperative. 2014. 'Lecongzhen Daduncun Zhengcun Gaizao Shishifangan'(乐从镇大墩村整村改造实施方案)['Implementation Plan of the Dadun Village Remake Project'].

Varshney, Ashutosh. 1998. *Democracy, Development, and the Countryside: Urban–Rural Struggles in India*. New York: Cambridge University Press.

Vijayabaskar, M. 2014. 'Tamil Nadu: The Politics of Silence', in Rob Jenkins, Loraine Kennedy, and Partha Mukhopadhyay, eds, *Power, Policy, and Protest: The Politics of India's Special Economic Zones*, pp. 304–31. New Delhi: Oxford University Press.

Wacquant, Loïc. 2010. 'Crafting the Neoliberal State: Workfare, Prisonfare, and Social Insecurity', *Sociological Forum* 25, no. 2: doi: 10.1111/j.1573-7861.2010.01173.x.

Wahi, N., A. Bhatia, D. Gandhi, S. Jain, P. Shukla, and U. Chauhan. 2016. *Land Acquisition in India: A Review of Supreme Court Cases from 1950 to 2016*. New Delhi: Centre for Policy Research.

Wahi, Namita. 2016. 'Property', in Sujit Choudhry, Madhav Khosla, and Pratap Bhanu Mehta, eds, *The Oxford Handbook of the Indian Constitution*, pp. 943–63. Oxford: Oxford University Press.

Wall, John. 1978. 'Foodgrain Management: Pricing, Procurement, Distribution, Import and Storage Policy in India', Occasional Papers, World Bank Staff Working paper No. 279. Washington, D.C.: World Bank.

Wang, Hui. 2013. *Zhongguo Tudi Zhengshou Zhidu Gaige: Lilun, Shishi Yu Zhengce Zuhe* (中国土地征收制度改革：理论, 事实与政策组合) [*Land Requisition System Reform in China: Theories, Facts and Policy Portfolio*]. Hangzhou: Zhejiang University Press.

Wang, Hui and Ran Tao. 2013. *Zhongguo Tudi Zhidu Gaige: Nandian, Tupo Yu Zhengce Zuhe* (中国土地制度改革:难点, 突破与政策组合) [*Chinese Land Institution Reform: Issues, Advancement and Policy Package*]. Beijing: The Commercial Press.

Wang, Shaoguang. 2008. 'Double Movement in China', *Economic & Political Weekly* XLIII, no. 52: url:http://www.jstor.org/stable/40278334.

Wassmer, Robert W. 2006. 'The Influence of Local Urban Containment Policies and State Wide Growth Management on the Size of United States Urban Areas', *Journal of Regional Science* 46, no. 1: 25–65.

White, Michael and Philip Allmendinger. 2003. 'Land-Use Planning and the Housing Market: A Comparative Review of the UK and the USA', *Urban Studies* 40, nos 5–6: 953–72.

Wilkinson, Steven. 2006. *Votes and Violence: Electoral Competition and Ethnic Riots in India*. Cambridge: Cambridge University Press.

Windsor Liscombe, Rhodri. 2006. 'In-dependence: Otto Koenigsberger and Modernist Urban Resettlement in India', *Journal of Planning Perspectives* 21, no. 2: 157–78.

World Bank. 2012. *India: Urbanization beyond Municipalities*. Washington, D.C.: World Bank.

World Commission on Dams. 2000. *Dams and Development: A New Framework for Decision Making*. London: EarthScan Publications, http://www.internationalrivers.org/files/world_commission_on_dams_final_report.pdf.

Yadav, Shyamlal. 2015. 'There's Pressure from Within Too: Red Flag from RSS Farm Chief', *The Indian Express*, 23 February.

Index

Editors and Contributors

THE EDITORS

Sanjoy Chakravorty is professor of Geography and Urban Studies at Temple University, and visiting fellow at the Center for the Advanced Study of India at the University of Pennsylvania, USA. He has published widely on urbanization, industrialization, urban development and policy, regional development and policy, land acquisition and land policy, location analysis, manufacturing clusters, international migration, and Kolkata and Delhi. He has written books on inequality (*Fragments of Inequality: Social, Spatial, and Evolutionary Analyses of Income Distribution*, 2006), industrialization (*Made in India: The Economic Geography and Political Economy of Industrialization*, 2007), land (*The Price of Land: Acquisition, Conflict, Consequence*, 2013), the Indian diaspora (*The Other One Percent: Indians in America*, 2016), and a novel, *The Promoter* (2015). His most recent book—*The Truth about Us: The Politics of Information from Manu to Modi*—is forthcoming in 2019; as is a coedited volume called *Colossus: The Anatomy of Delhi*. Professor Chakravorty writes occasional op-eds for leading newspapers in English and Bangla. His research has been funded by the US National Science Foundation, US National Institute of Justice, the World Bank, and other institutions.

Amitendu Palit is senior research fellow and research lead (Trade and Economic Policy) at the Institute of South Asian Studies (ISAS) in the National University of Singapore (NUS). He is an economist specializing in international trade policies, regional economic development, comparative economic studies, and political economy of public policies. He worked with the Government of India for several years, with his longest stint being in the Department of Economic Affairs in the Ministry of Finance. His current research focuses on economic and political implications of India's integration with the Asia–Pacific region, impact of mega-regional trade agreements, and various determinants of external trade and integration policies of China and India. His books include *The Trans Pacific Partnership, China and India: Economic and Political Implications* (2014), *China India Economics: Challenges, Competition and Collaboration* (2011), and *Special Economic Zones in India: Myths and Realities* (2008; co-authored). His most recent book is *Seven Decades of Independent India: Thoughts and Reflections* (co-edited with Vinod Rai). He has also published widely in peer-reviewed academic journals. He is a columnist for India's well-known financial daily, *The Financial Express,* and a regular contributor to the *China Daily.* He appears regularly as an expert on the BBC, Bloomberg, Channel News Asia, CNBC, Australian Broadcasting Corporation (ABC), Doordarshan (India), and All-India Radio.

CONTRIBUTORS

Abhirup Sarkar obtained his PhD from the University of Rochester and has spent most of his academic career at the Indian Statistical Institute, Kolkata. He has also taught and researched at various other places in India and abroad including the University of Florida, USA, Brigham Young University, USA, Concordia University, Canada, International Centre for Economic Research, Italy, and the Indian Institute of Management (IIM) Calcutta. The primary areas of his research are trade, development, and political economy. Apart from contributing to scholarly journals like *The International Economic Review, The Journal of Development Economics, The Journal of International Economics,* and *Economica,* he regularly writes popular pieces in dailies and periodicals. He was the Chairman of the Fourth State Finance Commission of West Bengal, and is the present Chairman of the Sixth Pay Commission of the state. He also chairs the West Bengal Infrastructure Development Finance Corporation, and is a member of the Technical Advisory Committee (Surveys) of the Reserve Bank of India.

K.P. Krishnan was educated in economics at St. Stephens College, and in law at the Campus Law Centre, University of Delhi. He obtained his

PhD in economics from IIM Bangalore. He belongs to the 1983 batch of the Indian Administrative Service (IAS). Before becoming Secretary, Ministry of Skill Development and Entrepreneurship, he served in various positions in the Government of Karnataka, Government of India, and the World Bank, primarily in the areas of economic affairs, rural and urban development. He has authored a number of reports and published many academic papers. In the year 2012, Krishnan held the BoK Visiting Professorship in Regulation in the University of Pennsylvania Law School. In 2017, Krishnan was conferred the Distinguished Alumni Award of IIM Bangalore.

Kala Seetharam Sridhar is professor, Institute for Social and Economic Change (ISEC), Bengaluru, India. Prior to this, she was with the Public Affairs Centre (PAC), where she was initially Ford Public Affairs Fellow, before which she was at the National Institute of Public Finance and Policy, New Delhi, and taught at IIM, Lucknow, as assistant and associate professor. She has been a visiting scholar at UNU-WIDER, Helsinki, a couple of times. She has authored and edited several books and has published papers in *Regional Science and Urban Economics, Urban Studies, Review of Urban and Regional Development Studies (RURDS), China Economic Review, Environment & Urbanization Asia,* and *Applied Economics,* among others. She is a referee for many journals, has won several international and national awards, and is in the top 10 per cent of authors on the Social Science Research Network.

Madalasa Venkataraman is a part-time researcher at the Real Estate Research Initiative at the IIM Bangalore. She obtained her PhD in management from IIM Bangalore in 2010. She is also a visiting faculty at IIM Indore and IIM Rohtak, where she teaches elective specializations in finance, valuations, and real estate. Her current research interests include real estate and urban economics. Prior to this, Madalasa was associated with the Centre of Excellence in Urban Development, Centre for Public Policy, IIM Bangalore, where she has worked extensively on the urban economics of Indian cities.

Manjusha Nair is assistant professor in the Department of Sociology and Anthropology at George Mason University, USA. Before this, she was assistant professor in the Department of Sociology at the National University of Singapore (2011–17). Her research is at the intersection of political sociology and development, with a comparative focus on land and labour politics in India, China, and South Africa. Her book *Undervalued Dissent: Informal Workers' Politics in India* (2016), undertakes a study of two different informal workers' movements, one that started in 1977, and became a success, and the other movement that began in 1989 and continues without success. She has also undertaken smaller research projects on automobile-worker unrest in India, and protests against land acquisition in India and China. She has published with the *Journal of Historical Sociology, International Labor and Working Class History*, and *Sociology Compass*. She is a visiting research affiliate with the Centre for Indian Studies in Africa, University of the Witwatersrand, Johannesburg, South Africa.

Ronojoy Sen is Senior Research Fellow and research lead (Politics and Governance) at the Institute of South Asian Studies and the South Asian Studies Programme, National University of Singapore. He has worked for over a decade with leading Indian newspapers, most recently as an editor for *The Times of India*. His latest book is *Nation at Play: A History of Sport in India* (2015). He is also the author of *Articles of Faith: Religion, Secularism, and the Indian Supreme Court* (2010), and has edited several books, the latest being *Media at Work in China and India* (2015). He has contributed to edited volumes and has published in several leading journals. He also writes regularly for newspapers. He has a PhD in political science from the University of Chicago, and studied history at Presidency College, Kolkata. He has held visiting fellowships at the National Endowment for Democracy, Washington, DC, the East–West Center Washington, and the International Olympic Museum, Lausanne, Switzerland.

Sai Balakrishnan is assistant professor of urban planning at Harvard University's Graduate School of Design. Prior to that, she was an assistant professor in international development at the Edward J. Bloustein School of Planning and Public Policy at Rutgers University, and served as a postdoctoral scholar at Columbia Law School's Center on Global Legal Transformations. She has also worked as an urban planner in the United States, India, and the UAE, and as a consultant to UN-HABITAT,

Nairobi. Through her research and teaching, Balakrishnan focuses on institutions for governing rapid urbanization, and on the spatial politics of land use and property. Her work has been published in *Pacific Affairs*, *Economic & Political Weekly*, and in edited volumes. Her book, titled *Shareholder Cities: Agrarian to Urban Land Transformations along Economic Corridors in Liberalizing India* is forthcoming. Balakrishnan holds a master's degree in city planning from MIT, a master's degree in urban design from the University of Michigan, and a PhD in urban planning from Harvard University, USA.

Sojin Shin is assistant professor in the Institute for International Strategy at Tokyo International University, Japan. Earlier she was Visiting Research Fellow in the Institute of South Asian Studies (ISAS) at the National University of Singapore (NUS) and taught South Asian Studies at NUS. Her research and teaching interests include international political economy and comparative politics in development with the particular focus on South Asia and East Asia. She authored *The State, Society, and Foreign Capital in India* (2018), which is a comparative case study examining how two select states in India, namely, Tamil Nadu and Odisha, have facilitated or regulated foreign direct investment (FDI) inflows in the relationship with both foreign capital and society through the lens of South Korean FDI projects. Her research articles and policy commentaries have appeared in *Economic and Political Weekly*, *Political Studies Review*, and *Oxford Bibliographies* among others.

Subhomoy Bhattacharjee is consulting editor at the *Business Standard* newspaper. He works on public policy, primarily finance, energy, and urban issues. His latest book, *India's Coal Story*, traces how India's coal reserves were at the centre of a major political scandal that nearly sent a prime minister to jail. It explores why since Independence, Indian business and government could not settle the rights on energy security, creating the murky politics of coal, and sketches the options for India's future energy security. His earlier book was *Special Economic Zones in India: Myths and Realities* (co-authored). He has studied economics at the Delhi School of Economics, Delhi University. He has worked in the Government of India as a senior officer, and has since moved to *The Economic Times*, *The Indian Express*, and *The Financial Express* newspapers. He is also a consultant with the think tank, Research and Information System for Developing Countries (RIS). He is a regular commentator on television channels for their business news programmes.

Subrata K. Mitra has a PhD from the University of Rochester, New York. He is emeritus professor of political science, Heidelberg University, Germany. He was visiting research professor at the National University of Singapore (NUS), and Director, ISAS, NUS (2015–18). He has taught in the Universities of Delhi, Hull, Nottingham, Paris, and Berkeley. Comparative politics, South Asian area studies, rational choice and game theory methods, citizenship, governance, and re-use/hybridity are among his main research interests. His publications include *Power, Protest and Participation* (1991), *The Puzzle of India's Governance: Culture, Context and Comparative Theory* (2005), *Kautilya's Arthashastra: An Intellectual Portrait: Classical Roots of Modern Politics in India* (2016), and *Politics in India: Structure, Process and Policy* 2017).

Venkatesh Panchapagesan is associate professor of finance and head of the Real Estate Research Initiative at IIM Bangalore. He has more than 22 years of experience in academia, and in the global financial services industry after finishing his PhD in finance from the University of Southern California. His current research interest includes real estate, market microstructure, and mutual funds. His prior experience includes senior management roles at some of the world's top hedge funds (Goldman Sachs Asset Management and Bridgewater Associates), and academic positions at the Olin School of Business at Washington University in St. Louis (full-time) and Stern School of Business, New York University (visiting). He has published in top peer-reviewed academic and practitioner journals of the world, and is qualified as a chartered accountant, a cost accountant, and is a post-graduate diploma holder from IIM Calcutta in India.

Yinghong Huang is associate professor at the School of International Relations, Sun Yat-sen University, P.R. China, and is joining Jindal Global University in 2019. He received his BA from Xiamen University, and MA and PhD from Sun Yat-sen University. He was a visiting scholar in the Harvard Yenching Institute (2017–18), a senior visiting scholar at the Asia Research Institute of the National University of Singapore (2014), and a visiting scholar at Jadavpur University (2015), Delhi University (2008 and 2011), and the Institute of Chinese Studies, Delhi (2013). He also served as an emerging scholar in the India–China Institute of the New School University (2014). His scholarly interests include Gandhian Satyagraha, comparative political studies of India and China, and the boundary dispute between India and China. His recent publications include a book, *The Politics to Convert Opponent: A Case Study of Mahatma Gandhi's Satyagraha Fastings* (in Chinese), and several academic articles. Currently, he is working on a project on land acquisition and development in India and China.